ORDNANCE:
WAR + ARCHITECTURE & SPACE

Ordnance: War + Architecture & Space

Edited by Gary A. Boyd and Denis Linehan
University College Cork, Ireland

ASHGATE

Published by
Ashgate Publishing Limited
Wey Court East
Union Road
Farnham
Surrey, GU9 7PT
England

Ashgate Publishing Company
110 Cherry Street
Suite 3-1
Burlington, VT 05401-3818
USA

www.ashgate.com

British Library Cataloguing in Publication Data
Ordnance : war + architecture & space.
   1. Architecture and war. 2. War--Environmental aspects.
   3. Military occupation--Environmental aspects.
   4. Memorialization.
   I. Boyd, Gary A. II. Linehan, Denis.
   720.1'03-dc23

Library of Congress Cataloging-in-Publication Data
Ordnance : war + architecture & space / edited by Gary A. Boyd and Denis Linehan.
      pages cm
   Includes bibliographical references and index.
   ISBN 978-1-4094-3912-7 (hbk) 1. Architecture and war. 2. Space (Architecture)--Social aspects.
3. Space (Architecture)--Psychological aspects. I. Boyd, Gary A., editor of compilation. II. Linehan,
Denis (Denis John) editor of compilation.
   NA2543.W37O73 2013
   720.1'08--dc23

2012027462

ISBN 9781409439127 (hbk)

Printed and bound in Great Britain by the
MPG Books Group, UK.

Contents

List of Figures

7.4   Plan for the camouflage of Bradley Field, Connecticut, 1941. Note that the three landing strips are barely visible. *Source*: Hoover Institution Archives, Edward Farmer Papers, Box 1.

7.5   John Claudius Loudon, sketches illustrating the 'gardenesque [top] and picturesque [bottom] way of planting trees'. *Source*: Loudon, 1838.

7.6   The camouflage planting on the right was considered more effective. Note the irregular groups of trees mask the rectangular building near the left edge of the illustration. *Source*: Breckenridge, 1942.

7.7   Sylvia Crowe, example of the unobtrusive integration of a transformer station into the landscape pattern. *Source*: Crowe, 1958.

7.8   Sylvia Crowe, landscape plan for Trawsfynydd nuclear power station, Wales, 1959. *Source*: Landscape Institute. Sylvia Crowe Collection.

7.9   Sketches illustrating views from roads approaching and passing Trawsfynydd nuclear power station, Wales. *Source*: Landscape Institute. Sylvia Crowe Collection.

7.10   Susan Jellicoe, aerial perspectives showing model of Geoffrey Jellicoe's landscape design for Oldbury nuclear power station on the River Severn. *Source*: Landscape Institute. Susan Jellicoe Collection.

8   The *Atlantikwall*: From a Forgotten Military Space Towards Places of Collective Remembrance

8.1   Northern France, Calais, *Atlantikwall* – Coastal artillery with camouflage nets and soldiers on patrol, April–July 1943. *Source*: Courtesy of German Federal Archives Koblenz. Bild 101I-293-1471-21A.

8.2   France, *Atlantikwall*, Mouth of the Gironde – Soldiers leaning over a map during a meeting at an inner court of a bunker. *Source*: Courtesy of German Federal Archives Koblenz Bild 101I-263-1581-10.

8.3   France, Lorient – General Field Marshal Erwin Rommel by the *Atlantikwall* inspecting an OT work place. *Source*: Courtesy of German Federal Archives Koblenz. Bild 101I-719-209-07.

8.4   Operation Overlord, D-Day invasion aerial photograph showing Normandy beaches. *Source*: Courtesy of United States National Archives at College Park, MD Aerial Photograph, 330/6/9/3-2 'Aerial Photograph of Normandy, June 1944'; Record Group 18, 8th Air Force.

8.5   Digging an antitank channel as part of the border condition of the *Sperrgebiet* in The Hague. *Source*: Photo taken by © Han Ketting, 18 March 1943.

8.6   The result of demolition works of entire urban quarters in The Hague. Shown here is the desolated street Goudsbloemlaan. *Source*: Photo taken by © Han Ketting, 20 February 1943.

8.7   France, Blanc Nez, *Atlantikwall* – Labourers building Coastal Battery 'Lindmann'. *Source*: Kuhn, Propaganda Kompagnie, Summer 1942. Courtesy of German Federal Archives, Koblenz. Bild 101I-359-2031-04.

8.8   Demolishing (antitank) obstacles from the German occupied beach of Scheveningen (The Hague). *Source*: Photo collection of Hydraulic Engineering Works of Delfland. Courtesy of Fotoverzameling Hoogheemraadschap van Delfland. Beeld a259_5.

8.9   Former U-Boat bunker 'Hornisse' in Bremen Germany. The bunker was converted in 1980 into roof-top car park while simultaneously serving as the foundations for a boat-like office building. A small memorial plaque that was placed on the eastern elevation reads: 'The U-boat bunker "Hornisse" was erected in 1944/45. This memorial plaque was erected to commemorate the suffering and death of the detainees deployed from the satellite Concentration Camps Riespott, Schützenhof and Blumenthal'. *Source*: Photo taken by © Daniel Sokolis, 2005.

8.10   *Train Tracks* – Part of the Wall Series taken along the French coastline. *Source*: Artwork by © James Morris, Photographer, 2005.

9   Military Intelligence: The Board of Ordnance Maps and Plans of Scotland, 1689–c.1760

9.1   The military landscapes of eighteenth-century Scotland. *Source*: Drawn by author.

9.2   John Henry Bastide, *A prospect of that part of the land and sea adjacent to ye barrack to be built in Glen Elg*, 1720. *Source*: Reproduced by permission of the Trustees of the National Library of Scotland.

10   Commanding the Rivers: Guarding the German Railway Network in Peace and War

About the Editors

Gary A. Boyd lectures in architecture at University College Cork and the CCAE: Cork School of Architecture. His first book, *Dublin 1745–1922: Hospitals, Spectacle and Vice* (Four Courts 2006), examines connections between medical institutions and the city's urban and social development. Current research activities include systems and manufactured landscapes, and housing design and its histories.

Denis Linehan is a graduate of the University of Nottingham. He joined University College Cork in 2000, having previously worked as a geographer at Swansea and Lancaster universities. His research is concerned with the relationships between print and visual culture and urban life, particularly in the contexts of modernity and social change. His other publications include *Atlas of Cork City* (CUP 2005) and *Spacing Ireland* (MUP 2013).

About the Contributors

Carolyn Anderson is a researcher and freelance editor. She completed her PhD on the Board of Ordnance military mapping of eighteenth-century Scotland in 2010; a collaborative project with the Institute of Geography at the University of Edinburgh and the National Library of Scotland Map Library. Prior to her studentship, she was Head of Cartography at Oxford University Press.

Peter Adey is Reader in Human Geography at Royal Holloway, University of London. He is interested in the relation between mobility, space and security and has published several books and research papers including *Mobility* (Routledge 2009) and *Aerial Life: Spaces, Mobilities, Affects* (Wiley-Blackwell 2010). Peter is the Director of a new MSc programme in Geopolitics & Security being launched by Royal Holloway in September 2012.

Garrett Carr is a writer and artist based in Belfast. To create maps, including The Map of Watchful Architecture, he walked the Irish border from end to end. He writes a blog on cartography at www.newmapsofulster.net.

Jonathan Charley lives in Glasgow and is currently Director of Cultural Studies in the department of architecture at the University of Strathclyde. He studied architecture in London and Moscow and works in a variety of media on the political and social history of buildings and cities.

Rebecca Lyn Cooper is a Cota-Robles Fellow and a PhD candidate in the Critical Studies in Architectural Culture programme at the UCLA Department of Architecture + Urban Design. Her forthcoming dissertation, "'Every Home a Fortress!': Militarization and Domesticity in Cold War America', examines points of connection between the post-war military-industrial economy and suburbanization during the period 1945 to 1962.

Sonja Duempelmann is Associate Professor of Landscape Architecture at Harvard University's Graduate School of Design. She is the author and editor of several essays and books on aspects of nineteenth and twentieth-century landscape architectural history, most recently of an edited volume, *The Cultural History of Gardens in the Age of Empire* (Berg Publishers, forthcoming 2012).

Reenie Elliott graduated from Architecture, University College Dublin in 1986. She has lived in New York, Paris and London, and worked in a range of architectural practices including Richard Meier, Jean Nouvel, and David Chipperfield. She started teaching architectural design part time in 1995. In 2004, she was appointed Academic Leader in Architecture at London Metropolitan University and runs the BA Architecture Degree Programme at the University of Greenwich.

Reenie Elliott is an architect and runs Invisible Architecture, a practice of mysterious proportions. Her current research interests are Contested Spaces, Berlin's Observation Towers, Histories of Architectural Technology, and the Collapse of Power and Vision in Architecture. She has worked in a range of architectural practices (including Richard Meier, Jean Nouvel and David Chipperfield), has taught architectural design since 1995 and has run architecture degree programmes at Oxford Brookes, London Metropolitan and Greenwich Universities.

Lisa Haber-Thomson is a PhD candidate in Urban Planning at Harvard University. Her research focuses on extra-territorial sites, and other spatial exceptions to political boundaries. She has a Masters in Architecture from the Harvard Graduate School of Design, and has worked as an architect and as a freelance animator.

Andrew Keating received his PhD in modern British history from the University of California, Berkeley in 2011. He is currently revising his dissertation on the politics and meanings of British war commemoration into a book titled *The Empire of the Dead*.

Volker Mende is a freelance building archaeologist and archaeological engineer, specialising in urban and industrial archaeology, fortifications and garden history. He has a Master of Arts in built heritage conservation from Brandenburg University of Technology, Cottbus and is currently a PhD candidate researching fortified railway bridges in Germany.

Peter Mörtenböck and **Helge Mooshammer**'s joint research is concerned with new forms of urban sociality arising from processes of transnationalisation, transient and informal land use, and changing regimes of governance. They both teach architecture and visual culture at Vienna University of Technology and at Goldsmiths College, University of London.

James Robinson is a doctoral candidate at the Institute of Geography and Earth Sciences, Aberystwyth University. His research focuses on the spaces and practices of camouflage during the Second World War, with particular emphasis on the concealment of industrial installations within the British 'Home Front' landscape.

Per Strömberg, art historian and Associate Professor at Norwegian Business School, has recently finished a Postdoctoral project at the Centre of Experience Economy focusing on the reuse of buildings as a cultural innovation strategy in tourism, event and retailing. In 2007, he defended his PhD thesis on the spatial connection and symbiotic processes between business and aesthetics in today's tourism industry.

Rose Tzalmona is engaged in exploring the relationship between contemporary architecture, memorial landscapes, war remnants and recovery. She is currently working on her dissertation where the central question addresses how the *Atlantikwall*, as a series of constructed buildings and infrastructure situated in the public realm, can be historically (re)defined and strategically (re)presented in terms of military, political, cultural and collective notions of space.

Nathaniel Walker's Master's Thesis, entitled 'Savannah's Lost Squares', won the Outstanding Graduate Thesis Award and was subsequently published in the Journal of the Society of Architectural Historians. He entered Brown University's PhD programme in the autumn of 2008 to work with Professor Dietrich Neumann on eighteenth- and nineteenth-century utopian literature and its reciprocal relationships with the 'aesthetics of progress' in architecture and urban planning.

Acknowledgements

For their immensely hard work, we would like the thank the book's contributors, who have not only produced a very fine series of engaging and original essays, rich in perspectives and critical in scope, but have also been singularly pleasant and amenable to collaborate with over the course of the book's development.

The institutions which have supported us in the production also deserve thanks, especially the Department of Geography, University College Cork and the CCAE: Cork School of Architecture (Cork Institute of Technology and University College Cork).

We would also like to thank Valerie Rose and Adam Guppy of Ashgate for making the task of producing the book an overwhelmingly positive experience.

Finally, we would like to thank our partners and families for all the support they have shown us throughout the process of editing *Ordnance: War + Architecture & Space*: Katharina and Emilia; and Anna, Elizabeth, James and Judith.

Introduction: A Place Called War

Gary A. Boyd and Denis Linehan

ON THE NATURE OF WAR

In his influential and celebrated nineteenth-century treatise, *On War* (1832), in a chapter entitled 'On Military Genius', Carl von Clausewitz describes the intimate and necessary connection between the mind of the commander and the often unseen and unknown physical landscapes in which he must conduct his warfare.

> *Terrain difficulties can be overcome only by a special faculty we can sometime call 'a sense of locality' [Ortsinn]. It is an ability to form an accurate mental picture of the country, and readily orient one's self with it. This sense of locality is largely imagination, coming in part from actual visual impressions, and part from a mental process which uses knowledge gained from study and experience to fill in missing points and make a complete whole of the fragments determined by physical sight. The power of imagination then brings this whole picture, or a mental map, and maintains it permanently present and unbroken.*

> Carl von Clausewitz, *On War*, 1832

Written in the first half of the nineteenth century by a Prussian military strategist, these observations provide unexpected insights into the complex, pervasive and enduring relationships between war and space. The term *ortsinn*, a sense of locality or place, translates the apparent precision of military logic into ambiguous realms of imagination, history and memory. This is also evident in von Clausewitz's most famous phrase 'the fog of war' where, as complex military systems meet in real places, event and decision oscillate between the rational and imaginative, between the precise and the perceived, between the systematic and the arbitrary. The functional ambiguity of the term *ortsinn* is mirrored in definitions of *ordnance*. The latter's duplicity is indicative of a relationship between military power and space which is often simultaneously affirmed and obscured. Today, its meaning is oblique. Most often it is attached to its apparently benign relationship to the *Ordnance Survey* and consequently to associations of travel, walking, rambling, tourism and leisure. This reification neglects its origins as a functional instrument in the geography of warfare in the service of the State, the control, management and storage of weapon systems and their relationship with visibility, territory, infrastructures and, ultimately, populations. Thus, the creativity emphasised by von Clausewitz, which we draw upon here, as being so necessary to the pursuit of war can be seen as a darker and more explicit iteration of the creative destruction in space necessary for the accumulation of capital or, indeed, the production of architecture.

LINES OF COMMUNICATION

> The formation flew backwards over a German city that was in flames. The bombers opened their bomb bay doors, exerted a miraculous magnetism which shrunk the fires, gathered them into cylindrical steel containers, and lifted the containers into the bellies of the planes.

Kurt Vonnegut, *Slaughterhouse-Five*, 1969

Ordnance: War + Architecture & Space brings together inter-disciplinary and international perspectives to critically engage with the social and cultural spatiality of warfare as it intrudes both ostensibly and stealthily into architecture and space. It seeks to illustrate how the pervasiveness of war reaches beyond physical contexts, to inform methods and memories, process and systems. There is no doubt that the events of 9/11 and the subsequent 'War on Terror' – stimulated new ways of thinking on the implications war has for architecture and the built environment and contributed to a paradigmatic shift in the ways in which both are conceptualised. These dynamics have fragmented the spatial composition and geographies of making war and drawn attention to the continuous presence of conflict at the centre rather than the edge of public life. Paul Hirst (2005) observed that the filtering out of violent conflict from the public mind-set through its separation over distance is increasingly more difficult to sustain, its representation less susceptible to State-media control and its impacts more difficult to ignore and supress.

The new spatialities of war partly result from the development of asymmetrical strategies from groups who have become dis-embedded from the containers of nations and moved into global networks and assemblages. The bombings in Mumbai, London and Madrid, violently illustrate the dissolution of the 'frontline' from the battlefield and its reconfiguration into the heart of the contemporary city. These threats – which included the stresses created by battlefield heterogeneity, the hybridisation of civilian and military populations, and increased ambiguity as to the origins and positions of the enemy – have changed the modes and means by which war is waged, the built environment securitized, its populations scrutinized and the risks of the urban sphere, imagined and governed. Today, a state of permanent and low-intensity siege defines every capital city which has engaged in the recent wars in Iraq and Afghanistan. There may be nobody at the gate, but the abstracted enemy lies everywhere, creating in its wake an architecture of paranoia.

Hence, the escalation in the intersections between the fabric of the landscape and the technologies of war and the extrusion and mutation of war from the battlefield into everyday life grow in significance. An extreme iteration of this tendency has been explored by Eyal Weizman who uncovered the genealogy and impact of the extensive network that has created the architecture of occupation in the Palestinian territories, with its systems of check-points, walls and tunnels, and its complex regime of surveillance and control. War is in flux, and its spatial signature is being rewritten, affecting the mobility of the population and the disposition of architecture (Weizman 2007). Within this *zeitgeist*, the once cosmopolitan spaces of railway stations, airports and city centres are now shrouded with the aura of threat. This is well represented in the installation of surface to air missiles on blocks of flats and the mooring of a giant warship on the River Thames to securitize the 2012 London Olympics.

UNIFICATION OF FORCES IN TIME

> *As I write, highly civilized human beings are flying overhead, trying to kill me.*

> George Orwell, *The Lion and the Unicorn*, 1940

Presupposing a relationship with the transformations that have characterized war in the present, this collection of essays explores the condition of warfare within the time-frame of modernity, tracking its role in the formation of the built environment and the human landscape (Bacon Hales 1990, Light 2003, Lotchin 2003). In *War and Modernity*, Hans Joas argues that war, and especially its powerful creative and destructive relationship with modernity, has been neglected in classic social theory (Joas 2003). A number of critics, however, have excavated how liberal democracies in the West are founded not just on consensus and utopian principles, but also on the appropriation and control of violence. 'Humanity', writes Michel Foucault '… does not gradually progress from combat to combat until it arrives where the rule of law replaces warfare'. Instead, '… humanity installs each of its violences in a system of rules, and thus proceeds from domination to domination' (Foucault 1994: 378). The bleak result, as is proposed by the *Dictionary of War* collective, is that '… there is no difference between war and non-war: war is perpetual and everywhere' (Dictionary of War 2012). Together with the unrelenting and atrocious impacts war has on people – 'War tears, war rends. War rips open, eviscerates. War scorches. War dismembers. War ruins' (Sontag 2003: 8) – these processes also have inexorable implications for architecture and space. Paul Virilio was not the first to realize that the city itself originates as a defensive entity, a logistical system embedded in a culture of war. By extending this thesis into the Cold War, Virilio concluded that the total war machine built around the project of deterrence enveloped the whole basis and logic of city life. This is what he called the perpetuation of 'Pure War, war which is acted out … in infinite preparation', woven into the fabric of cities and the practices of architects, city planners and other experts (Virilio and Lotringer 1983: 92).

From these perspectives, the emblematic building of modernity is arguably not so much the skyscraper or the department store, but rather the bunker, the aerodrome, the munitions factory or the Satellite Receiving Station. Consequently, for Stephen Graham, the very notion of the 'good city' is difficult to sustain. No ordinary and peaceful life, he writes, can be lived '… at the heart of metropolitan complexes in which the economy and politics are sustained by military atrocities against far-off cities' (2010: 381). Beatriz Colomina has mapped war and violence in the elemental structuring of public and private space and the domestic realm (1996, 2001, 2004). In considering the creation of boundaries and the definition of public space, she recalls an analogy prepared by the Spanish philosopher Ortega y Gasset, who suggested that the most precise explanation to describe the emergence of the city can be found in the manufacture of the cannon. 'You take a hole' he suggests:

> *wrap some steel wire tightly round it, and that's your cannon. So, the urbs or the polis starts by being an empty space, the forum, the agora, and all the rest is just a means of fixing that empty space, of limiting its outlines (Ortega y Gasset 1930: 82).*

From this insight, Colomina maintains, it is incumbent on architects to realize that '… the *urbs* is "like" a cannon. The city is "like" a military weapon'. The disciplines of geography and architecture have been associated with the prosecution of warfare, through the manipulation of the built environment – which major city built before 1800 is without a fortress? – and the creation of maps and intelligence systems (Heffernan 1996, Farish 2010, Gregory 2010, 2011).

While Robert Bevan's *The Destruction of Memory: Architecture at War* elucidates how place and architecture become targets and victims of violence, it is also the case, that the modes of thinking often mobilized to wage war – concepts devised to control territory, assess sites strategically or gather intelligence – resonant deeply within geographical traditions and architectural methodologies (Vanderbilt 2003). As Yves Lacoste made clear: 'geography serves, first and foremost, to wage war' (Lacoste 1976). Critically however, these connections can be uncloaked and interventions in architecture can contest its own history of violence. The strategies taken in Berlin at the Holocaust Memorial by Peter Eisenman and at the Jewish Museum by Daniel Libeskind to repel the emancipating comforts of memorialization, illustrate what James Young has identified as a mode of architecture that refuses to domesticate terror and '… never makes people at home with them, never brings them into the reassuring house of redemptory meaning' (2000: 3).

THE CONCENTRATION OF FORCES IN SPACE

The scales that preoccupy the essays here are intentionally diverse, moving through realms of the body to the landscape, from the domestic to the infrastructural and so on. The synthesis and juxtaposition of scales is driven, as is argued above, by our contention that war's place in modernity has been centrally implicated in the project of architecture and resonates through the spatial arrangements of everyday life. Inevitably, the many ways in which these processes intersect presupposes a response which needs interdisciplinary lens.

And, while there is an extensive literature in political science that explores war, society and governance – one of the distinctive contributions of *Ordnance* is perhaps its focus on space and the multiple and mutable physical imprints war leaves on society through architectural artefacts. Across these interventions a non-linear narrative begins to emerge – war's dark shape moves in and out of the frame. These investigations into the multiple forms of militarism, is focused by ensuring that within each chapter – and across the collection – special attention is placed on the intimate qualities of site, built form and context. Where the potential exists to do so – through the use of original archival material, the production of new architectural drawings or artwork – the contributors focus on the artefact: the landscape, the bunker, the museum, the stadium, the railway, the ruin, the speech, the gesture, the feeling.

Accordingly, the essays are arranged under a series of four territorial sub-themes. In 'Urban Orders: Militarised Terrains in the City' the dialectical relationship between conflict and urban form is examined over a series of points in time. Walker's examination of eighteenth-century Savannah excavates ambiguities within the form, space and organisation of an apparently martial plan. The connections between aesthetics and securitization in the design of contemporary public space and the evolution of a British football stadium are explored by Moosehammer and Mortenbock while Adey traces the impact of the ephemeral spaces of morale in the urban environment of Second World War Liverpool. The next section, 'The Invisible Front: Domesticity and Defence', explores the conscious and unconscious techniques by which war penetrates everyday spaces and surroundings. Stromberg's essay interrogates the re-use of Cold War bunkers and their re-calibration as spaces of amusement for the leisure industries, while Cooper maps the impact of the Second World War on the American home and especially its kitchen. Duempelmann and Robinson, meanwhile, investigate the invention and proliferation of camouflage in the First and Second World Wars. For Duemplemann the military methods and intents of strategic concealment become normalised in the post war period in the development of landscape architecture techniques designed to subdue the visual impact of large infrastructural works. Robinson, meanwhile, provides a close reading of the design guidance on combatting 'vertical visualities' offered to potential camoufleurs by the British State in Second World War.

'War in the Landscape: Infrastructures and Topology' delineates the architecture and legacies of efforts to control border areas and large territories through the use of connected systems and networks. Haber-Thomson and Tzamolna investigate some the largest pieces of infrastructure of the Second World War – the Maginot Line and the Atlantic Wall respectively. Their work not only concerns the concrete physicality of these structures but also the ephemeral social and political landscapes which inspired their building and the on-going yet often obfuscated meaning their residues continue to produce. The role of the State in the strategic production of networks and representations is also explored by Anderson and Mende. Anderson's evocation of the Board of Ordnance's operations in eighteenth-century Scotland provide an early example of the links between the visualisation and mapping of space and its physical control. Mende's insights into the development of the railway network in nineteenth and early twentieth-century German, meanwhile, provide another series of moments where notionally civilian space is interrupted by and infused with the exigencies of war.

The final section, 'Trauma: Spaces of Memory', extends an engagement with the emotive and psychological legacies of the physicalities of conflict. Carr's overlaying of the historical and contemporary methods of defining and controlling the borders of Ulster expose continuities across centuries of the meanings attached to contested spaces. Keating's essay explores the origins of the modern military cemetery in the British graves of Crimea where, he argues, for the first time sites of war became recast as sacred and national spaces of commemoration. Challenging the mechanisms through which sites of trauma are conceived, remembered and constructed is a central concern of Eliot's essay which examines the possible roles of architecture in re-negotiating these territories. Finally, Charley re-examines the omnipotence of war as it travels from space to psyche, culture to infrastructure, practice to theory, in a perpetual cycle of creative destruction, amnesia and memorial.

INTELLIGENCE IN WAR

The original purpose of the Ordnance Survey was to map that which could not be seen. This was a means of understanding territories and prefiguring the tactical engagements that might, in future, take place there. An analogy can found in the increasingly interrogation of the culture, artefacts and spaces of war within the Humanities. Evocations range from the research of Derek Gregory or Stephen Graham on the embedded spatial and abstracted systems of warfare to recent works by Eyal Weizman, Beatriz Colomina or Jean-Louis Cohen on the designed aspects of war and the recycling of its architectures throughout public and private space. These perspectives, to which this book contributes, continue to map war's pervasive qualities: both its brute force and its ability to manifest itself in unexpected locations in hitherto unforeseen forms. The fog of war may never be fully dissipated, but a critique which brings the relationships between the arts and the acts of war to account, must become a necessary part of the critical spatial imagination.

REFERENCES

Bacon Hales, P. 1990. *Atomic Spaces: Living on the Manhattan Project*. Chicago: University of Illinois Press.

Bevan, R. 2005. *The Destruction of Memory: Architecture at War*. London: Reaktion Books.

von Clausewitz, C. (1830) 1976. *On War*. Edited and translated by M. Howard and P. Paret. Princeton: Princeton University Press.

Cohen, J.L. 2011. *Architecture in Uniform: Designing and Building for World War II*. Montreal: CCA.

Colomina, B. 1996. Battle Lines: E.1027, in *The Sex of Architecture*. Edited by D. Agrest, P. Conway and L.K. Weisman. New York: Harry N. Abrams, Inc., 167–82.

Colomina, B. 2001. *Domesticity at War*. New York: Actar.

Colomina, B., Kim, J. and Brennan, A-M. (eds) 2004. *Cold War Hothouses: Inventing Modern Culture from Cockpit to Playboy*. Princeton: Princeton Architectural Press.

Dictionary of War. 2012. 'Idea'. Available at: http://dictionaryofwar.org/idea [accessed 12 December 2011].

Farish, M. 2010. *The Contours of America's Cold War*. Minneapolis: University of Minnesota Press.

Foucault, M. 1994. Nietzche Genealogy, History in *Michel Foucault Aesthetics Essential Works of Foucault 1954–1984*, Vol. 2. Edited by J.D. Faubion. London: Penguin Books, 369–92.

Gasset y, O. 1930. *The Revolt of the Masses*. New York: New American Library.

Gregory, D. 2010. War and Peace. *Transactions of the Institute of British Geographers*, 35(2), 154–86.

Gregory, D. 2011. The Everywhere War. *The Geographical Journal*, 177(3), 238–50.

Graham, S. 2010. *Cities Under Siege: The New Military Urbanism*. London: Verso.

Heffernan, M. 1996. Geography, Cartography and Military Intelligence: The Royal Geographical Society and the First World War. *Transactions of the Institute of British Geographers*, 21(3), 504–33.

Hirst, P. 2005. *Space and Power: Politics, War and Architecture*. Cambridge: Polity.

Lotchin, R.W. 2003. *The Bad City in the Good War: San Francisco, Los Angeles, Oakland, and San Diego*. Bloomington: Indiana University Press.

Joas, H. 2003. *War and Modernity*. Cambridge: Polity Press.

Light, J. 2003. *From Warfare to Welfare: Defence Intellectuals and Urban Problems in Cold War America*. Baltimore: John Hopkins University Press.

Sontag, S. 2003. *Regarding the Pain of Others*. New York: Farrar, Straus and Giroux.

Weizman, E. 2007. *Hollowland: Israel's Architecture of Occupation*. London: Verso.

Young, J.E. 2000. Daniel Libeskind's Jewish Museum in Berlin: The Uncanny Arts of Memorial Architecture. *Jewish Social Studies*, 6(2), 1–23.

Vanderbilt, T. 2010. *Survival City: Adventures Among the Ruins of Atomic America*. Chicago: University of Chicago Press.

Virilio, P. and Lotringer, S. 1983. *Pure War*. Translated by M. Polizzotti. New York: Semiotext.

Part I
Urban Orders: Militarised Terrains in the City

1

To Gather in War and Peace: The City Squares of Savannah, Georgia

Nathaniel Robert Walker

INTRODUCTION: A CITY OF TWO MINDS

In February of 1733, the British North American colony of Georgia was founded on the banks of the Savannah River, roughly ten miles from the sea. That same year the colony's London-based leaders, a group of philanthropists known as the Georgia Trustees, published a tract entitled *Reasons for Establishing the Colony of Georgia*. The opening statement was written by General James Edward Oglethorpe (1698–1785), the experienced military officer and vocal social reformer who had personally led the settlers to their new home south of the Carolinas, and who was instrumental in nearly every aspect of the venture:

> The first Honours of the ancient World were paid to the Founders of Citys; they were esteemed as the Parents from whose Wisdom whole Nations had their being and were preserved (Oglethorpe ca. 1730: 3).[1]

It was the city of Savannah that Oglethorpe, after years of preparation, had finally begun to carve out of the hot, humid pine and palmetto forests of the coastal Low Country. This city contained, and contains, all the complexity of the both the man and his mission: the precision and foresight of an experienced warrior tasked with establishing a defensive bastion of British imperial might, and the generosity of a progressive advocate for social and political change who was personally committed to establishing a haven for the downtrodden.

As a result, the first city of Georgia has one of the most remarkable town plans in modern colonial history – and as another result, this plan has been a source of nearly perpetual controversy ever since its execution. This is not least because Oglethorpe, despite writing about nearly everything else pertaining to the founding and nurturing of colonies, wrote almost nothing regarding the physical layout of Savannah, the design of which he is virtually guaranteed to have assisted, if not performed outright (Reps 1984: 166). The question has been asked repeatedly over the past two centuries, by persons as diverse as federal judges, automobile advocates, and urban historians: was the stunningly meticulous Savannah plan designed as the stage for an ideal civic society or as a utilitarian fortress? With Oglethorpe uncharacteristically silent on the matter, the town as a physical artefact, as a manifestation of

1.1   Portrait of
James Edward
Oglethorpe,
ca. 1720.

its social and military missions, was eventually left to grow and evolve without the guidance of its founder. The city's urban plan has, as a result, often become a site of conflict in which its past and residual meanings are contested – not merely as academic curiosities, but also as legal precedent for the status of its public spaces, and as cultural inheritance. Rarely amidst this uncertainty has the debate turned to the possibility that the squares of Savannah were meant to be *both* engines of war and of civic community. If these purposes can indeed be located concurrently in the intentions of the city's founder – a possibility that some architectural

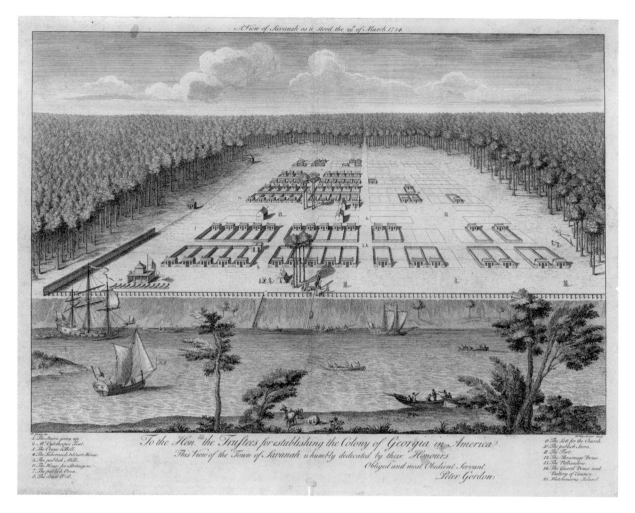

1.2   The first four wards of Savannah are laid out on a high bluff of the Savannah River.

historians, such as Turpin Bannister (1961) and John Reps (1965, 1984), have suggested, but none have fully explored – then the city's grid truly represents a unique adaptation of late-Renaissance military planning to accommodate a progressive social reform scheme that was civic in character and utopian in scale. It may also provide insight into the ways that, in this crucial period of foreign expansion, many British minds understood the connections between military rigor and social cohesion – between the perfect soldier and the ideal citizen.

The city of Savannah is made up of a series of neighbourhoods called wards which are carefully designed to accommodate both public and private lives of a seemingly communal and egalitarian character. Every ward has at its centre a square of approximately 60 by 75 meters (with greater variation in newer wards on the fringes of the town's historic centre). To the east and west of this square are two Trust Lots (for a total of four), prestigious public building sites meant for churches, schools, and other civic institutions. To the north and south are 20 Tything Lots (for a total of 40 in every ward), laid out in long rows ten apiece and reserved for private homes with rear gardens. This ensemble of private buildings, public buildings, and public space, laced with an intricate network of streets and lanes, is modular in the truest sense and endlessly

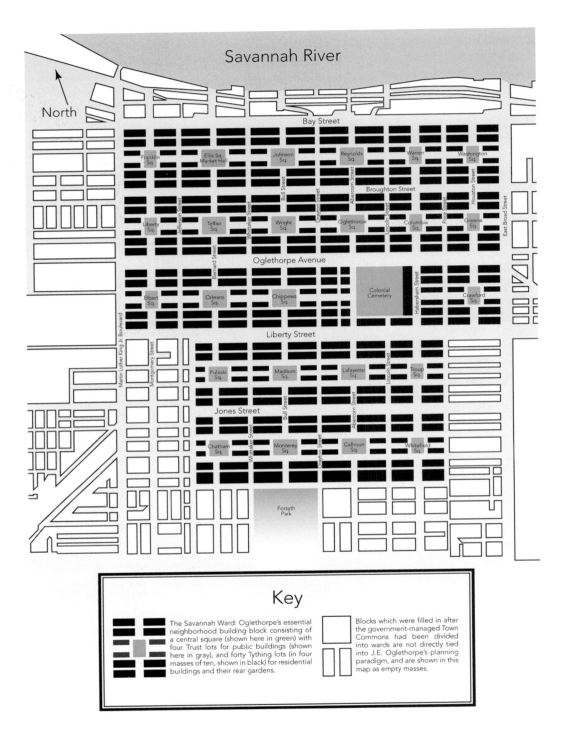

Savannah River

North

Bay Street

Franklin Sq.   Ellis Sq Market Hall   Johnson Sq.   Reynolds Sq.   Warren Sq.   Washington Sq.

Broughton Street

Liberty Sq.   Telfair Sq.   Wright Sq.   Oglethorpe Sq.   Columbia Sq.   Greene Sq.

Jefferson Street   Whitaker Street   Bull Street   Drayton Street   Abercorn Street   Lincoln Street   Price Street   Houston Street   East Broad Street

Oglethorpe Avenue

Elbert Sq.   Orleans Sq.   Chippewa Sq.   Colonial Cemetery   Crawford Sq.

Barnard Street   Habersham Street

Liberty Street

Pulaski Sq.   Madison Sq.   Lafayette Sq.   Troup Sq.

Lincoln Street

Jones Street

Martin Luther King Jr. Boulevard   Montgomery Street   Bull Street   Abercorn Street

Chatham Sq.   Monterey Sq.   Calhoun Sq.   Whitefield Sq.

Whitaker Street   Drayton Street

Forsyth Park

Key

The Savannah Ward: Oglethorpe's essential neighborhood building block consisting of a central square (shown here in green) with four Trust lots for public buildings (shown here in gray), and forty Tything lots (in four masses of ten, shown in black) for residential buildings and their rear gardens.

Blocks which were filled in after the government-managed Town Commons had been divided into wards are not directly tied into J.E. Oglethorpe's planning paradigm, and are shown in this map as empty masses.

1.3   A conventionalized map of the ward-based historic centre of Savannah as it stood ca. 1920.

repeatable. As the city expanded following the initial layout of four wards, it simply built more modules to the south, east, and west – and the large Common reserved by Oglethorpe and the Trustees as public property ensured that Savannahians were able to continue adding square-filled neighbourhoods well into the nineteenth century, resulting today in a total of 24 wards (Reps 1984: 106–7, 120).[2] Together this series of squares provides a rich fabric of public outdoor living spaces which accommodate trees, fountains, monuments and, above all else, people. It is this final point that has proven most controversial among both scholars and Savannahians whose opinions, as described above, so often gravitate to one of two polarized positions: were these squares intended as the spaces in which a new, charitable community might enact the pageantry of civic life, or were they simply utilitarian marshalling grounds for a colony always on the brink of war?

OF MORE ADVANTAGE THAN A CONQUEST

A brief account of how James Edward Oglethorpe came to find himself the leader of a new colony may provide a suitable starting point for an investigation into the competing and/or complimentary values that course through the squares of Savannah. On March 20, 1728, the general stood in front of the House of Commons in Westminster, England and read a document entitled *A Report from the Committee appointed to Enquire into the State of the Goals of this Kingdom* (Baine 1994: 48). In it he offered sordid details of the abuse and corruption that then filled the prisons of England, whose victims included not only criminals and vagrants but also otherwise law-abiding subjects whose tenure in irons, sunk with rapists and murderers into dark and disease-ridden cells, was their reward for having fallen into debt.

Among the stories illuminated by Oglethorpe was that of his good friend Robert Castell. Castell was an architect and a scholar of some note – he had translated the work of Vitruvius into English and written a volume entitled *Villas of the Ancients Illustrated*, published the very year he was incarcerated in the notorious Fleet Prison for his debts (Baine 1994: 49, 362). It was there that he was consigned to perish by the warden Thomas Bambridge, who deliberately exposed the architect to smallpox for failing to provide a steady stream of so-called 'presents' (Oglethorpe 1729: 63–4). Oglethorpe was furious upon hearing this news, and took it upon himself not only to lead an official Parliamentary committee to inquire into the plight of debtors in the United Kingdom, but also to prosecute the most grievous perpetrators of these hitherto invisible abuses, and to demand systemic reform. Bambridge became infamous throughout London for his cruelties after the publication of the committee's reports, and was so shamed by Oglethorpe's dogged pursuit that he eventually cut his own throat (Beckett 1948: 222). But deep and meaningful reform was harder to come by – the House of Commons was too familiar with too many financiers – so James Oglethorpe, long a man of action, conspired with a group of well-heeled, like-minded reformers and philanthropists to establish a new colony abroad that would act as a haven for English debtors, as well as for persecuted Protestants from Continental Europe. He and the other Georgia Trustees hoped that this haven would in time become a shining example to an England that seemed unwilling to change, declaring that it would be 'an Asylum of the Unfortunate', and of 'more advantage to Britain than the Conquest of a Kingdom' (Spalding 1984: 65).

But Britain was in the conquest business, not the asylum business. Oglethorpe and his allies would need to integrate their new haven with the strategic interests of an expanding empire if they hoped to gain official sanction and support for the project. They needed a site that could harbour utopia while still serving the interests of King and Country. Sub-tropical North America, it seemed, offered just such a place: in the vast lands between British Carolina and Spanish Florida there existed no European settlement of any note. It was disputed territory, and as such was perpetually subject not only to the ravages of war between two rival Old World powers, but was also a bubbling cauldron of turmoil among the regional Native American nations whose allegiances to each other and to their mutually resentful white neighbours were constantly shifting and moving in response to strategic needs as well as to personal affections and antagonisms (Corry 1936). For years, strategic thinkers in Britain and its colonies had been calling for a new settlement in these lands. As far as the royal government was concerned, a permanent outpost below Carolina would consolidate their claims to the area. For the Carolinians, a friendly neighbour installed south of Charleston would act as a buffer between themselves and their Floridian enemies – a first line of defence not only against the Spanish Men-of-War but also against Spain's Indian allies, as well as Spanish efforts to incite slave rebellion on Carolina plantations (Oglethorpe 1740: 253, Coleman 1994: 4).

And thus it was that the founding of the colony of Georgia, named after the King who offered it his support, was set in motion: it was to be both a haven of charity and a fortress of war. As the project acquired its complex, potentially conflicting purposes, James Oglethorpe seemed increasingly perfect as its leader. Before becoming a reformer, he had long been a soldier and a somewhat notorious scrapper, having served as a volunteer in the war between Austria and the Ottoman Empire under the command of Prince Eugene of Savoy, and having fought Spaniards in Sicily. After returning to England, he had found himself in some trouble after a 'warm answer' from an associate during an after-church stroll resulted in a bloody swordfight (Oglethorpe 1722: 5–6). But his willingness to act was not limited to violent impulse. He was also a voracious reader and an astute intellectual thinker. By the time he and his associates had drawn up their plans for the new colony, he had become an expert on American and European colonial history and theory and a published writer on the subject, promoting and defending his unique ambitions all over the kingdom in search of investment (Spalding 1984: 65). His desire was to leverage the wisdom of his predecessors in the fields of colonial settlement and social reform in order to establish an ideal society of equality and prosperity that would lend itself to the best natures of people whose spirits would otherwise be crushed by misfortune and tyranny (Oglethorpe 1732a: 6).

Today it may seem counter-intuitive to imagine a deliberately non-profit colony, but this is exactly what Oglethorpe (along with the Georgia Trustees) worked to establish, forswearing any personal economic benefit and even ownership of Georgian property (Coleman: 10). This ensured that they were sufficiently disinterested to promote honourable prosperity, protecting the colony and its spiritual fibre from the sort of economically motivated moral compromises already common in other American colonies. In a time when rum was commonly used to sedate unruly, do-nothing colonists and lubricate the seduction of Native Americans into poor business deals and subject them to other 'degrading effects', the Georgia Trustees explicitly forbade it (Corry 1936: 26, Spalding 1984: 68). In a time when African slaves were considered the single most indispensable asset to a North American and Caribbean colonial plantation system based upon large land holdings and enormous crop yields, a total prohibition of chattel slavery was, in the words of historian Betty Wood (1989: 67), 'the cornerstone of the Georgia Plan'. In addition, the institutional tools perceived by Oglethorpe and his comrades as indispensable to the abuse of the working poor were broken early and totally: Georgia was to have no lawyers and therefore no profit-driven litigation, no rural or urban real estate speculation, and no massive landholdings either gathered or inherited (Spalding 1984: 67–9). All of this was unheard of in England, let alone the colonies. Georgia was, without question, a rather daring experiment.

IN CASE A WAR SHOULD HAPPEN

Proposed design precedents and sources of inspiration for the Savannah town plan vary to an extraordinary degree, ranging from a seventeenth-century representation of Beijing (Bell 1964), Masonic interpretations of Biblical cities (Reinberger 1997), and the geometry of Renaissance gardens (Anderson 1993). Urban historian John Reps offered a thoughtful and certainly influential argument that ultimately positions the Savannah plan as a Baroque composition, a direct descendant of the elegant and refined residential squares then very popular in London, such as St. James Square or Hanover Square (1984: 120–38). He notes the interesting fact that a number of the wealthy Georgia Trustees were known to have lived on these squares, and points out that some of these spaces were developed in coordination with one another and sewn together with streets in a way that is somewhat similar to the Savannah plan. Of course, London's famously complex development environment meant that large swathes of the city could never be remade along grand formal schemes as executed in cities more convivial to the powers of absolutism – say, Rome, Turin, or Paris. This does not mean, of course, that nobody fantasized about how the city might look if its residential squares were built along monumental lines. A few schemes for comprehensive urban reform in London featuring rational grids and regularly distributed public spaces, tentatively drawn up by a number of different designers after the Great Fire of 1666, have also been pointed out as possible sources for the Savannah plan (Bannister 1961: 55–6). Perhaps Oglethorpe and his fellow Trustees did in Savannah what any number of architects and developers might have done in London at the time, given the chance.

Historians have usually offered these aesthetically grounded planning paradigms as counterpoints, however, to the traditionally dominant attribution of lineage for the Savannah plan: military camps and fortified outposts. There is no doubt that Oglethorpe gave a great deal of thought to architectural and urban responses to conditions of war and conflict. While he praised the grid-planned, square-punctuated city of Philadelphia for its ability to host public institutions and accommodate growth (Oglethorpe 1732b: 171), he spent much more time waxing lyrical about the success of Londonderry and Coleraine in the north of Ireland, commending their planners for providing them with the means to withstand sieges and produce wealth in hostile territory (Oglethorpe 1732c: v–vi). As Reps has pointed out, both of these imperial power centres are largely defined by prominent squares. Additionally, in a compendium of colonial theory edited and published by Oglethorpe in 1732 entitled *Select Tracts Relating to Colonies*, there is a passage by Machiavelli (1517: 181–2) describing Roman *castrum* towns – fortified colonies which often functioned as imperial points of control at least as much as they did hubs of social or cultural life, and whose central squares were a defining feature. That the regular open spaces of such towns and camps were understood as possessing great martial value was illustrated more than a century earlier by the engineer Robert Barret whose 1598 drawing of an ideal riverside army encampment bears, as noted by Turpin Bannister (1961: 61), a striking resemblance to the later plan of Savannah. This resemblance is made even more striking when Barret's drawing is graphically simplified and turned 45 degrees to reflect

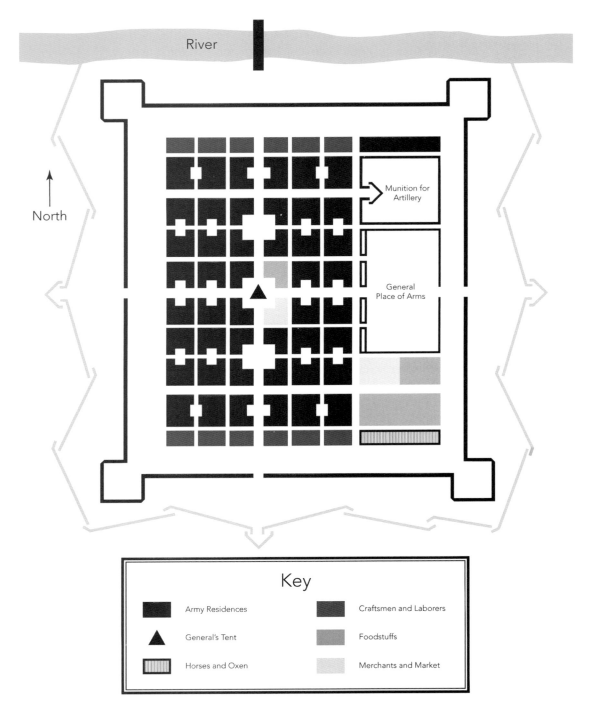

River

North

Munition for Artillery

General Place of Arms

Key

Army Residences

General's Tent

Horses and Oxen

Craftsmen and Laborers

Foodstuffs

Merchants and Market

1.4   Robert Barret's scheme for an ideal military camp from his 1598 volume *The Theorike and Practike of Modern Warres*, redrawn and rotated to reinforce its resonance with the Savannah plan.

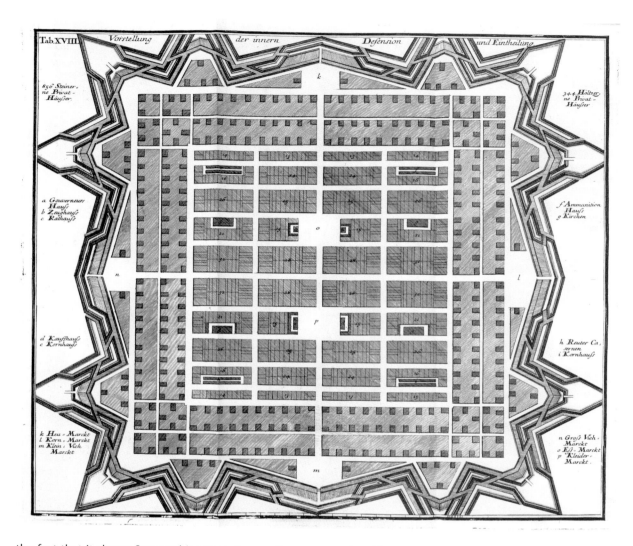

the fact that it shares Savannah's orientation on the compass (see Figure 1.4). Bannister also noted the intriguing fact that Oglethorpe may have experienced first-hand a physically realized ideal garrison town while serving on campaign against the Ottomans with Prince Eugene of Savoy. The town of Palma Nova, a famous fortified settlement laid out in radial, wheel-like symmetrical order and punctuated by orthogonal open spaces, was specifically designed to buttress Western Christendom against its would-be conquerors, and was in many ways an ideal model for the Georgia Trustees' ambitions in their own border country (Bannister 1961: 56). The obvious fact that, due to its circular layout, this town was 'irrevocably bound by its ambitious geometrical outline' (Pollak 2010: 160) – and as a result faced serious impediments to future growth – seems sufficient to explain how Oglethorpe could have been inspired by elements of Palma Nova's plan and yet felt compelled to reject the radial mode of their implementation.

There is another ideal military town plan, however, that due to its relative obscurity has escaped the notice of previous Oglethorpe scholars – despite the fact that it bears striking

1.5   Leonhard Christoph Sturm's vision of an ideal fortified town as influenced by George Rimpler.

similarities to the Savannah plan. Leonhard Christoph Sturm (1669–1719), a mathematician as well as an architect and urban planner, published in Augsburg in 1718 a book partially entitled *Freundlicher Wett-Streit der französischen, holländischen und teutschen Krieges-Bau-Kunst* [*A Friendly Competition Between French, Dutch, and German Military Architecture*]. This compared the ideas of Vauban, Coehoorn, and Rimpler, and contained an abundance of mathematical calculations formulated to guide the designer of fortifications. Among the many detailed engravings is plate XVIII, a 'Presentation of inner Defenses and Divisions' of an ideal German fortified town (see Figure 1.5). Its central core consists of two identical modules featuring squares flanked by small blocks to the east and west and long blocks to the north and south. It is not an exaggeration to say that the geometry and indeed the scale of this layout are almost exactly the same as those of the Savannah ward, save Oglethorpe's inclusion of alleys between the rows of Tything Lots and streets between the Trust Lots. Furthermore, the blocks to the north and south are entirely residential – just like the Tything blocks of Savannah – and the faces of the small blocks lining the east and west sides of the squares are given to public purposes: the Governor's House, the armoury, the town hall, and the *Kauffhaus* or store. This makes these publicly aggrandized building sites comparable to Savannah's Trust Lots. There are no spaces on the squares for the community's churches, however, which are instead tucked away on side streets along with a few storehouses, cavalry barracks, etc. This notable difference might have been avoided if Sturm's plan was bigger and featured more square-and-block modules to accommodate more civic structures. But even considering this divergence, Sturm's module and the Savannah ward are still nearly identical in geometric composition and extremely similar in their allocation of public and private space.

While no proof has yet been uncovered that Oglethorpe had access to Sturm's book, it is significant that the German architect dedicated his volume to 'The Most Serene Prince and Lord Eugenio Francisco, prince of Savoy and Piedmont' (Sturm 1718). This is the same prince Oglethorpe served as an adjutant general while fighting the Ottomans under whom Oglethorpe both learned military science (Baine 2000: 200–202) and probably his knowledge of German (Jones 1996: 848). Additionally, the publication date of 1718 comes right at the end of Oglethorpe's service on the Austrian frontier and at the beginning of his service in Sicily. Last but not least, two of the famous military architects discussed by Sturm were of clear significance to Oglethorpe: Vauban was a source for the designs of the Georgian fortress settlement of Frederica (Baine 2000: 200), and Rimpler had himself perished while fighting the Turks on the Austrian front in 1683. All of this anecdotal evidence, together with the obvious formal and functional similarities of the plans, suggest that this overlooked ideal fortified settlement could very well have been a key source, if not *the* key source, for Oglethorpe when he was designing Savannah.

With or without knowledge of Sturm, potential military applications for Savannah's open spaces were intuited by Georgians and their guests almost from the beginning. This is evidenced by the published opinion of a contemporary of Oglethorpe, a traveller named Francis Moore, who in 1744 declared that Savannah had been given its open public spaces 'in case a War should happen, that the Villages without may have Places in the Town, to bring their Cattle and Families into for Refuge' (1744: 29, Bannister 1961: 46–50). Nonetheless, as subsequent developments and debates reveal, there remained ample room in the squares for a non-martial interpretation regarding their original intent and ultimate purpose. An unstable tension existed between the civic and the military, the enduring and the provisional, the utopian and the pragmatic. This split personality (or at least the perception of one) nurtured a persistent ambivalence that the rediscovery of Sturm's ideal settlement cannot alone resolve, not only due to that ideal fortification's own seasoning of its martial fabric with civic gestures, but also, and more importantly, due to the fact that there are clearly significant differences between the social visions of the military mathematician and the humanitarian reformer. The former calculated to fortify the existing European order while the latter dreamed of empowering downtrodden souls under the palmettos of Georgia in a new and altogether reformed order.

THE PRECAUTION OF FORM

There is another vision of an ideal settlement that, as urban historian John Reps (1965: 199) has pointed out, was 'almost certainly an influence', and which may shine light on the social motivations behind the Savannah plan to an extent that has been hitherto unrecognized. In 1717, 16 years before Oglethorpe planted his boots on the banks of the Savannah river and one year before Sturm presented his *Friendly Competition*, a Scottish nobleman named Sir Robert Mountgomery published a book optimistically entitled *A Discourse Concerning the Design'd Establishment of a New Colony to the South of Carolina, in the Most Delightful Country of the Universe*. It was written in support of his dream to colonize the lands between Carolina and Florida as the new 'Margravate of Azilia' (1717: 2–3). Following an assertion that chaotic and dispersed settlement patterns lead to impotence and vulnerability, Mountgomery went on to propose a solution in the form of a dense, centralized, urban community populated by poor English labourers rather than mutinous slaves or Indians (1717: 14). Importantly, Mountgomery's vision of an ordered colony went beyond this urban core to exert itself over the entire landscape. He called for a huge defensive enclosure that would have taken in not only a main town but also dozens of fortified villas, as well as agricultural lands and hunting grounds. This conglomeration of urban artisan, agricultural labourer, and landed gentry, reveals the Margravate of Azilia not as some mere outpost or military camp, but rather as an entire social and geographic order positioned defensively against a hostile world – particularly the disorder of the wilderness, and the rival order of the Indians. It is a *hortus conclusus* of national proportions, a microcosm of British social fabric that has been idealized, miniaturized, militarized, and deployed. It requires an understanding of the social and the military as one and the same and an admission that the right sort of citizen must be present if the right sort of soldier is to be called upon. This vision of the successful colony prescribes, in short, a civil as much as it does a military fabric, blurring the distinctions drawn by past historians of Georgia between the social and martial in their quest for the sources of the Savannah plan.

It is not hard to imagine why Mountgomery failed to rally sufficient support for such an ambitious scheme. But it is also not hard to imagine Oglethorpe giving some thought to his arguments, taking inspiration from this vision of a physically rationalized colony composed of carefully arranged buildings and open space – and perhaps even deciding upon a tightly packed and ordered urban settlement and a ban on slavery in part because of Mountgomery's suggestions. Oglethorpe (ca. 1730: 14) certainly criticized the colony of North Carolina in resonant terms, saying that its 'people on their first establishment for their present conveniency dispersed themselves into Country Plantations so that there is no Town of any consideration and very little Trade there'. He also included in his *Select Tracts Relating to Colonies* an eloquent and revealing argument by Machiavelli (1525: 174) that colonists must be kept together in sufficient numbers to create meaningfully dense and lively towns, because urban populations

1.6   Sir Robert Montgomery, the Margravate of Azilia, 1717.

A Plan representing the Form of Setling the Districts, or County Divisions in the Margravate of Azilia.

not only provided 'Beauty and Ornament' but were also more dutiful to their leader, more apt to grow, and better prepared to spring into military action due to their orderly lifestyles.

In the case of Sir Robert Mountgomery's so-called 'unformidable Indians', however, he and Oglethorpe could not have disagreed more. Indeed, the latter (1762: 297) made clear his appreciation for the prowess of Native American warriors in a statement published in England in 1762 entitled 'Some Account of the Cherokees'. There were not 'any people in the world braver', he wrote, 'or more dexterous with the use of their arms and manner of fighting among woods and mountains, none more patient of labour, or swifter on foot'. Indeed, one of his first acts as the founder of Savannah was to befriend a local Yamacraw Indian chief named Tomochichi, a relationship that would have important effects on the urban fabric of Savannah (Coleman 1994: 14). Oglethorpe acquired the chief's permission to settle on the high bluffs of the Savannah River, and then worked tirelessly to secure his affection and loyalty, enhancing Tomochichi's prestige with gifts and public displays of support at every opportunity (Corry 1936: 71–2,

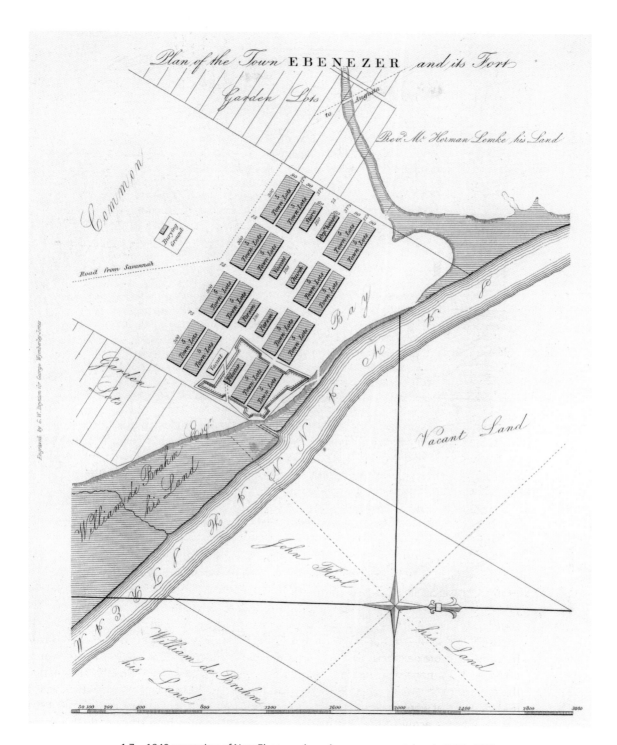

1.7   1849 engraving of New Ebenezer based upon a survey taken in 1751–1771.

1.8   A modern rendering, based on archaeological and historical evidence, of the fortified, frontline settlement of Frederica as it was designed and developed under Oglethorpe's leadership.

Coleman 1994: 14). Later, one of the first great civic gestures conducted by Oglethorpe in his new city was prompted by the death of Tomochichi. As one of the pallbearers, the general bore the corpse of the chief through the town, and laid him to rest under a prominent mound in the heart of one the city's most central squares (Stevens 1847: 158). This tomb, together with a sundial placed by the Oglethorpe in Johnson Square, marked a central axis through the town's heart. For a military settlement, the city of Savannah was taking a surprisingly diplomatic route regarding the surrounding territory – filling its so-called marshalling grounds with memorial mounds, and treating the native peoples as neighbours to be courted rather than as subjects to be subdued. Indeed, one of Savannah's first settlers later reported that bonds with Tomochichi's people and 'all the *Indian* Nations bordering round us' were gained early 'by our good Conduct, and steady Justice … so that we never lost a Man by their Means' (Christie 1741: 62). The city was conspicuously devoid of any but the most rudimentary fortifications, revealing the fact that its inhabitants had 'no fears of Indian troubles', evidently as a result of their leader's success with the complex array of important local figures, as well as his insistence that all colonists give guarantees of fair treatment towards the members of native nations (Coleman 1994: 14, Spalding 1984: 68–9).

Monumental investments of meaning into the city's public spaces such as the burial of Tomochichi weaken the argument that Oglethorpe's designs for Savannah were primarily military. Another important point to this end is offered by John Reps as a footnote in his volume *The Making of Urban America*. He points out that more than one central Georgia settlement featured the square-and-ward model of development, including the Savannah contemporary New Ebenezer (see Figure 1.7), but that the heavily fortified towns founded by Oglethorpe on the fringes of friendly territory, such as Frederica – where a violent confrontation with the Spanish actually did occur, at the Battle of the Bloody Marsh – were essentially devoid of open public space (Reps 1965: 199). Indeed, the squares of New Ebenezer were considered by the early colonists to be so removed from possible conflict that a contingent of German pacifists insisted upon going there rather than to Frederica, where 'they apprehended Blows might happen' (Moore 1744: 21–2). There was more than one urban planning paradigm in early Georgia, and the layout of Savannah is certainly not the one most obviously postured for war. Perhaps Bannister and Reps were correct to suggest the potential relevance of other, more 'civilized', socially and aesthetically oriented architectural paradigms such as the squares of Mayfair, despite the obvious resonance between Savannah and Sturm's fortress city, let alone Barret's army camp. Surprisingly, however, neither they nor most Savannahians noticed or remembered that Robert Mountgomery and Machiavelli, at least, drew no hard distinction between the ready soldier and the ideal citizen. Consequently, the binary, either-or understanding that locates utilitarian Roman military camps on one end of a spectrum and aesthetically rich, leafy residential squares on the other – assuming all the while an inherent incongruity – would in coming decades polarize Savannah's increasingly fractured and incomplete understanding of its built legacy.

SHADOWS ON THE SQUARES

The Spanish threat from Florida eventually diminished to nothing, and Savannah achieved a measure of prosperity. As it grew in safety and security, its colonists began to resent the restrictions placed upon them by the Georgia Trustees. Despite unequivocal moral condemnation of slavery by Oglethorpe and a petition declaring African solidarity written by Scottish Highlanders from the Georgia town of Darien (New Inverness),[3] the 'Malcontents' of the colony pressed their case until the British crown took the reigns of the colony away from the increasingly slack hands of the Trustees in 1752, and ended the ban on rum and slavery (Wood 1989: 76). Almost overnight, it seems, the city of Savannah was transformed. A precipitous decline in Indian relations, brought on at least in part by the 'blunt and tactless' royal governor John Reynolds and his successors, necessitated a greater investment in fortifications (Corry 1936: 134, de Brahm 1849: 38–9). New regulations were drawn up and hastily adopted to manage the sudden flood of enslaved peoples to the fields and cities of Georgia, transforming the squares of Savannah into whipping grounds and filling them with conscripted patrols brandishing guns and cutlasses (Acts passed 1755–1761: 9–15). With every white male required by law to carry a weapon and ammunition to church, Sunday mornings in particular must have brought the sights and sounds of armed conflict to the town's public spaces with a previously unknown regularity (Acts passed 1755–1761: 15). The colony had in effect declared martial law to establish, in perpetuity, a conspicuously displayed apparatus of force against a self-inflicted invasion of unwilling enemies, transforming the squares into venues for legally mandated separation and difference. As the Highlanders of Darien predicted in their anti-slavery petition of 1739:

> [Slavery] would oblige us to keep a Guard Duty at least as severe as when we expected a daily Invasion … how miserable would it be to us, and our Wives and Families, to have one Enemy without, and a more dangerous one in our Bosoms! (Parker 1997: 126).

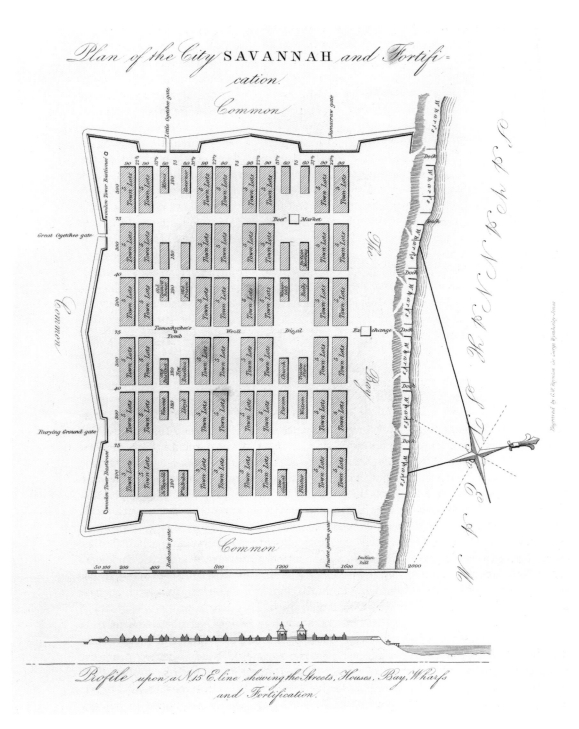

1.9   1849 engraving of Savannah based upon a survey taken in 1751–1771, revealing the
dramatic increase in fortification required after the Royal takeover of Georgia.

To reinforce the necessary regime of difference separating Georgians from their enslaved captives, acts were passed providing separate race-based codes dictating the behavior of whites and blacks in the public realm. For example, in 1758 it was legislated that a white Savannahian caught galloping his horse in the streets or squares would be subject to a fine 'not exceeding five shillings', while a black offender, free or enslaved, would be publicly lashed 'on the bare back, in the manner as is directed for the better ordering and government of negroes and other slaves' (Acts passed 1755–1761: 34).

While the Revolution of 1776 first brought terrible war to all and then the benefits of liberty to some, tyranny remained blanketed over the squares for the disenfranchised and the enslaved. That this outcome was a sore disappointment to Oglethorpe there is no doubt. From his home in England he stated his belief that the painful divorce between Britain and America, as well as the catastrophic Lisbon earthquake of 1755, were divine 'retribution to those who fat their luxuries on the labors of wretched slaves', and mused prophetically that Paris would be the next to suffer (Oglethorpe 1776: 155–6). Sadly, his haven of the downtrodden had at last fully committed both its urban spaces and the civil society that had grown up within them to the paranoid surveillance, bodily regulation, and armed comportment of a slaveholding martial state. Even as all of Savannah's squares were demarcated with chain fences as green oases accessible only to pedestrians – giving the town an 'enchanting' appearance no later than 1810 (Mackay 1810: 92) – Savannah entered a prosperous and vibrant nineteenth century as a city afraid of its own people.

The Civil War brought both economic collapse and the conciliation prize of survival to Savannah as General Sherman, at the terminus of his infamous March to the Sea, decided to present the charming city to President Lincoln 'as a Christmas gift' rather than torch it as he had Atlanta and countless other Southern towns (Stanton 1864). Shortly thereafter, however, the newly liberated community would have to wage battles of a non-military variety in order to protect their squares from a myriad of intrusions and abuses (Walker 2011). Amidst the incompetence and corruption of post-war Reconstruction, a state judge ruled against the city's lawyers and declared the squares open to the private exploitation of mule-driven streetcar operators, based upon the notion that the spaces had, ever since the city's founding, always been purely utilitarian and never intended as 'parks or … pleasure grounds' (Molony 1937). Both this decision and its rationale infuriated the citizens of Savannah who watched helplessly as most of their spaces were pierced first by rails and later by electric lines. By the close of the nineteenth century, many of the squares had fallen on hard times, particularly on the fringes of town where industrial infrastructure and racial ghettos insured a measure of civic neglect. Telfair Square was used, perhaps ironically, as the site for a temporary barracks during the Spanish-American war of 1898 – insuring for a brief instant that the Savannah squares were in fact used both for civic and military purposes simultaneously.

Ensuing decades saw local advocates of civic beauty, pedestrian rights, and architectural tradition fighting relentlessly to save the squares from being demolished for automobile routes against mostly white, male, business-centric advocates of 'modernity' and 'progress'. Throughout these so-called 'Battles of the Squares', combatants on both sides frequently appealed to history, arguing that the squares either were or were not ever meant to play a civic role as social gathering places (Bishop 1988). The idea that 'they were designed for military purposes only' and that their subsequent beautification was a departure from Oglethorpe's intentions was a powerful rhetorical weapon for those who believed the spaces should be paved over (Anon. 1921). While most of the city's citizens rejected this logic outright, they rarely

1.10   1898 photograph of Spanish-American War tent barracks on Telfair Square, Savannah.

managed to articulate a historically grounded counter-argument, perhaps because they were unfamiliar with Oglethorpe's published appreciation for social cohesion expressed as 'Beauty and Ornament'. Nonetheless, the city's preservationists managed, with much effort, to protect most of the squares, losing only three of them to automobile interests in 1935 (Walker 2011). One of these, Franklin Square, was restored in the 1980s. Ellis Square, which since Oglethorpe's day had been the site of a covered market, was buried under a multi-story parking garage from 1954 until 2010, when it too was pulled back into the domain of the pedestrian.

A STRONG AND MAGNIFICENT CITY

Following the end of his tenure as the leader of Georgia, the architectural legacy of James Edward Oglethorpe faded into obscurity and myth. The sundial he placed to mark the primary central axis of the town was removed and Tomochichi's mound was flattened. More importantly, the dark shadow of slavery, the strife of Civil War and corruption of Reconstruction, and the slow agony of postbellum decline partially obscured the social egalitarian character of the squares. Even today, with almost all the squares restored and flourishing, there is more disagreement than one might expect regarding their original intents and purposes.

Ultimately, when considering the influences cited by Oglethorpe and his description, if not of Savannah's town plan then of the community he hoped it would contain, there is good reason

1.11 Photograph of recently renovated Ellis Square taken in February of 2011.

to believe that, for him, there was no contradiction present within, and no tension between, the health of a civic community as a public body and its ability to mobilize and preserve itself in times of crisis and upheaval. Perhaps it seemed intuitively obvious that a city worth defending was more likely to be defended, and that a tight-knit social network of citizens whose relationships were cast and tempered in a functioning civic realm were more likely to protect and care for each other. From such a perspective, the collusion between the military and the civil seems less like a reconciliation of opposites, or even a compromise between dissimilar elements, and more like a mutually reinforcing marriage of concurrent purposes, each strengthening the other. The much more unequal partnership of civic and military purposes in Sturm's strikingly similar urban plan also expresses, to a certain degree, such reciprocities of purpose, although of course he did not set out to populate it with a reformed and more equitable society. This difference in final ends could alone account for Oglethorpe's apparent decision to literally multiply the civic quality of Sturm's vision while subtracting the martial, and as a result achieve a more perfect union between the two.

In his 1732 pamphlet *Select Tracts Relating to Colonies*, Oglethorpe explicitly linked the promotion of public wealth with the formation of a militarily powerful community, citing Machiavelli's declaration that, 'to keep the Publick rich, and the Private poor, and with all possible caution to keep up a well Disciplined and orderly Militia are the Ways to make a Commonwealth formidable and great' (1517: 182–3).[4] It is significant for the public spaces of Savannah that its maker put faith in the argument that public wealth was the best kind of wealth to summon a public defence. This is a social expression, perhaps, of the Vitruvian architectural principles of

firmitas, utilitas, et venustas: strength, utility, and beauty. Oglethorpe himself declared that the architec
expression of such classical values, when deployed in hostile or contested territory, would be 'a st
convenient, and magnificent City' (ca. 1730: 36). Perhaps he had his ill-fated friend Robert Barret's transl
of Vitruvius in hand when he sat down to draft the Savannah plan.

The on-going search for meaning in the Savannah squares has been at least somewhat frustrat
the past by the arbitrarily hard line many modern thinkers draw between utility and beauty, structure
ornament, readiness of arms and refined civility. Bannister, for example, worked to reconcile these 'oppo
by suggesting that Oglethorpe may have imagined the squares being given over to civic purposes
their martial calling was fulfilled (1961: 62). But in 1742, on the eve of the first and final Spanish inva
of Georgia, General James Oglethorpe declared that his men 'held the spade in one hand and the swo
the other and both successfully' (Spalding 1984: 70). Their call to arms *and* to the spade, was more tha
expedient rallying call to shore up the shifting frontlines of empire; this was the start of a sacred campai
create a city on a hill, a bastion of social justice with a destiny reaching far beyond its rough palisades (o
was hoped). The rational transformation by the early Georgians and their allies of this piece of the New V
was indisputably an act of defiance against Spain – but it was equally an act of defiance against the c
and ugliness of a broken English legal system, the predations of other colonists on Indians and Africans
ultimately each other and themselves, and a whole host of other intolerable ills that Oglethorpe hop
shame out of the world. He began by working, however unsuccessfully, to gather free and virtuous cit
soldiers in the squares of Savannah.

ACKNOWLEDGMENTS

I would like to thank the Architectural History faculty at SCAD, particularly, David Gobel, Robin Williams
E.G. Daves Rossell. I would also like to thank the wonderful staff at Brown University's John Carter B
Library, the Special Collections Library at the University of Michigan, the Hargrett Rare Book & Manus
Library at the University of Georgia, Oglethorpe University, the Georgia Archives, the US National
Service, and the Georgia Historical Society.

NOTES

1   While the 1733 tract was, and still is, usually attributed to Benjamin Martyn, it draws heavily from a then-
     unpublished document written by Oglethorpe probably in late 1730, which in 1990 was edited and republish
     R.M. Baine and P. Spalding.

2   Initially, only four wards were demarcated and built upon the settlers' arrival, but as John Reps noted, there is '
     reason to believe that [Savannah's] early expansion by two additional wards was envisaged from the day of its
     founding'.

3   Clause 5 of the 'Darien Antislavery Petition' of 1739 reads: 'It is shocking to human Nature, that any Race of Ma
     and their Posterity should be sentenc'd to perpetual Slavery; nor in Justice can we think otherwise of it, than t
     they are thrown amongst us to be Scourge one Day or other for our Sins: And as Freedom must be as dear to t
     as to us, what a Scene of Horror it must bring about! And the longer it is unexecuted, the bloody Scene must b
     the greater'. To his Excellency General Oglethorpe. The Petition of the Inhabitants of New Inverness (cited in P
     1997).

4   In his 2000 volume, *The Ideological Origins of the British Empire*, historian David Armitage discusses the importa
     of Machiavellian philosophy not only to British efforts to reconcile *imperium* and *libertas* generally, but also to
     Oglethorpe's specific desire to form a colony based upon 'Religion, Liberty, good Laws, the Exercise of Arms, a

Encouragement of the Arts (168–9). Unfortunately, however, the unique and meaningful Savannah town plan did not figure into Armitage's discussion.

REFERENCES

Anon. 1921. Favors Opening of Streets in Squares, W.W. Gordon Gives Views. *Savannah Morning News*, 6 February, 6.

Acts passed 1755–1761 which were in force when printing was introduced (archival folio compilation in the John Carter Brown Library, Providence, Rhode Island), Georgia.

Anderson, S. 1993. Savannah and the Issue of Precedent: City Plan as Resource, in R. Bennett (ed.), *Settlements in the Americas: Cross Cultural Perspectives*. Newark, Delaware: University of Delaware Press, 110–44.

Armitage, D. 2000. *The Ideological Origins of the British Empire*. Cambridge: Cambridge University Press.

Baine, R.M. (ed.) 1994. *The Publications of James Edward Oglethorpe*. Athens, Georgia: University of Georgia Press.

Baine, R.E. 2000. General Oglethorpe and the Expedition Against St. Augustine. *The Georgia Historical Quarterly*, 84 (2), 197–229.

Bannister, T.C. 1961. Oglethorpe's Sources for the Savannah Plan. *The Journal of the Society of Architectural Historians*, 20 (2) (May), 47–62.

Beckett, R.B. 1948. Hogarth's Early Painting: III 1728/9: The Gaols Enquiry. *The Burlington Magazine*, 90 (545), 222–6.

Bell, L.P. 1964. A New Theory on the Plan of Savannah. *The Georgia Historical Quarterly*, 48 (2), 147–65.

Bennett, R. (ed.). 1993. *Settlements in the Americas: Cross Cultural Perspectives*. Newark, Delaware: University of Delaware Press.

Bishop, G.J. 1988. The Battles of the Squares, folder Squares: Miscellaneous, Historic Savannah Foundation, Savannah.

Brahm de, J.G.W. 1849. *History of the Province of Georgia: With Maps of Original Surveys* (taken 1751–1771), edited by G.W.J. De Renne. Wormsloe, Georgia.

Christie, T. 1741. *A Description of Georgia, by a Gentleman Who Has Resided There Upwards of Seven Years, and Was One of the First Settlers*. London: C. Corbett.

Coleman, K. 1994. The Founding of Georgia, in H.H. Jackson and P. Spalding (eds), *Forty Years of Diversity: Essays on Colonial Georgia*. Athens, Georgia: University of Georgia Press, 4–20.

Corry, J.P. 1936. *Indian Affairs in Georgia, 1732–1756*. Philadelphia, Pennsylvania: University of Pennsylvania, doctoral dissertation.

Jackson, H.H. and Spalding, P. (eds). 1994. *Forty Years of Diversity: Essays on Colonial Georgia*. Athens, Georgia: University of Georgia Press.

Jones, F.J. 1996. Bringing Moravians to Georgia: Three Latin Letters from James Oglethorpe to Count Nicholas von Zinzendorf (translated by David Noble). *The Georgia Historical Quarterly*, 80 (4) (winter), 847–58.

Machiavelli, N.B. 1517. Discourses upon Titus Livius, in *Select Tracts Relating to Colonies*, edited by J.E. Oglethorpe, 1732, in Baine (ed.), 177–83.

Machiavelli, N.B. 1525. Some Passages taken out of the History of Florence, in *Select Tracts Relating to Colonies*, edited by J.E. Oglethorpe, 1732, in Baine (ed.), 169–99.

Mackay, R. 1810. Robert Mackay to Eliza Anne Mackay, April 2, 1810, in *The Letters of Robert Mackay to His Wife*, edited by W.C. Hartridge, 1949. Athens, Georgia: University of Georgia Press.

Molony, C. 1937. Savannah's Famed Squares Did Not Always Enjoy Full Serenity. *Savannah Morning News*, 12 February, 16.

Mountgomery, R. 1717. *A Discourse Concerning the Design'd Establishment of a New Colony to the South of Carolina, in the Most Delightful Country of the Universe*. London.

Moore, F. 1744. *Voyage to Georgia Begun in the Year 1735*. London: Jacob Robinson.

Oglethorpe, J.E. 1722. A letter 'To the Author of the Daily Journal' (A Duel Explained), in Baine (ed.), 5–6.

Oglethorpe, J.E. 1729. A Report from the Committee Appointed to Enquire Into the State of the Gaols of this Kingdom: Relating to the Fleet Prison, in Baine (ed.), 48–82.

Oglethorpe, J.E. ca. 1730. *Some Account of the Design of the Trustees for Establishing Colonys in America*, edited by R.M. Baine and P. Spalding, 1990. Athens, Georgia: University of Georgia Press.

Oglethorpe, J.E. 1732a. To the Author of the London Journal (Appeal for the Georgia Colony), in Baine (ed.), 159–66.

Oglethorpe, J.E. 1732b. Introduction, in *Select Tracts Relating to Colonies*, 170–72, in Baine (ed.), 169–99.

Oglethorpe, J.E. 1732c. *A New and Accurate Account of the Provinces of South-Carolina and Georgia*. London: J. Worrall, v–vi.

Oglethorpe, J.E. 1740. An Account of the Negroe Insurrection in South Carolina, in Baine (ed.), 252–5.

Oglethorpe, J.E. 1762. Some account of the Cherokees, as given by Lieutenant General Oglethorpe, in Baine (ed.), 296–7.

Oglethorpe, J.E. 1776. Letter to Granville Sharp received 26 September, in *Memoirs of Granville Sharp, Esq.*, vol. 1, edited by P. Hoare. London: Henry Colburn and Co., 155–6.

Parker, A.W. 1997. *Scottish Highlanders in Colonial Georgia: The Recruitment, Emigration, and Settlement at Darien, 1735–1748*. Athens, Georgia: The University of Georgia Press.

Pollak, M. 2010. *Cities at War in Early Modern Europe*. Cambridge: Cambridge University Press.

Reinberger, M. 1997. Oglethorpe's Plan of Savannah: Urban Design, Speculative Freemasonry, and Enlightenment Charity. *The Georgia Historical Quarterly*, 18 (4), 839–62.

Reps, J. 1984. The Origins of Savannah's Town Plan, in Jackson and Spalding (eds), 101–51.

Reps, J. 1965. *The Making of Urban America: A History of City Planning in the United States*. Princeton, New Jersey: Princeton University Press.

Spalding, P. 1975. James Oglethorpe and the American Revolution. *The Journal of Imperial and Commonwealth History*, 3 (3), 396–407.

Spalding, P. 1984. James Edwards Oglethorpe's Quest for an American Zion, in Jackson and Spalding (eds), 60–79.

Stanton, E.M. 1864. Savannah Ours. Sherman's Christmas Present. *New York Times*, 26 December, 1.

Stevens, W.B. 1847. *A History of Georgia from its First Discovery by Europeans to the Adoption of the Present Constitution*. New York: Appleton and Co.

Sturm, L.C. 1718. *Freundlicher Wett-Streit der französischen, holländischen und teutschen Krieges-Bau-Kunst, worinnen die Befestigungs-Manier des Hrn. von Vauban an Neu-Breisach, die beste Manier des Hrn. von Coehoorn, und zweyerley Vorstellungen der von L.C. Sturm publicirten, und nach des weit-berühmten Hrn. George Rimplers Maximen....* Augspurg: In Verlegung J. Wolffens, daselbst gedruckt bey P. Detleffsen.

Vitruvius Pollio, M. First century BC. *The Ten Books on Architecture*, translated by M.H. Morgan, 1960. New York: Dover Publications, Inc.

Walker, N.R. 2011. Savannah's Lost Squares: Progress *vs.* Beauty in the Depression-Era South. *Journal of the Society of Architectural Historians*, 70 (4), 512–31.

Wood, B. 1989. Oglethorpe, Race, and Slavery, in *Oglethorpe in Perspective: Georgia's Founder After Two Hundred Years*, edited by P. Spalding and H.H. Jackson. Tuscaloosa, Alabama: The University of Alabama Press, 66–79.

2

The Political Aesthetics of Counter-Terrorism Design

Peter Mörtenböck and Helge Mooshammer

INTRODUCTION: GUNNERS AND RUNNERS

On 12 May 2006 the Gunners, as the world famous London football club Arsenal is often nick-named, played their last home game at Highbury Stadium, a venue steeped in tradition. The name Gunners stems from the site on which the club was founded, the former Royal Arsenal munitions factory in the London suburb of Woolwich near the Thames, which in the nineteenth century was one of England's most important armaments production facilities. Its riverside location led to the Royal Arsenal becoming the most important military supply centre for the expansion of the British Empire. The factory workers' football team, which was founded in 1886 at the height of the expansion of the Royal Arsenal into Europe's largest military industrial complex, represented an extension of military rivalry into civilian rituals of competition and domination. Initially playing on a piece of open ground on the Isle of Dogs, which some described as a ditch or open sewer, the football club moved from one nearby site to another until finding a long-term base for its activities in North London. Highbury Stadium, the home of the Gunners from 1913 to 2006, grew up around a playing field situated between gardens and backyards and was integrated seamlessly into the small-scale contours of a Victorian residential neighbourhood where on match, days kiosks takeaways and souvenir stands were unceremoniously set up in front gardens and driveways. Every home game at the 'Home of Football' thus constituted an extravagant staging of the homeland: an opulent theatre of British culture that spilled out from the stadium into the neighbourhood and was perpetuated in numerous myths and legends.

In the weeks leading up to the closure of the stadium in May 2006, British newspapers such as *The Evening Standard* and *The Guardian* devoted entire extra supplements to

2.1 The 'Infant School' gun foundry, Woolwich Arsenal, 1874.

2.2   The Home of Football – entrance to the North Bank stand of Arsenal's old Highbury Stadium, 2006.

wistful obituaries for this historic London venue: 'Highbury wasn't just any stadium, Highbury was a cathedral of football'. The end of 'Highbury' also brought to an end the sacral practices with which the stadium was staged as a representation of British community. In Ashburton Grove, 500 metres away from the old venue, there is now a new stadium complex equipped with VIP lounges, luxury restaurants and a multimedia infrastructure that has been co-financed by Emirates, the state airline of Dubai, United Arab Emirates. The switch to the Emirates Stadium became 'necessary' in order to be able to continue competing in the premiere league of global media presence. This transition from a cathedral of football to a cathedral of consumption marks not only a local but also a cultural change: from community-based pubs and fish-and-chip stalls to the comprehensive commercial use of multifunctional stadium structures, from a locally orientated, English working-class culture to a globalized world of flows. The upper end of this transformation is served by the convenient flows of capital, the lower end by the more ambiguous flows of migration. Thus, two geographies of upheaval meet directly at the intersection point constituted by North London's Finsbury Park: the world of football and the postcolonial world of Islamic cultures in Europe. If the demolition of Highbury Stadium was mourned as the loss of a piece of British culture, it also constituted the loss of a monument that helped mask the realities around the stadium that had long exhibited a different image of 'Britain today'. Arsenal's move to the Emirates Stadium did not simply signify that a local population lost 'its' urban backyard stadium but that a stadium also lost 'its' population.

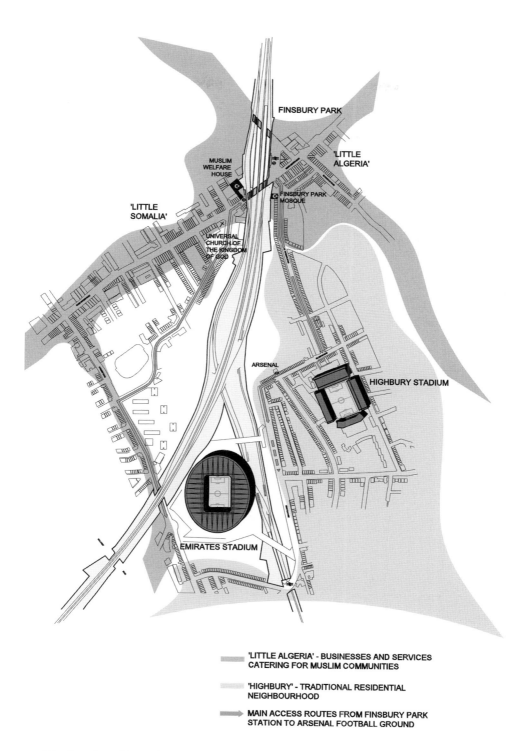

FINSBURY PARK

'LITTLE ALGERIA'

MUSLIM WELFARE HOUSE

FINSBURY PARK MOSQUE

'LITTLE SOMALIA'

UNIVERSAL CHURCH OF THE KINGDOM OF GOD

ARSENAL

HIGHBURY STADIUM

EMIRATES STADIUM

'LITTLE ALGERIA' - BUSINESSES AND SERVICES CATERING FOR MUSLIM COMMUNITIES

'HIGHBURY' - TRADITIONAL RESIDENTIAL NEIGHBOURHOOD

MAIN ACCESS ROUTES FROM FINSBURY PARK STATION TO ARSENAL FOOTBALL GROUND

2.3   Location of Arsenal's Highbury and Emirates stadiums near Finsbury Park, North London.

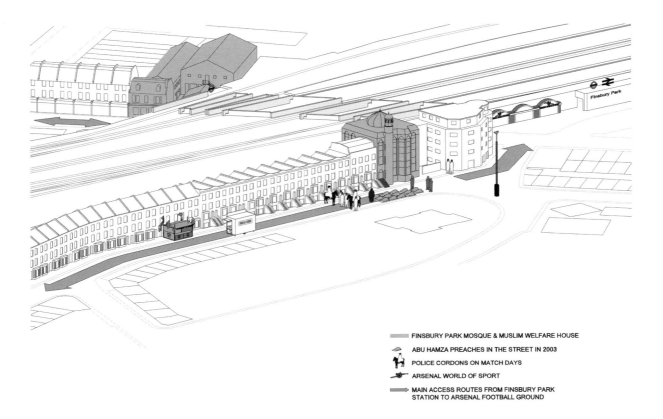

FINSBURY PARK MOSQUE & MUSLIM WELFARE HOUSE
ABU HAMZA PREACHES IN THE STREET IN 2003
POLICE CORDONS ON MATCH DAYS
ARSENAL WORLD OF SPORT
MAIN ACCESS ROUTES FROM FINSBURY PARK
STATION TO ARSENAL FOOTBALL GROUND

2.4 Encounters between football and faith communities in Finsbury Park, North London.

This atomization of an unambiguous relationship between sociality and space is taking place on two levels simultaneously. One level involves the confrontation of a locally shaped football culture with globally operating finance capital. This includes the purchase of naming rights for the stadium by the Dubai-based Emirates airline as well as the expectations linked with the stadium relating to London's claim to a place in the league of global cities. The other level concerns the intermixing of an introspective English residential neighbourhood with the networks of the global *jihad*. Nearby the stadium stands the Finsbury Park Mosque, which was opened in 1990 by Prince Charles and King Fahd of Saudi Arabia and which, between 1997 and 2003, served as a gathering point for supporters of Islamic extremism inspired by the teachings of the resident radical cleric Abu Hamza al-Masri. It was during the run-up to the Football World Cup in Paris in 1998 that calls were first heard for Abu Hamza to be banned from the Finsbury Park Mosque due to fears of possible terrorist attacks (O'Neill and McGrory 2006). The events of 9/11 accelerated the investigation of possible subversive activities connected with the mosque. In January 2003 a raid by British anti-terrorist units uncovered not only fake passports and credit cards but also CS gas, hunting knives and hand guns. Conservative newspapers reacted by describing the mosque as a 'honey pot for terrorists' and as an 'arsenal for Islamic terror'.

After being stripped of his status as an imam, Abu Hamza continued to preach to his supporters in front of the mosque on St. Thomas's Road, on the very stretch of street used by Arsenal fans on their regular pilgrimage to their stadium. In the spring of 2006, recordings of these street sermons led to Abu Hamza's arrest and conviction for incitement to racial hatred and incitement to murder. Now under new leadership, the Finsbury Park Mosque – which was renamed the North London Central Mosque in 2005 – currently enjoys a high level of attendance, and the local network of businesses and facilities for immigrants from various parts of the Islamic world is growing rapidly. On match days the Arsenal fans now make their way to 'their' club through a multi-ethnic neighbourhood in which more than 120 languages are spoken, passing mosques and Muslim welfare houses, Halal butcher shops, internet cafés, Maghrebi snack bars and cafés with names like Salam, Aladdin and Paradise, specialized travel agents and bedsit agencies, Islamic bookshops and scarf shops. These concentrated financial and migratory links with the Mahgreb and the Near and Middle East in Finsbury Park have led to a cultural and economic coexistence of religion and football, prayer rituals and pre-match anthems, international financial operations and local street culture. In the encounters and intermixing of English football fans with the migrant population, the urban space becomes a stage for the ambiguities of prosperity, legality and security with which the neo-liberal transformation of western society operates. The path that these encounters take is never prescribed, for outside an accidental confrontation on the street there are no roles or channels of coalescence for these separately existing spheres. Rather than generating a field of clear identitary positions, the different flows of cultural affiliations in Finsbury Park mark a departure from the belief in a stable concept of Britishness.

It is not only football but culture that is no longer, as the 1996 football hymn *Three Lions* put it, 'coming home'. The mourning of Arsenal's Highbury Stadium opened up a space for a more reaching farewell, a farewell to the idea that access to the understanding of culture is to be found in identitary configurations. The wistful final salute to the old Arsenal stadium signalled a transformation that all European cultures are experiencing: a shift from an unambiguous socio-cultural belongingness and security experienced as familiar and homelike to a fragmented, kaleidoscopically refracted world in which urban space is no longer defined and shaped 'by ourselves' but in an interplay with the conditions and prescriptions of global capital. The uncontrolled acting out of this drama, with all its potential for deviation from prescribed patterns of behaviour, is not taking place in organized political rallies but in marginal actualities such as the encounters of massing football fans with radical Muslims praying on the street in St. Thomas's Road in Finsbury Park.

CULTURES OF SECURITIZATION

The case of Arsenal provides an example of an increasingly expanding geography of parallel worlds that are organized via networks and that become interwoven with other networks through situative opportunities. The dependence of these interactions on the interests of the global market raises the question as to whether its politics of diffusion, segmentation and splintering is rendering it impossible to share cultural values or whether life in parallel universes is capable of generating new forms of sociality and solidarity. In particular, as the logic of globalization seems to prevent any kind of cultural, political and indeed material bridge being built between the different characteristics of this landscape (Castells 2000: 458): While the neoliberal economy orients itself to financial risk taking, those who enjoy its benefits seek shelter in communities of securitization, which are deliberately detached from the risks of the surrounding society and from market fluctuations. That way, risk management and safety concerns have become top priorities in programming urban environments. Closer attention to this dynamics is all the more urgent, as, from the perspective of the global market economy, cities are increasingly becoming

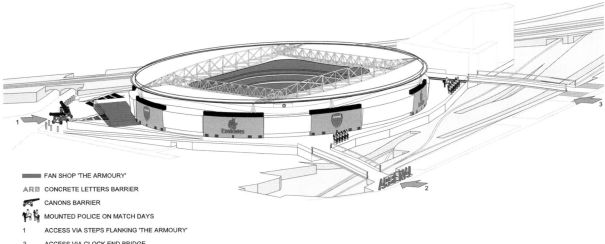

FAN SHOP 'THE ARMOURY'
ARS   CONCRETE LETTERS BARRIER
CANONS BARRIER
MOUNTED POLICE ON MATCH DAYS
1   ACCESS VIA STEPS FLANKING 'THE ARMOURY'
2   ACCESS VIA CLOCK END BRIDGE
3   ACCESS VIA STEPS TO NORTH STAND BRIDGE

2.5   Location and surroundings of the new Emirates Stadium in North London.

a commercial formula, spatial products that can be assembled, dismantled and relocated to a new place. Entrepreneurial risks are often avoided by locating economic activities wherever a community is willing to safeguard the business, while labour disputes result in outsourcing abroad. Replacing the city, the much more flexible concept of community is now capturing our attention as the new level of reference. This transformation is critically advanced by a new culture of security-conscious planning which designs fear into our cities.

Less than a year after the opening of Arsenal's Emirates Stadium, the newly built structure formed the backdrop for an international meeting of political leaders: a UK-France summit attended by French President Nicolas Sarkozy and the then British Prime Minister Gordon Brown. This first state visit by a French President in Britain in the twenty-first century took place at what the British government has recently hailed 'a prime example of elegant counter-terrorism design'. A number of anti-terrorism measures are in place to meet new national security strategies for public buildings: CCTV and a high tech security system control every way in and out of the stadium. But the real strength of the new stadium is that it offers limited access to vehicles. Situated on a triangular piece of land that on two sides is completely engulfed by the spaghetti of criss-crossing railways, the stadium sits virtually on an island, cut off from the adjoining neighbourhoods and accessible only at three points via bridges and flights of steps. Its apron is surrounded by subtle obstacles, concrete planters and benches that are strategically placed to prevent cars from getting anywhere near it. Large concrete letters displaying the name of the football club Arsenal outside the stadium are built to block vehicle-borne bombs. Similarly, two cast iron guns on garrison carriages, part of the club's insignia, are not just there for nostalgic reasons – weighing several tons each, they can stop moving vehicles at a critical access point. Given this whole gamut of aesthetic deceit, it may come as no surprise that the stadium's fan shop is proudly labelled, in bold letters, as an 'armoury'.

With its clever use of masquerades to conceal the true nature of its deterrents, the Emirates Stadium has been promoted as a showcase building to demonstrate the high level of quality design that can be achieved when incorporating urban safety guidelines in the training of design professionals. The aim of such training programmes is to implement anti-terror measures without affecting the aesthetic appeal of the urban environment. In 2008, the Home Office

launched a national scheme to train all key designers of major public buildings in counter-terrorism.[1] 'Argus Professional', a National Counter-Terrorism Security Office initiative, and which is part of the programme, is aimed at encouraging architects, developers and designers to consider counter-terrorism protective security in the concept design stage of their projects. These training measures have not remained undisputed, though. As one commentator put it: 'The government wants major new buildings to be designed with panic rooms, truck-bomb barriers and limited glazing to counter terrorist attacks in a policy which architects have warned would blight the attractiveness of towns and cities' (Booth 2008). These warnings notwithstanding, in its 2008 National Security Strategy the Cabinet Office promised to 'work with architects and planners to "design in" safe areas, and blast-resistant materials and enhanced physical protection against vehicle bomb attacks' (Cabinet Office 2008: 26). Work on fortification of the Treasury against the threat of car bombers is now underway. Likewise, retrofitting work at railway stations, airports and other public transport hubs is being accelerated. Some of the most striking effects of these security efforts can been seen in the winning entry of an international competition for the new US embassy building in London by Kieran Timberlake architects, which some critics have portrayed as a cross-breed between an International Style corporate headquarters and a medieval keep. The *New York Review of Books* went so far as to refer to it as 'a twenty-first century avatar of the Tower of London' (Filler 2010). This comparison with the Tower of London is premised on cleverly worked out security measures that dominate the design of the 12-storey cube-shaped structure: to begin with, its position atop a bunker-like platform, then its dense landscaping with grassy berms, trenches and a moat-like water feature

2.6   Concrete letters barrier at the clock end bridge access to Arsenal's Emirates Stadium, London, 2006.

2.7   Arsenal's iconic cannons in front of the fan shop 'The Armoury' at the new Emirates Stadium, London, 2006.

surrounding the building and, last not least, the large expanses of glass treated with polymer plastic to lessen the projectile force in case of an explosion.

Following in the footsteps of such eminent security-led design, the Royal Institute of British Architects and a number of partners, including the Royal Society of the Arts and the Home Office, jointly launched an educational initiative – a competition that asked architecture students to think creatively about counter-terrorist features as integral parts of building blueprints. 'Public Spaces, Safer Places: Designing in Counter-Terrorism' called for design responses for a public space in the aftermath of a fictitious terrorist attack in the centre of a major European city. Backed by the Design Against Crime Research Centre at Central St Martin's College, London, the competition pleas for paying more attention to pro-active counter-terrorism planning so that security is built in rather than bolted on: Terrorism security is to be validated as a design challenge along with place-making and aesthetics, as an answer in equal measure to the specifications of elegant, busy and animated public space, with the winning entry to this competition being praised for combining 'inspiring symbolism with an ingenious, tactical organization of space' (RIBA 2009). In an ironic portrait, the online magazine *Bad Idea* has described this 'Dove and Olive Branch' design as an emblem 'of peace, both literally, with giant letters that spell out 'PEACE', and more subtly, with cosy curling nooks laid out across the square for people to relax in, or hide in if a shooter attacked' (Beaumont-Thomas 2010).

FEAR(ED) BY DESIGN

In fact much of the European debate on counter-terrorism planning is not new at all, but has been well rehearsed in the USA, not least in the wake of 9/11. Joseph Masco (2010) has argued that the transformation of the USA from a counter-communist to a counter-terrorist state formation in the late twentieth century has been facilitated by the deep structure of a public/secret divide that is managed by the mobilization of threat. US government agencies, including the Department of Homeland Security and the Department of Justice, have provided references for building owners, developers, architects, and engineers seeking to manage the terrorist threat to buildings. Recommendations on how to prevent and mitigate the effects of a terrorist attack on a building include vehicle threat vector analyses and the incorporation of hard perimeters into design plans, the design of effective access control, screening, and monitoring systems as well as the use of protection against emerging threats from chemical, biological, and radiological weapons (New York City Police Department 2009: iv–viii). A prime example of the implementation of these design principles into the urban fabric is the Staples Center, a privately financed and controlled multi-purpose arena in Downtown Los Angeles, which manifests the new understanding of urban spatial organization: Dozens of large-scale sculptures and an uninterrupted sequence of some hundred man-sized planters surrounding the building's apron regulate the stream of visitors and defend the arena against the threat of an attack. What at first sight may look like decoration is the minutely calculated camouflage of crisis planning hidden behind a normalizing façade. The Staples Center is a showcase project of

2.8   Cordon of vehicle barriers surrounding the Staples Center, Los Angeles, 2009.

US-American terrorism prevention in the urban realm and as such has been hosting numerous conferences on technologies for homeland security. This liaison between military organization and urban aesthetics has come to epitomize the twofold transformation of urban public culture underway in the Western world: first, on the level of political agitation, and second, on the level of practical manifestations in architectural design as they have been brought forth in particular historical, cultural and social contexts. Aesthetic adornment has clearly become a strategic instrument of the politics of normalization and naturalization in support of the invisible city of privatized infrastructures and technological flows.

The increasing implementation of prevention-oriented counterterrorism in urban environments also has to be seen against the backdrop of policies dating back to the 1970s which aimed at regulating urban behaviour through specialized design strategies, in particular the American 'defensible space' concept, a design manual that has been strongly backed by the insurance industry, the police and politicians, and has been adopted by many European governments as tool in aid of safe urban environments (Minton 2009: 71–4). Focusing on ownership and control of the environment, the concept basically marks out clear territorial boundaries and renders strangers a source of danger for 'vulnerable' places. Since the early 1990s, Secured by Design, the influential UK Police flagship initiative supporting the principles of 'defensible space', has been a major force to transform thousands of commercial, housing and public sector developments into high-security enclaves. While the USA maintain specialized national training centres, such as the disaster centre facilities at Camp Dawson, West Virginia, to stage terrorist situations against the backdrop of a replica three-block urban landscape, the European logic of action – military, political or architectural – seems to lie in an implementation

2.9   Oversized planters with Chinese Cypress trees placed as vehicle bomb barriers in Canary Wharf, London, 2009.

of replica military elements in real urban space. Its artful disguise of mock urban features is to propagate a visual culture of innocence: barriers that double as planters, concrete bollards in the shape of giant letters and Chinese Cypress trees of the kind planted at Canary Wharf in London. Instead of making the environment look sinister, they are said to foster a 'feeling of well-being' – a term that is now regularly woven into government rhetorics when promoting security-led design. In more technical terms, such trees are planted to regulate the 'standoff space' between a building and where an explosive could go off. Their main virtue is that they are exceptionally good at absorbing the kinetic energy of a bomb blast.

If we were to trust the narratives evoked by blending such deterrents into the landscape, we would have to assume that the threat of world-wide terrorist networks has gradually come to expand to the whole of the Western world, seeking to produce micro-conflicts for communities everywhere, so that defences have to be put up in an ambivalent and all-encompassing terroristic situation. The omnipresent enemy generated through these stories figures as the actuator of an ever more restrictive politics of social-based 'urban security' (in government lingo: 'community-based justice'). Bluewater, Britain's largest shopping mall, for instance, is claiming to crack down on vicious attacks by issuing guidelines which are set to regulate social behaviour on its premises, including bans on clothes which obscure the face such as hooded tops, baseball caps and headscarves. In the heat of a national moral debate in Great Britain in summer 2005, this move was backed by the then Deputy Prime Minister John Prescott, who himself reportedly almost fell victim to a happy slapping attack by a group of teenagers in a motorway café.

These developments in the United Kingdom exemplify the exploitation of safety concerns arizing from a governmental approach that seeks to regulate what is regarded as a growing climate of cultural disrespect. Reminiscent of the earlier ill-fated 'Back to Basics' campaign run by the former Conservative administration, New Labour initiated so-called Anti-Social Behaviour Orders (ASBOs) introduced by the Crime and Disorder Act immediately upon taking office in 1998. These by-laws define anti-social behaviour as acts likely to cause 'harassment, alarm, or distress to one or more persons not in the same household'. What qualifies as anti-social behaviour, though, remains unclear and dependent on what counts as 'proper' or 'poor' urban conduct in the eye of the beholder. Unsurprisingly, examples are on record of ASBOs preventing people from sleeping rough, fly-posting, street begging or illegal parking.[2] These measures produce a worrying cartography of Britain: while public space becomes hyper-regulated and homogenized in the interest of middle class life-styles, private space mutates into home detention zones. It is this new biased and unbalanced demarcation between private and public realms which in the 1990s Rosalyn Deutsche has described as characteristic of the evictions taking place in the name of restoring what is in popular political terminology now called 'culture of respect'. The public sphere is instituted as a means for class-related private interests to control public activities, while conflicts are being homogenized by privatizing whole aspects of urban life (Deutsche 2002: 58). Homogenization as in the case of the 'essential decency of the British character' praised in the former Home Office minister's pamphlet *The Politics of Decency* (Blears 2004) is only effected by exclusions and evictions. Hand in hand with the accelerated privatization and bureaucratization of the urban space, legislation and jurisdiction assist in justifying exclusions as natural benefit for 'the public'. The means taken to achieve this end is to single out and tackle those groups of individuals and those urban areas whose existence, according to standards of 'decency', disrupt citizenship and community values. Feeling the urge to appeal to Middle Britain anxieties, politics buys into the logic of urban eviction and presents itself willing and able not only to stamp out unruly behaviour through issuing bans on individuals, but also the potential of terroristic attacks through designing terror-proof buildings.

'VICTORIA CONCORDIA CRESCIT' – VICTORY GROWS OUT OF HARMONY

The current quest for civilian 'decency', 'security' and 'well-being' and its legitimization through a heightened perception of urban violence mobilizes a form of biopower which reinforces social hierarchies along prevalent value systems and opinion polls. Just remember the 'The rules have changed' campaign of the British government after the bomb attacks in London in July 2005 and the political reactions to the riots in the French Banlieues in November of that year that quickly delegitimized the violence by dismissing it as the work of 'voyous' or thugs. In the light of these developments it may come as no surprise that, in the mind of authorities and security officials, the urban landscape looks like a product catalogue of items that can be assembled into a harmonizing weapon system to ward off any sense of threat or danger. 'Victoria Concordia Crescit' has not only been a long standing motto to adorn the crest of London's Arsenal football team from the post-war period to the end of the last century, it is also the battle cry of an almost unmappable intrusion of security-oriented forces into our lives and into the structure of urban cohabitation. Combating terrorism fear in every corner of the public realm, everything that is pleasing to the eye is being turned into the 3D interface of a much more powerful command line operating in the background.

Fear is the ultimate mobilizing principle in a 'global' society without overt political struggle. In asserting the legitimacy and authority of this ideological structure, the use of the 'network' concept and the myths of its all-pervasiveness cleverly disguise a global policy of expert administration that attempts to control network dynamics on the one hand but must provide space for its expansion on the other to uphold its mobilizing powers and to achieve its own goals. To distract attention away from the ambiguity of this situation, war and terrorism anxieties are recast as non-ideological issues that need comprehensive technical solutions to achieve a greater sense of urban security. Political statements are thus readily based on the premise of an uncontainable threat and the necessity to plan territorial security far beyond the actual target. In the widespread talk of a 'war on terrorism', the focal idea of a global terrorist network has become an instrumental notion to give fear a place. Of infinite scope, this place can be experienced everywhere – which is why it must also be reorganized, monitored and protected everywhere by political leaders. This shift of scale and perspective demonstrates how in the war against abstract enemies the limits of security measures are rendered indeterminate, both spatially and temporally. Wars against abstract concepts or social practices are acts of governmentality, indistinguishable from other forms of political activity. Reproducing all aspects of social life, they can be extended anywhere (Hardt and Negri 2005: 14).

The pervasive rhetorics of counter-terroristic measures evoke a certain proximity of today's urban security policies to a more general complicity of contemporary visual culture and urban warfare. It is not without reason that cities are entrenched in military imagery and that the resurgence of this imagery comes at a time of social deregulation. From battle fields to strategic lines, from frontier areas to the hostile urban wilderness, the combined ideologies of social orchestration and urban planning have always conjured up a language of military warfare to legitimate violent acts of urban transformation and eviction. There is a close, even symbiotic relation between social conflict and the way cities have been built as sites of warfare. In taking up different roles looming on the horizon of conflict, the forces of war and the institutionalization of military apparatuses have shaped the urban in an enduring battle against what might be called spectral incursions. Fresh incidents and happenings have constantly reoriented the public mind on new framings of what gets to count as a 'menace to society' or as a 'terroristic threat'. These range from the civil defence measures taken in response to the threat of nuclear attacks in the Cold War period to an increasingly safety-conscious urban design that reacted to the civil rights uprizings in the 1960s and the rescripting of internal 'enemies' – often immigrants from the Arab world – as really external and foreign in the 1980s and 1990s (Smith 1996: 213–15). As new conflicts emerge from this complicated fabric today, they direct the public conscience towards the new ways in which the presence of social exteriority is constituted and expressed.

In this militarized urban landscape, the state of being human is defined by a matrix of inclusions and exclusions in which spectral existences justify an endless warfare against the phantasmal infinity of the enemy. Judith Butler (2004: 33) has noted that in the light of such exclusionary practices it:

> is not a matter of a simple entry of the excluded into an established ontology, but an insurrection at the level of ontology, a critical opening up of the questions, What is real? Whose lives are real? How might reality be remade? Those who are unreal have, in a sense, suffered the violence of derealization. ... Violence renews itself in the apparent inexhaustibility of its object.

It is therefore indicative that, although the debate on the use of rights performs a central ethical and political function, the relationship between law and justice has no greater meaning in the expanding discussions on political and economic spatial control (Besson 2005). The apparatus underlying a legal practice is not the result of its own nature; it is a changeable, contingent construct of political and theoretical engagement. There is an idiosyncratic commonality between the denial of this connection and the denial of the link between the organization of violence and urban life: their construction as incompatible zones and the consciousness this creates (i.e. that there can be no place for dissent in the law and no place for conflict in the city) are related to a particular conception of culture in which difference poses a danger. The ideological function of the agreement between law and justice therefore coincides with the normative organizational design of the city as a non-violent zone of civilization.

If conflict is declared to be something that cannot be fit into twenty-first century terms of civic conduct, it is defined as a state of exception that exists outside the bounds of urban society. 'In the decision on the state of exception', as Agamben (2005: 36) has argued, 'the norm is abandoned or even annulled; ... the state of exception separates the norm from its application in order to make its application possible'. That way, scenario planning, a critical technique for effective counter-terrorism design, is not about predicting the future. It is about exploring the future. Scenario thinking promotes a system whose goal is to pro-actively preserve power, one that is rooted in two seemingly antithetical initiatives: the deliberate provocation of conflict and the simultaneous exclusion of conflict as a public sphere. This double-edged strategy aims for protective control following the triggering of the conflict – control that can be used to 'resolve' the conflict and take the transformation process in the desired direction. Conflict and the exorcism of conflict are thus both intrinsic components of the urban condition and embedded in its spectrum of political action. What is at issue is the creation of a situation that makes the application of the legislated norm possible. That way, the war ideology of the city, as described by Anthony Vidler (2001: 35–45), is not emanating from an external evil, but part of a programme that is transforming urban life under the aegis of safety.

Instead of engaging with a geopolitical situation that cuts across separate categories of violence and peace, the city of fear seeks to isolate and ghettoize zones of unregulated violence from purified and patrolled zones of harmony. This practice, which operates on a discursive and material level, results not only in the growing fragmentation of spatial co-existence, but also in the institutionalization of conflict in a policy of global division. Conflicts become the dominant framework for determining the way a certain territory and a certain population are to be perceived and governed. Using data from the US National Counterterrorism Center's Worldwide Incidents Tracking System, the UK has recently been rated as at 'medium risk' in the 2011 Terrorism Risk Index published by Maplecroft (2011), a UK-based risk advisory company. Taking these kinds of assessment down to a smaller level, property management companies in London have started to introduce terrorism insurance fees for leaseholders in areas where terrorist activity has in the recent past been present. Interestingly, the focus of attention here is less directed towards areas in which acts of terrorism have been carried out than towards neighbourhoods where people accused of these acts have been residing. Urban hotspots of terrorist activity are thus marked out by linking residents charged with planning acts of terrorism to the more general character of the urban area in which they live (Jones 2011). That way, pebble-dash fronted terrace houses in suburban England have, in the public imagination, become a surprisingly iconic image of global terrorism. Less controlled and bastioned than the dense metropolitan environments that are deemed to be vulnerable to terrorist attacks, suburban single-family homes, like the ones around the former Arsenal stadium in North London, are now regarded as hideout, breeding ground and launching pad of terrorist networks.

In the transition from the resourcefulness and self-made character of a working-class football club to a globally financed sports and media business, the hands-on involvement of local populations – the wooden gates squeezed between simple Victorian terrace houses, hand-made boards to announce the next match, hawking on sidewalks and driveways in which parked burger vans have to be accessed across neighbouring garden walls by climbing up and down household ladders – had to give way to the militarized logic of mass control and securitized corporate space. In a perverse twist of logic, the unregulated appropriation of the built environment through local people – urban spatializing practices that once formed the spiritual backbone of the British empire when predominantly Scottish workers at the Woolwich Arsenal Armament Factory founded the Arsenal Football Club – is now recast as its most feared enemy. Once an expression of the homely attachment of a local population to its football club, the merging between private ingenuity and public sphere is rendered one of the most challenging theatres for security policies. In this scenario, the formerly safe haven of the domestic turns into an impenetrable cell of suspect coalescence vis-à-vis the uncanny emptiness lurking beneath the surface of high-security public spaces. The safety upgrading and military build-up of the urban environment is thus an ever-changing platform for articulating conflicts – a very concrete form of conflictual practice that, at its worst, actively destroys risk-taking: not the speculative risk of economic transactions but the fundamental risk that lies at the heart of open-ended spatializing practices in the urban field. The tenacity of such risk-taking manifests the fact that there is no environment shapeable via counter-terrorism design which could take the sting out of the exposure to the unknown and the uncertain. Architecture can neither circumvent nor plan this experience just as it cannot fully condition an optimal structure of urban cohabitation. The way we live together is not a state that can be determined through security planning and therefore is available not as a blueprint but only as a political possibility.

2.10   Burger van selling from a front yard on one of the last match days at Arsenal's old Highbury Stadium, 2006.

FLAG STALLS AND FOOD VANS SET UP IN FRONT GARDENS

ARSENAL UNDERGROUND STATION

MOUNTED POLICE ON MATCH DAYS

1   'WELCOME TO HIGHBURY - THE HOME OF FOOTBALL'
     ACCESS TO NORTH BANK STAND

2   ACCESS TO WEST LOWER

3   ACCESS TO WEST UPPER

2.11   Neighbourhood of Arsenal's old Highbury stadium on match days prior to the move to the Emirates Stadium.

NOTES

1   The Home Office is the British government department responsible for leading the national effort to protect the public from terrorism, crime and anti-social behaviour.

2   The extended powers of the Anti-terrorism, Crime and Security Act 2001 were even used to freeze British financial assets in a failed Icelandic bank to recover depositors' money during the financial crisis in 2008.

REFERENCES

Beaumont-Thomas, B. 2010. London's New US Embassy Shows How Far Counter-Terrorist Architecture Has Come. *Bad Idea Magazine* [Online 24 February]. Available at: http://www.badidea.co.uk/2010/02/londons-new-us-embassy-shows-how-far-counter-terrorist-architecture-has-come/ [accessed: 26 September 2011].

Besson, S. 2005. *The Morality of Conflict: Reasonable Disagreement and the Law*. Oxford: Hart Publishing.

Blears, H. 2004. *The Politics of Decency*. London: Mutuo.

Booth, R. 2008. Home Office urges architects to design terror-proof buildings. *The Guardian*, 22 March, 18.

British Cabinet Office March, 2008. *The National Security Strategy of the United Kingdom: Security in an Interdependent World*. London: TSO.

Butler, J. 2004. *Precarious Life: The Powers of Mourning and Violence*. London and New York: Verso.

Castells, M. 2000. *The Information Age: Economy, Society and Culture*, Vol. I, 2nd edition. Oxford: Blackwell.

Deutsche, R. 2002 (1969). *Evictions: Art and Spatial Politics*. Cambridge, MA: MIT Press.

Filler, M. 2010. The New Tower of London. *The New York Review of Books* [Online 8 March]. Available at: http://www.nybooks.com/blogs/nyrblog/2010/mar/08/the-new-tower-of-london/ [accessed: 26 September 2011].

Giorgio Agamben, G. 2005. *State of Exception*. Chicago, IL: University of Chicago Press.

Hardt, M. and Negri, A. 2005. *Multitude*. London: Hamish Hamilton.

Jones, R. 2011. Residents face demand for terrorism insurance. *The Guardian* [Online 15 July]. Available at: http://www.guardian.co.uk/money/2011/jul/15/residents-terrorism-insurance [accessed: 26 September 2011].

Maplecroft 2011. Newly formed South Sudan joins Somalia, Pakistan, Iraq and Afghanistan at top of Maplecroft terrorism ranking – attacks up 15% globally [Online 3 August]. Available at: http://maplecroft.com/about/news/terrorism_index_2011.html [accessed: 26 September 2011].

Masco, J. 2010. Sensitive but Unclassified: Secrecy and the Counterterrorist State. *Public Culture*, 22(3), 433–63.

Minton, A. 2009. *Ground Control: Fear and Happiness in the Twenty-First-Century City*. London: Penguin.

New York City Police Department, Counterterrorism Bureau 2009. *Engineering Security: Protective Design for High Risk Buildings*.

O'Neill, S. and McGrory, D. 2006. *The Suicide Factory: Abu Hamza and the Finsbury Park Mosque*. London: Harper Perennial.

RIBA 2009. Winner of RIBA counter terrorism design competition announced [Online 8 May]. Available at: http://www.architecture.com/NewsAndPress/News/PolicyNews/Press/2009/WinnerOfCTDesignCompetitionAnnounced.aspx [accessed: 26 September 2011].

Smith, N. 1996. *The New Urban Frontier: Gentrification and the Revanchist City*. London and New York: Routledge.

Vidler, A. 2001. Photourbanism: Planning the City from Above and Below, in *A Companion to the City*, edited by G. Bridge and S. Watson. Oxford: Blackwell, 35–45.

3

Protecting the Population: Bureaucracy, Affectivity and Governing the Liverpool Blitz

Peter Adey (with Barry Godfrey and Dave Cox)

INTRODUCTION

From the first to the seventh of May 1941, bombing raids of varying intensity were made on Liverpool in the Luftwaffe's aerial campaign over Britain during the Second World War (Garnett 1995, Hughes 1993, Whittington-Egan 1987). The extent of the raids, wrote the Chief Constable in his final and overall report to the Watch Committee following the war, can be judged from the total destruction of 4,400 homes, serious damage to 16,400 homes and the slight damage to a further 45,000. Water was affected to such an extent that over 700 repairs were necessary, and there were 80 cases of damage to sewers. In the city alone, there were 235 unexploded bombs, causing 300 roads to be closed to traffic. And that was just Liverpool. Altogether the Blitz had 'left some 70,000 homeless people in the Merseyside region, almost 4,000 people were killed outright with a further 3,489 seriously injured' (Watch Committee 1945). Over 2,300 high explosive bombs had been dropped as well as a further 119 landmines, countless incendiary bombs, leaving 40,000 tonnes of shipping lying on the port's sea bed. Constituting another component of British 'blitz' experience (Gardiner 2010, Gardiner 2005, Calder 1991), Liverpool had gone through a particularly concentrated and intense period of destruction (Figure 3.1).

3.1   The effects of the Blitz on Liverpool.

Reports such as these scratch the surface of a raft of indexical measures to ascertain the material urban damage inflicted on the city. The product of an array of statistical measures and forms of knowledge capture, the numbers express a plethora of bureaucracy aimed at knowing the impact of the Blitz upon objects that were almost unknowable, resisting this gaze. This essay considers how such techniques, among with others, came to compose a kind of architecture. This was not simply in the concrete forms of bunkers or shelters, but as an apparatus of urban protection whose task was to ensure that the city would live on (Gollin 1984, Charlton 1935, Billing 1916).

Reversing the targeting of where to send a bomb, protection was a calculus whose variables included a range of geographical imaginations as well as contextual and conceptual narratives of human behaviour. These would drive a series of practices and bureaucratic techniques aimed at knowing and coordinating the most minute detail of the city's fabric and its people. The protecting apparatus of civil defence, air raid precautions, police, and war-time regulations grappled with the object of their focus: the population and particularly its morale. As an excess that appeared to escape the calculative rationalities of governance, morale was a dangerous remainder the local state attempted to colonise. More-than individual, morale seeped through and across collectives of people, but also formed an aspect of the stuff of life, as a 'thing-power' (Bennett 2010) of emotion and affect that was related to the intimate association between people and buildings, objects, food and fuel, but also the skein of bureaucracy and defence regulations intended to manage them (Woodward 2009). In other words, the apparatus took form, coalescing in hard materialities, a morass of paper work and correspondence, drawings of bureaucratic organisational connections – all embodied in fleshy feelings, urges and emotions.

MORALE, TARGETING AND PROTECTION

The manner of population protection describe here is many ways an inversion of the kinds of the matrices of representation, measurements and abstraction we are presented within scholarly discussions of the target and targeting. These are the mediated kill-chains Derek Gregory (2007) has explicated, processes through which the apparatus of aerial targeting builds and assembles an object identified within a population. The kind of aerial reconnaissance performed on Liverpool which enabled the Luftwaffe to target the city's ports and industrial buildings was one step in a chain of processes that would render a distanced place or thing legible. Within this 'chain', reports, detailed maps and plans, models, mosaics and prints would be circulated throughout the intelligence network allowing targets to be decided-upon (Ehlers 2009). For Gregory, what was performed through these processes was a 'concatenation of aerial views produced through a process of calculation that was also a process of abstraction' (Gregory 2011).

The Luftwaffe's aerial reconnaissance aircraft had taken large amounts of imagery of the UK from 1935, although following the war it was shown that their techniques of analysis were remarkably unsophisticated in relation to their Allied counterparts. Photos were compiled with already selected *Zielraume* or target areas of Liverpool which had been drawn from intelligence surveys and the 1928 Ordnance Survey Half-inch series maps of the area. In one series of targets the city's iconic Liver building, Cunard building and Dock Boarding Office were located, identified and marked as targets. Of course the traffic between processes of understanding the impact of bombing at home in order to predict what one might inflict abroad was also quite evident, and this process went two ways.[1] Eminent scientist Solly Zuckerman's studies on home morale in the wake of bombing in Birmingham and Hull are now famous in their mobilisation of Britain's 'morale' bombing strategy in Germany (Grayling 2006, Rau 2005, Zuckerman 1988).

The German bombers did not necessarily employ terror bombing tactics on Liverpool, as had been seen in parts of London and, of course, the retributive and vengeful British attacks on Hamburg and Dresden (Friedrich 2008), the zenith of Trenchard's colonial experience bombing villagers and villages in Persia (Satia 2008, Meilinger 1995, Omissi 1990). Liverpool was targeted in an effort to destroy the city's infrastructure and thus disrupt the nation's imports, exports and its ability to make war. This meant that the docks and their nearby worker housing came under an inevitable heavy and concentrated bombing. The means with which the city prepared and reacted to aerial bombardment saw the population identified not as an object of aggression, but as the subject of protection. Within Liverpool and elsewhere, this kind of calculus underpinned an architecture of preparedness, coordination and response. Unlike the gun batteries, balloon barrages and air force pilots, preparedness was not about stopping a bomb from falling, but the preparation of the ground for the event of if and when it would. Within protection, bombing census data, home intelligence reports, mass observation surveys, local press media bulletins, crime statistics and police constable reports, along with situation assessments, city engineer surveys, emergency committee actions, all fed into the wider analysis and understanding of the population's life and their way of life (see the Chart Room below, Figure 3.2).

Protection was concerned with the smooth running of essential services, stopping blockages in the network of communications, saving lives, preventing energy supplies being cut off or road networks damaged (O'Brien 1955). But it was understood that something held these infrastructures together, that enlivened material things with a manner of security (McCormack 2006). For food planners considering stockpiles of commodities across the city and boroughs, the news that 'corned beef' and 'condensed milk' was readily available and deliverable anywhere within the 'area within a few hours' – was considered especially 'good news' (Anon. 1940a). The same thing could also threaten with surprise, its unpredictability and its negativity – food's mobility could help prevent, for instance, the 'menace' of civilians attempting to get to their

3.2 The chart room of Liverpool's main control centre.

parents or friends bombed house. Residing somewhere within the relations between entities, this was morale: an object of governing that bore a very fuzzy relation to materials, infrastructure and the productive life of the community (Jones, Woolven et al. 2006, Mackay 2002).

Seeking to open up how morale is assembled as a target within contemporary military violence within the so-called 'war on terror', from Shock and Awe to counter-insurgency strategy, Anderson illustrates morale's duplicitous role as an assembled object of power (in his context as a target of aggression), and as 'a placeholder for the aleatory dynamics of living, a pre and post personal force that interrupts, perturbs and troubles fixed subjects and objects' (2010: 222). Morale may then work to enforce its relation as an object of power, or simultaneously unsettle and ultimately erode it.

AMBIGUITY AND THE POPULATION AS AN IDEA

Later in the war chief scientists such as Solly Zuckerman and colleagues at the Oxford Extra Mural Unit. under the auspices of the Ministry of Home Security would describe morale as an object which was 'not entirely a mathematical one …' an entity which 'should be considered from all angles and not merely the point of view of the statistician. Their main problem was morale's ambiguity and one of the case-studies they actually used was Liverpool, or more precisely Bootle. In fact, Liverpool's 1941 May Blitz and the huge damage of Bootle became one of the Ministry's case-studies under Dr Emmens' review of morale following the Baedeker raids in the middle of the war (Rothnie 1992). Bootle, while not part of these raids in 42 and 43, was compared to Greenock, York, Canterbury, Norwich, Exeter, and Clydebank. Although Emmens does not go too much into its rationale, it appears Bootle was identified as a place of bad morale and susceptibility, even though the boundaries between Bootle and Liverpool were readily slipped over in the official study.

Morale was both an 'an object distinct though necessarily related to, material damage' (Investigation of Moral and Industrial Effects). It was impossible to be more or 'less certain as regards morale, for we are still without definite knowledge of the point' the scientists would write in a Ministry of Home Security report. Directed 'for the purposes of its measurement and the application of knowledge concerning it', those who considered morale, were 'largely in the dark as to which analytical methods are likely to yield reliable quantitative estimates of air-raid morale. It seems unlikely that any simple index will be found, or than any very reliable single method ill be evolved, for the problem is composite' (Anon. 1941a). Turning morale into an object of understanding and eventual governance was understandably not that easy. And its objectification through these analytical processes of abstraction is perhaps more closely reflective of Anderson's (2010) concern to conceptualise how morale has become an 'object of power' that frustrates its submission to a 'passive, reduced, terminus of processes of abstraction and reduction'. Morale actually behaved far more unruly in the sense of object as obstacle.

These kinds of interpretation are clear to see within the debates that circulated through the British ministries and their scientists (Anon. 1944a, McLaine 1979). What the scientists could agree on, however, was that morale was about response to external potential or real threats.[2] According to Emmens' report, it was a 'a factor which influences the response of towns to air attack apart from the direct physical damage which they suffer', even if it was effected by that physical damage. But the ambiguity continues, for while morale is drawn quite apart from physical damage in Emmens' last sentence, in the next the puncture of a raid on morale was seen to be 'bound up with its other effects, and the relations between damage, number of casualties, etc'. Along with morale itself, all this had 'also to be considered' (Emmens 1943a). This gave towns such as Liverpool a kind of constitution, a dispositional propensity becoming subject to governmental intervention and modulation, even if it cannot be directly and distinctly touched (Massumi 2005). And the biophysical overtones scream loudly here, as raids would not then be understood to have caused certain symptoms of weakened morale, but rather to have acted as the stimulus that would reveal a pre-existing condition or potential weakness (Emmens 1943b).

Underpinning Liverpool's and the nation's debates over morale's malleability were conceptions of the population broken up into various types and groupings. As a geographic imaginary the population cannot be separated from the social context in which such imaginaries were born (see also Gregory 2004). Several social historians have shown how psychoanalysis became a dominant frame through which the social could be viewed in populist and more official public discourses (Overy 2009, Jones and Wessely 2005). While the official reports were careful not to attribute any kind of 'morale depression' to the 'inferiority' of a town's people', they express a certain analysis of certain cities and their populous as potentially dangerous. The treatment of Liverpool inherited the overtones of suspicion at migrant Dockers and unruly delinquents.

Newly introduced regulations and juridical discourse anticipated wide spread panic, deviancy, criminality and social disorder. The individual seems bifurcated into either the position of one who flees, or one who is shocked. Take the conversations of the judiciary, where it was not unusual for magistrates and local judges to rely upon an informal typology of the citizen, stigmatised and criminalised according to new regulation orders under the Air Raid Precautions Act, Civil Defence regulations and the Defence of the Realm (DORA). In the *Justice of the Peace*, one of the main venues for court discussion, the index of the citizen was conjured up, imagined and rendered according to speculations on the impact of legislation or experiences of cases passing through the courts. An idea of the individual was drawn here. The separation of the problematic population from the 'brave' or useful citizen was particularly fine. Take the description of the 'overbold' and selfish person':

> who will vitiate the air in a shelter with tobacco smoke he feels unable to do without. The drunkard in the shelter is worse still ... It is, however, comforting to find that pickpockets who plied their light fingers while the sirens are sounding have gone to prison to reflect on their sins. Air raids account for much. It now appears that bombs will affect cows and reduce the fatty content of their milk (Anon. 1940b: 480).

An amplification or exacerbation of already existing social stigmas, 'another troublesome person is the hunter of souvenirs', they wrote describing the looting of materials from crashed aircraft such as bombs and other munitions. These were 'unthinking fellows [who] rush in and destroy or purloin the evidence' such as a petrol gauge stolen from a crashed plane. The culprit, 'certainly ought to have known better, but there is a sad want of reflection in many people of adult age'. A more paternalistic kind of State is evoked here, necessary for the governing of its child-like population, unable to control their own whims and urges that impel them to act and to 'to cope effectively with the thoughtless conduct complained of' (Anon. 1940b). In Liverpool this kind of population threat was combined with the complexities of an incredibly mobile workforce of sailors, dockworkers, migrants, and the shadow of Irish Republican violence.

The threat of childhood delinquency, already an Edwardian suspicion of urban pollution and racial degeneracy (Thompson 1992), took particular hold in Liverpool. Research from the Tavistock clinic would emphasise the separation and uncertainty of the children's environment of school or home, which could be expressed through social delinquency. Directed curfews, confined only to Liverpool's children, was proposed in the House of Commons (*Hansard* 1940), while in the juvenile courts indictable offenses rose dramatically as did repeat offending. The threat was ever present but also inhabiting in futurity – a social problem which would grow up to become an even broader social nuisance were it not nipped in the bud.[3] Children and young people were a portion of the population perceived to be susceptible and of easy 'influence' from others in the darkened and hidden atmospheres of the Blitz (Gardiner and Imperial War Museum (Great Britain) 2005). A 14 year old girl is found paralytic, drunk in a shelter with an eighteen year old friend. They were said to have 'got into conversation in a shelter with two sailors'. Offered a bottle, 'she did not remember any more'. The Chairman of the court would remark, 'we are having quite a lot of trouble with girls who go into shelters and talk to soldiers, sailors and strange men' (Anon. 1940c).

Incidents including children often revolved around the literal architectures of protection of public shelters and war materials designed to safeguard Liverpool's citizenry, and constituted as places both meaningful and integral to the wider national war effort. Offences such as shelter hooliganism and damage were often reported (Anon. 1940d). The theft of the sorts of materials intended to shore-up public shelters was common place. Examples included children stealing sandbags, which were later found on their own home shelter roofs (Anon. 1940e), and the very bricks and mortar from shelters – the bricks valued at around 1d each. Tried in the juvenile courts, the theft of building materials on sites in-progress was commonplace (Anon. 1940f), as was a so-called 'outburst' of juvenile delinquency for whom the 'terrors' of the court and probation were no longer proving an effective remedy to the problem. With examples of boys breaking into factories and smashing machines and stories of boy gangsters armed with razor blades threatening shop staff, Liverpool's atmosphere of juvenile lawlessness was said to 'strike at the root of our national war production' (Anon. 1940g, Anon. 1940h, Anon. 1940i). Serious offences, particularly stealing for many children resulted in enforced corporal punishment. In one example, three boys aged between eight and eleven were ordered to receive six strokes of the birch (Anon. 1940j).

NETWORKS, ASSEMBLY AND THE AFFECTS OF BUREAUCRACY

In 1935 Liverpool's city representatives had come together for a conference with the Assistant Under Secretary of State in charge of Air Raid Precautions: The conference goers were advised that they should 'consider how organisations in their areas could be adapted to meet various emergencies in time of emergency' (Anon. 1935).

In many narratives of the Blitz and indeed within Liverpool we hear how the air raid warden was one of the key nodes of a hub and spoke network of preparation (see below). This was a figure that sought to hold the community together by their example. As a heroic and particularly emotionally controlled individual these subjects would regulate and perform the maintenance of morale – the collective affects – of the household or neighbourhood (see Adey 2010, Ministry of Home Security 1938). But in the raft of preparations under Civil Defence, Air Raid Precautions and other defence regulations, how 'to meet various emergencies in time of emergency' (Anon.

1935) was also the task of the city leaders and other civic personnel and public servants from the local authority. It is in this context where the logic of the heroic individual acting within the apparatus of urban protection is blurred. Instead it is the bureaucrats who gain the unlikely status as the heroes. They are portrayed as civic leaders ready to forge on, wielding the network of preparedness together by leadership and coordination. Doing battle against the evils of bureaucracy. Although as with the wardens (Figure 3.3), these figures also gained a status of antagonism too.

Before the bombing on Merseyside began, Liverpool's arrangements for preparedness meant encouraging inter-authority and organisational working, drawing on existing networks of relationships and building new ones. The balance seemed to be heavily in favour of a 'local solution', government empowering local authorities with the 'responsibility for the restoration of the life of the community', local context taking favour over an attempt to 'meet the needs of every situation' with pre-arranged national plans (Anon. 1941b). Certainly, all response could

3.3   Liverpool's civic leaders were often pictured as beacons of coordination.

not be 'improvised on the spur of the moment', wrote the Birkenhead Town Clerk as the town drew up its Air Raid Precautions document for approval, and so huge quantities of advance plans would be made (Anon. 1938a). Many of these drew upon the strength of Liverpool's existing relationships, such as its Mutual Assistance Pacts already forged within the Co-Operative Movement and its network of suppliers and distributors, wholesalers and retailers of food and clothing, in the Merseyside region (see also Birchall 1994). Those pacts would be drawn into plans for food security at wider city and county level planning for the event of the necessary coordination. This was 'not for emergency purposes', but 'EXTREME EMERGENCY PURPOSES' read one report, anticipating a wide-level attack on Liverpool and its surrounding borough's and pre-empting the actual raids that would follow a year later (Anon. 1940a).

Developing their own procedures and training suitable for the geographic, administration and organisational context, however, was a duel against a bureaucratic machine. 'It has been said', wrote one report that:

> 'The hour produces the man', That was true in Liverpool, for no sooner was it apparent that the danger of enemy air raids was no longer remote in time, than the leader of the City council, Alderman A.E. Shennan J P, took upon his shoulders the responsibility for cutting the Governmental 'red tape' which had hitherto hampered the actions of our ARP Committee (Anon. 1938b).

Held back by non-decisions and the hesitations of central government, it was the timely and decisive civil servant who battles the bureaucracy and release the ties that bind the hands of local organisation and response.

The heroes of preparedness were those who would not shrink from cutting red tape, acting speedily, making good decisions. Emphasis is played on the assembly of Liverpool's protection network, the speed of the assemblage to come together within reports which focused on the complexity of the logistics operations in delivering services to the citizens of Liverpool or distributing objects for the war-effort. The way in which these cold and logistical forms of mobility and coordination, seemed to stand for the promissory speed and assembly of a more general protection effort in the face of an emergency. Take the way gas masks were discussed in one press article:

> the government had millions of these in store at Aintree for the inhabitants of the north-west region, which covers a wide area. First of all, it became necessary to transport from the stores at Aintree the 800,000 masks which our citizens required. This task was performed by the Corporations own vehicles, and they were conveyed to the Lister Drive Power Station. It is natural to assume that these masks, which were in three sizes, were all ready to be handed out. Nothing of the kind. The parts of which each individual mask is constructed had to be assembled, and the organisations of that task fell upon our Civic rulers … The parts of which each individual mask is constructed had to be assembled, and the organisations of that task fell upon our Civic rulers. Speed in assembly was vital, and machinery had to be constructed to enable the assembly of the masks to be accomplished in the shortest possible time (Anon. 1938b).

Through the logic of protection-as-assembly, protection was more than putting gas-masks or Anderson shelters together, it also involved the right sort of speed and energy.

Like most cities, Liverpool's response was organised into seven separate services operated by Air Raid precautions organisations, they were: first aid parties, ambulance, ambulance cars, light rescue parties, heavy rescue parties, decontamination squads and gas identification

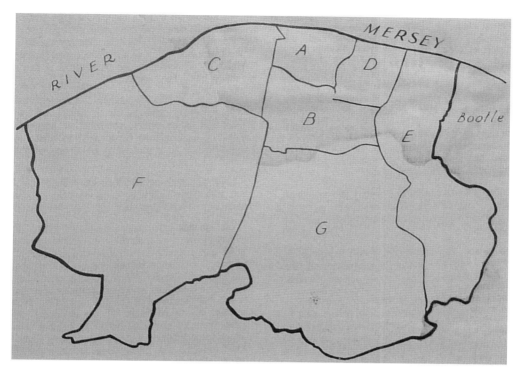

3.4 Liverpool's area of emergency coordination

squads. These would be overseen by the city's Emergency Committee and operationally by a main control centre. The city was divided geographically into divisional report and control centres which had sector posts within those divisions and with an average of 12 sector posts per square mile of the city with many more in the highly populated ones (Figure 3.4). Each divisional control centre had a fixed line telephone to the local headquarters of each service and the main control centre which was divided into three: a main control room, chart room, and a message room (Figure 3.5, see also Anon. 1940k).

Overseeing all of this, the emergency committee and its sub-groups saw their primary concern to be that of coordination. Coordination and yet more coordination. And even while, 'considerable coordination had already taken place … it was necessary, in view of the great urgency of the matter, to explore the subject still further', explained one spokesperson to the *Liverpool Daily Post* (Anon. 1939a). Outside of the city, the smaller towns and boroughs of Bootle and Birkenhead, for instance, had their own Emergency Committees who would work in tandem with Liverpool's. Backup services were required should the communication networks breakdown. In Liverpool even 'cyclist citizens' were proposed to form a squad of cyclist messengers who would maintain communications should others fail (Anon. 1939b).

Of course the techniques or technologies of coordination did not necessarily amplify but were required to subdue response and did so through their considerable abstraction of the intelligence they gathered and distributed. Between these organisations, huge flurries of situation reports would be generated and passed on to pinpoint locations of incidents, for instance, a railway cutting between Overbury Street and Kingslake. Hit by a high explosive bomb, the main railway line traffic was suspended. Evacuation was unnecessary. In another message, a foot has been found on the corner of Fisher and Grafton. In the following

3.5 The 'nerve centre' of Liverpool's chartroom, where clerks focussed intently on the 'disposition' of the personnel.

sentence, a street lamp at the corner of Brindley Street and Grafton is damaged, a pipe is fractured. In these evaluations of damage circulated through the network of coordination and response, the technologies restrict information to a minimal humanism, flattening out an equivalence between the body of the population and the infrastructure and urban fabric it has become inseparable from. As an immediately more fleshy, yet less human form of reporting, the feeling of death, or loss, or the mess and rubble experienced at the site, is engineered into a distinctively colder and more abstract manner of affective materiality – now made graspable and communicable through the city's networks of communications.

The coldness of these messages has to be then compared with the wider strategy of censoring news of air-raids from many provincial cities such as Liverpool. This was a strategy that during the May raids led to wild rumours that the city had submitted to the destruction and a state of martial law was in place. The rumour led to one man being sentenced to a month's imprisonment (Anon. 1941b). Indeed, with almost 18 per cent of the population of Bootle, only four miles north of the city, having been reported to have trekked at some point during the raids, Emmens' reports on morale, suggested that morale 'was said to be good, but … it should be watched' (Emmens 1943a).

With the sombre tones of the communiqués other areas of the city's response had to enliven and ignite the city and its people to the principles of preparing for the emergency of aerial war. This was particularly the case when the city had to repeatedly rehearse and repeat the performance of just how these networks could come together, demonstrating what Kathleen Woodward describes as the two main oscillating affects of modern bureaucracies: urgency and its partner, boredom. Exercises over bombing raids and their response would walk a shaky path between being too urgent (see Figures 3.6 and 3.7), or slipping from exigency into fatigue precisely because of the procedural nature of their activities. The city's training centre for air raid precautions designed and ran numerous exercises that were very careful not to bore their participants should they lose interest in the process. Turning the approved protocols of putting out a fire, or even putting on a gas mask or decontamination suit into a staged performance, the repetition of the exercise would threaten to lose the attention of its players, which could harm their training. 'Every endeavour', wrote one report, 'is made during the course of instruction to capture and hold the attention of the trainees by appealing to their imaginations'. The goal was to set about 'impressing upon their minds that this is not mere play-acting but something real and of vital importance', 'the sense of realism' is introduced at this point in order to combat the monotony of the work'.

Exercises were also held outside Liverpool and Merseyside, the North West performing its role within a wider network of regional preparedness. Located at the regional war offices situated in Manchester's underground regional control room, preparedness – complete to the last detail, could be practiced. In the position to potentially form an embryonic government should it be needed the regional offices acted similarly to Liverpool's control centre but just at a higher scale. The centre was able to coordinate all actions and make decisions, allowing any events that would overcome the capacity of Liverpool to deal with, to be escalated upwards to larger and more resource laden scales of authority.

During one exercise of the regional control room, the reported descriptions of the process of receiving and recording messages and relaying others which would have been practiced by the players, is accentuated by descriptions of the complexities of the processes, and the manner in which the exercises were designed to ramp up stress and tension (see Davis 2007 for exercises in a cold war setting; and Anderson and Adey 2011 for exercises in today's context of Civil Contingencies). The exercise produced what a report called a 'desperate complication' as mutual assistance was required for medical aid in Chester, 'to test reactions during the stress of events in Liverpool a message was sent at once to the local control in that city requesting the dispatch of six ambulances'.

Attention was maintained by the possibility of surprise, mimicking the uncertainties of a real raid. Although 'the wardens knew that something would happen' they were explicitly given 'no knowledge of what they might be expected to do until the very moment they received their instructions' (Anon. 1940l).

3.6   Trainees learn to use stirrup pumps at the fire service training school.

3.7   Fire-bomb fighting at the pier-head.

CONCLUSION: ARCHITECTURES OF PROTECTION

Protection happened through morale and on morale. Protection was not meant to stop the bomber, but to act upon an interval within which preparations that were intended to avoid the 'crippling of the nation's war efforts' and the 'paralysis of the life of the community' could be performed (Report of Committee on Evacuation 1937–1938). Acting on those 'collective, ambiguous and indeterminate' affects of morale through the systems of response and preparedness was to construct an environment which could support life and the war effort.

How did they do this? In the example of Liverpool it seems clear that what was at stake for civil protection schemes was how to grapple with their population indexed with two inseparable values. Firstly of affect: the populations feelings, moods and sentiments that made up other collectives of feeling known as morale. The question was how to manage these sentiments often set against dominant imaginaries or typologies of the population expected to behave and respond in different ways. Second, these were in-turn inextricably linked, albeit imperfectly measured, in relation to the city's capacities of material production, mobility, distribution and its ability to provide essential services. Circulations had to keep on going. The port needed to keep on moving. Feeling and infrastructural mobilities become indistinct as the material labour of felt emotion and affectivity.

We might see the techniques of protection as an apparatus or perhaps an architecture, both literal and metaphoric, that can be characterised by three interrelated elements. First, the architecture produced an envelopment of safety dominated by several kinds of geometry; it was portrayed as a safety net, a blanketing wealth of bureaucracy; it distributed help through networks and systems, and it coordinated activity by hierarchies and strong leaders at the helm of those networks. Second, the architecture involved literal spaces and buildings made meaningful in the context of the blitz, as shelters became dark and dangerous in some areas, and sacred places of withdrawal and safety in others. Finally, the civil protection architecture was about assembly and enactment. It was built, and as a building is built and constructed by morale boosting activities, it was maintained through repetitive acts, supporting and sustaining the apparatus. All these elements could be seen as abstractive and statistical, taking the form of procedural spaces of plans, reports, regulations and protocols, which to use Julian Reid's terms, see human life as 'logistic' (2007). But they were particularly expressive too; affective and connective energies that made relations concrete and new interactions possible.

NOTES

1   Official social historian Richard Titmus would comment on the expertise sought from the Colonial Office, requisitioning their knowledge of crowd control for the Committee of Imperial Defence in the middle of preparations for the Second World War (Titmuss 1950).

2   Within the Ministry of Information surveys on morale and public opinion, morale mattered because of what it could do. For Stephen Taylor, director of the Home Intelligence department, measuring morale was thus 'ultimately measured not by what a person thinks or says, but by what he does and how he does it'. Morale itself was understood to be completely unimportant unless it stimulated action and movement. According to Ian McLaine, various Ministry psychologists defined morale to be 'of value only insofar as it facilitates or promotes favourable action' (McLaine 1979: 8).

3   So concerned were the city's leaders and philanthropists at the future of Liverpool's youth, that they setup the country's first Civil Defence Cadet Corps in Liverpool, an organisation that took particular care over disciplining its cadets and inculcating the collective spirit of the war effort.

REFERENCES

Adey, P. 2010. *Aerial Life: Spaces, Mobilities, Affects*. Oxford: Wiley-Blackwell.

Anderson, B. 2010. Morale and the affective geographies of the 'war on terror'. *Cultural Geographies*, 17(2), 219–36.

Anderson, B. and Harrison, P. 2010. The promise of non-representational theories. B. Anderson and P. Harrison (eds), *Taking-Place: Non-Representational Theories and Geography*. London: Ashgate.

Anderson, B. and Adey, P. 2011. Affect and security: Exercising emergency in 'UK civil contingencies'. *Environment and Planning D: Society and Space*, 29(6), 1092–109.

Anon. 1938a. Draft: Air Raid Precautions Scheme, The Town Clerk, County Borough of Birkenhead, Birkenhead Archives.

Anon. 1938b. How crisis needs were dealt with in Liverpool. *The Liverpolitan*, October.

Anon. 1935. Air raid measures. *Liverpool Post*, 8 November.

Anon. 1939a. Emergency committee: Conference on coordination. *Liverpool Daily Post*, 9 September.

Anon. 1939b. Corps of Cyclist messengers. *Liverpool Daily Post*, 12 October.

Anon. 1940a. Instructions Regarding a Combined Blitz on Birkenhead and Liverpool: Emergency Precautions, December, Birkenhead Archives.

Anon. 1940b. Justice of the Peace, 31 August: 480.

Anon. 1940c. Girls in shelters. *Liverpool Echo*, 11 November.

Anon. 1940d. Shelter hooligans. *Liverpool Echo*, 6 December.

Anon. 1940e. Boys take sandbags. *Liverpool Echo*, 23 August.

Anon. 1940f. Boys who stole bricks. *Liverpool Echo*, 2 August.

Anon. 1940g. Sabotage by boys. *Liverpool Echo*, 8 August.

Anon. 1940h. Juvenile crime. *Liverpool Echo*, 8 August.

Anon. 1940i. Boy gangsters with razors. *Liverpool Echo*, 15 August.

Anon. 1940j. Boys to be birched. *Liverpool Echo*, 24 October.

Anon. 1940k. The civil defence of Liverpool. *The Liverpolitan*, January: 10–11.

Anon. 1940l. Down in the war room. *Liverpool Daily Post*, 1 April.

Anon. 1941a. The total effect of air raids. Ministry of Home Security Report 2770, HO 199/453 TNA.

Anon. 1941b. Lying war rumours. *The Guardian*, 17 May.

Anon. 1941c. Coordinating Action After a 'Blitz'. *Government Chronicle*, 6 September.

Anon. undated. Home intelligence reports on opinion and morale 1940–1944. London: Ministry of Information.

Anon. undated. Investigation of Morale and Industrial Effects of Enemy Bombing. Ministry of Home Security, HO199 453.

Bennett, J. 2010. *Vibrant Matter: A Political Ecology of Things*. Durham, NC: Duke University Press.

Bialer, U. 1980. *The Shadow of the Bomber: The Fear of Air Attack and British Politics, 1932–1939*. London: Royal Historical Society.

Billing, N.P. 1916. *Air War: How to Wage It*. London: Gale & Polden, 74.

Birchell, J. 1994. *Co-op: The People's Business*. Manchester: Manchester University Press.

Calder, A. 1991. *The Myth of the Blitz*. London: J. Cape.

Charlton, L.E.O. 1935. *War from the Air, Past, Present, Future*. London: T. Nelson & Sons.

Coaffee, J. 2009. *The Everyday Resilience of the City: How Cities Respond to Terrorism and Disaster*. Basingstoke: Palgrave Macmillan.

Collier, S.J. and Lakoff, A. 2008. Distributed preparedness: The spatial logic of domestic security in the United States. *Environment & Planning D: Society & Space*, 26(1), 7–28.

Davis, T. 2007. *Stages of Emergency*. Durham, NC: Duke University Press.

Ehlers, R. 2009. *Targeting the Third Reich: Air Intelligence and the Allied Bombing Campaigns*. Lawrence, KS: University Press of Kansas.

Emmens, C. 1943a. A note on the meaning and measurement of the morale of towns in relation to air-raids, HO 199 4563, The National Archive (TNA).

Emmens, C. 1943b The Assessment of Air-Raid Morale From the Local Press Home Intelligence, Social Survey and Damage Reports in Britain. HO 199/4563, TN: 1.

Friedrich, J. 2008. *The Fire: The Bombing of Germany, 1940–1945*. Chichester; New York: Columbia University Press.

Gardiner, J. 2010. *The Blitz: The British Under Attack*. London: Harper Collins.

Gardiner, J. 2005. *Wartime: Britain 1939–1945*. London: Review.

Gardiner, J. and Imperial War Museum (Great Britain) 2005. *The Children's War: The Second World War Through the Eyes of the Children of Britain*. London: Portrait in association with the Imperial War Museum.

Garnett, R. 1995. *Liverpool in the 1930s and the Blitz*. Preston: Palatine.

Gollin, A. 1984. *No Longer an Island: Britain and the Wright Brothers 1902–1909*. London: Heinemann.

Graham, S. 2010. *Cities Under Siege: The New Military Urbanism*. London; New York: Verso.

Grayling, A.C. 2006. *Among the Dead Cities: Was the Allied Bombing of Civilians in WWII a Necessity or a Crime?* London: Bloomsbury.

Gregory, D. 2011. 'Doors into nowhere': Dead cities and the natural history of destruction. P. Meusberger, M. Heffernan and E. Wunde (eds), *Cultural Memories*. Heidelberg: Springer Verlag.

Gregory, D. 2007. 'In another time-zone, the bombs fall unsafely': Targets, civilians and late modern war. *Arab World Geographer*, 9, 88–112.

Gregory, D. 2004. *The Colonial Present: Afghanistan, Palestine, and Iraq*. Oxford; Malden, MA: Blackwell.

Hansard. 1940. Children (Curfew) 9 July, vol. 362: 1082.

Hughes, J. 1993. *Port in a Storm: The Air Attacks on Liverpool and its Shipping in the Second World War*. Birkenhead: Merseyside Port Folios.

Jones, E. and Wessely, S. 2005. *Shell Shock to PTSD: Military Psychiatry from 1900 to the Gulf War*. Hove: Psychology Press.

Jones, E., Woolven, R., Durodié, B. and Wessely, S. 2006. Public panic and morale: Second World War civilian responses re-examined in the light of the current anti-terrorist campaign. *Journal of Risk Research*, 9(1), 57–73.

Lakoff, A. 2008. The generic biothreat, or, how we became unprepared. *Cultural Anthropology*, 23(3), 399–428.

Mackay, R. 2002. *Half the Battle: Civilian Morale in Britain During the Second World War*. Manchester: Manchester University Press.

Massumi, B. 2005. Fear (The Spectrum Said). *Positions*, 31(1), 31–48.

Massumi, B. 2002. *Parables for the Virtual: Movement, Affect, Sensation*. Durham, NC: Duke University Press.

McCormack, D. 2006. For the love of pipes and cables: A response to Deborah Thien. *Area*, 38, 330–32.

McLaine, I. 1979. *Ministry of Morale: Home Front Morale and the Ministry of Information in World War II*. London: Allen and Unwin.

Meilinger, P.S. 1995. Trenchard and 'morale bombing': The evolution of Royal Air Force doctrine before World War II. *The Journal of Military History*, 60, April, 243–70.

Ministry of Home Security. 1938. *The Duties of Air Raid Wardens*. London: HMSO.

O'Brien, T. 1955. *Civil Defence*. London: HMSO.

Omissi, D.E. 1990. *Air Power and Colonial Control: The Royal Air Force 1919–1939*. Manchester: Manchester University Press.

Overy, R.J. 2009. *The Morbid Age: Britain Between the Wars*. London: Allen Lane.

Rau, E. 2005. Combat science: The emergence of Operational Research in World War II. *Endeavour*, 29(4), 156–61.

Reid, J. 2007. *The Biopolitics of the War on Terror: Life Struggles, Liberal Modernity and the Defence of Logistical Societies*. Manchester: Manchester University Press.

Report of Committee on Evacuation', 1937–1938 CMD 5837, HMSO.

Rothnie, N. 1992. *Baedeker Blitz: Hitler's Attack on Britain's Historic Cities*. London: Ian Allen.

Satia, P. 2008. *Spies in Arabia: The Great War and the Cultural Foundations of Britain's Covert Empire in the Middle East*. New York; Oxford: Oxford University Press.

Thomas, D. 2003. *An Underworld at War: Spivs, Deserters, Racketeers and Civilians in the Second World War*. London: John Murray.

Thompson, P.R. 1992. *The Edwardians: The Remaking of British Society* (2nd edn). London; New York: Routledge.

Thrift, N. 2004. Intensities of feeling: Towards a spatial politics of affect. *Geografiska annaler*, 86(B) 1, 57–78.

Titmuss, R.M. 1950. *Problems of Social Policy*. London: HMSO.

Watch Committee for the City of Liverpool. 1945. Report of the Police Establishment and the State of Crime for the Severn Years Ending 31 December, 1945. Liverpool Chief Constable's Office, Liverpool. LRO. 353 WAT.

Whittington-Egan, R. 1987. *The Great Liverpool Blitz*. Parkgate: Gallery.

Woodward, K.M. 2009. *Statistical Panic: Cultural Politics and Poetics of the Emotions*. Durham, NC; London: Duke University Press.

Zuckerman, S.Z. 1988. *From Apes to Warlords: The Autobiography (1904–1946) of Solly Zuckerman*. London: Collins.

4

Funky Bunkers: The Post-Military Landscape as a Readymade Space and a Cultural Playground

Per Strömberg

INTRODUCTION

With the move of Western hemisphere industries to other parts of the world in the 1960s, vacant factories, industrial ruins and disengaged waterfront areas became desirable urban areas. In the 'post-industrial society' of today, reusing buildings is a widespread strategy to create attractive and exciting urban environments for trendy citizens. Old industrial buildings such as factories, mines and warehouses have become the new temples of culture, creating space for art and cultural events such as galleries, concert halls, amphitheatres and museums, as well as commercial activities for marketing, shopping centres, restaurants and lifestyle hotels. Place-making and staging based on the principle of expressive creativity through reuse and recycling are critically important to the cultural economy.

Similarly, since the end of the Cold War deserted bunkers from different periods of time have become a cultural playground for tourism and the creative industries. At Gotland, Sweden, an old bunker has been turned into a design hotel while in Stockholm, a Cold War bunker functions as a setting for archaeological exhibitions. The 'Bunker' as a building and heritage type seems as much a spatial resource for the growing cultural economy as the 'Factory' is. The principle of this transformation act is more or less based on appropriation. This is a well-established art practice of borrowing or stealing, making new uses for and changing the meaning of the objects, images and artefacts of a culture. But even if the creative reuse of worn-out buildings and waste spaces is a common strategy today, few scholars have theoretically considered the spatial aspect of such aesthetical appropriation, especially concerning military bunkers. Accordingly, using a series of converted military bases and bunkers in Scandinavia as case studies, this chapter explores the role, conditions and techniques of creative reuse, the nature of aestheticization processes and the compulsion, within a contemporary consumer society, to transform the built legacies of the Cold War into 'funky bunkers'.

As art is a fundamental aspect of aestheticization processes in society (Welch 1996: 2), art theory is useful as a tool to explore the cultural alchemy of appropriation. It can be said that the appropriation techniques of converted buildings begin to resemble some of the means used by the modernist avant-garde to express new meanings and revolt against the art of the bourgeoisie in the beginning of the twentieth century. Today, appropriation is central to artists' critique of the contemporary world and their visions for alternative futures. Arguably the notion of 'readymade space', or alternatively 'found space', is useful as a theoretical metaphor in order to describe, categorize and analyse practices of creative reuse and, more precisely, to explain how, by playing with the original contexts, worn-out everyday spaces can acquire new functions, meanings and appearances in the cultural economy.

'POST'-SOCIETIES

One of the preconditions in the creative reuse of buildings is structural changes in society in which previous functions take new objectives. Reuse of buildings is not an utterly new phenomenon: temples, fora and amphitheatres, for example, were commonly reused in Rome as dwellings after the fall of the Roman Empire. Historically speaking, crisis and structural change are the common reasons such reuse. The de-industrialization of the last decades is an example of such fundamental change. Daniel Bell coined the notion of 'post-industrial society' to describe the economic changes in which he saw a transition from a manufacturing-based to a service-based economy, a diffusion of national and global capital, and mass privatization (1973: 14).

In many ways, the 'post-military society' parallels the post-industrial condition to become a defining characteristic of the end of the twentieth century: a structural transition from the Cold War era. But just as post-industrialism does not abolish industry, or post-modernism modernity, so post-militarism, while it transforms the military and militarism, does not remove them from central positions in the social structure (Shaw 1991: 184–5). The contemporary war on terrorism has led to a 'new military urbanism' for which emerging anti-terrorism infrastructures are implemented. There is, however, no longer the constant military preparation for total nuclear war (Graham 2010). One consequence of these structural changes is the large quantities of buildings which have become vacant after being shut down, with their functions replaced and relocated to other geographical areas of the world. This vanishing process, the ethnographer Robert Willim stresses, creates a mental distance from the former activities. This is a crucial condition for processes of aesthetization, where former activities are redefined to relate to condition of consumption, entertainment, excitement, joy and recreation. A new culture heritage has gradually been established by heritage institutions in conjunction with a romantic approach and an aesthetic predilection for decay, decline and the rustic. These processes imply a kind of 'cultural sorting': practices of choosing and extracting positive qualities from their contexts (Willim 2008: 123–4). The post-military landscape of bunkers and rusting barbed wires is often regarded with the same romanticism and with similar preservation ideologies and economic interests as the post-industrial landscape (Strömberg 2010).

As perhaps exemplified in Paul Virilio's (1975/1995) seminal text *Bunker Archaeology*, the military-historical landscape of bunkers has in many ways been rediscovered and explored in the same way as abandoned industries. The industrial as well as the martial materiality of such landscapes contain many connotations which today are aesthetically explored and exploited in new, fancy contexts. As Nikos Papastergiadis remarks, the dustbins of history have become the key sites for cultural renewal (2006: 466). Thus, the 'com-post-modernism' of today provides an alternative type of innovation.[1]

THE BUNKER AS A FUNKY MAKEOVER

The fortress of Fårösund illustrates how bunkers and military spaces can be modified in one way or another: the bunker as a 'makeover'. The fortress was originally built in 1886 as a battery with the purpose to secure the northern part of Gotland from being occupied or used as a shelter by any other nation during the English-Russian war. The battery was one of three that were finally taken out of service in 1936, but continuously served as a military depot until 1993. After ten years of decay, two entrepreneurs proposed a luxury conference hotel with security classification for summits, reachable by private plane or helicopter in less than an hour from the entire Baltic Sea area, in the unique environment of a nineteenth-century fortress and battery (interview with Hammerstedt). They were supported by the building's owners the Swedish State's National Property Board (SFV) whose aim was not only to make the building available as a heritage site but also, and more importantly, to support local business initiatives – part of a series measures to counteract the unemployment caused by the closing of the military bases on the island (Göthe 2003: 2).[2] A condition for the reuse of the historic building was that it must be completely reversible. Therefore, the hotel was extended with removable corridors of glass and metal with adjoining parts of the batteries connected by a central annex. Today, you can sleep in one of the former bomb shelters furnished as fancy hotel rooms and enjoy a gourmet dinner prepared by fashionable chefs at the place where artillery pieces once were positioned to command the sea. The whole concept is adapted to a military theme. Everything is low-key in colour, scale and finishes: grey and green. Raw materials of local limestone and steel, articulated in a severe minimalism, arouse 'post-military' relaxation in the bunker lounge.

4.1   The fortress of Fårösund as a funky makeover. Rusted barbed wires and deserted defense obstacles still encircles the fortress as a part of the design scenery.

4.2   Post-military relaxing in the bunker lounge.

The bunker is embedded with grass growing on the top of the surrounding embankments. Rusted barbed wires and deserted defence obstacles encircle the whole fortress. There is an exchange of aura in the aesthetic interplay between the martial hardware and the arty software as the designed minimalism merges with fossils from the military era. The bunker is converted into a stylish coulisse for the hotel business where designer products become aesthetic weaponry and branding ammunition. The cultural alchemy of the makeover mixes the high with the low, exclusivity with military severity. The point of departure for this whole venture is an aesthetically-grounded postmodern neo-romanticism which turns rust and concrete into appealing gestures of victory over the site's former activities.

Another illuminating example of bunkers as makeovers are the architectural installations created by *Bunkerologi,* a group of artists and architects, on the Lista peninsula in southern Norway. At Lista, there are approximately 400 mass-produced military structures of the Atlantic Wall dating from the German occupation during the Second World War. In recent years, some of the bunkers have been reused as tool sheds, stables, vegetable stores or playhouses, incorporated into new built structures, or granted preservation status. *Bunkerologi's* projects are based on the principle of adding; by simply adding new elements they hope to bring out new dimensions at the same time as the historical building is preserved, an exploration of the post-military landscape as a future resource for new purposes and new architecture.

In the spring of 2005, *Bunkerologi* designed what is today *Field Station Nesheim*, a new structure attached to the top of a military sand silo. The field station is an alternative kind of heritage attraction in the post-military landscape. Over time, it has become a popular shelter

4.3   A former German sand silo turned in to a bunkerological 'field station' at Lista, Norway.

for hunters and local hikers visiting the beach next to the site. Like the many of their other bunkerological projects, the installations invite visitors to climb and physically experience the bunkers in new ways. The added wooden structure was built in collaboration with the local landlord and sponsored by local businesses and authorities. Indeed, the group's method is to work closely with local groups. According to Alf Waage, one of the *Bunkerologi*'s members, people's reactions to the bunkers reflect the duality of the projects themselves: a fascination for the unusual forms and an awareness that they once have been instruments of war. He regards *Bunkerologi* as a comment on current preservation practices; a combination of preservation and pedagogical aspects of heritage and regional development and future use. Finally, it is about local communication, local initiative and changing local habits and attitudes (interview with Waage 2010; see also *Byggekunst* 2006: 48–53).

Both projects, *Bunkerologi* and the bunker-hotel at Fårösund, are based on reversibility. The makeovers are provisional, but might also become permanent. While the bunker-hotel has an entrepreneurial venture character, the *Bunkerologi*-project is thus far based on an artistic idealism. The point of departure is, however, quite similar, namely to find new objects and different atmospheres to profile both of their businesses: the bunker environment offers a unique hotel concept which is hard to copy, while the projects of *Bunkerologi* occupy an experimental niche for the members which promotes *Stiv kuling*, an architecture practice run by three of the group's members. Their common interest in the post-military landscape could

4.4   Bunkerological
construction works.

also be regarded in the light of an over-exploitation of reused industrial environments. There is always a risk of aesthetic inflation; that 'industrial cool' becomes trivial in view of constantly shifting cycles of taste. 'Funky bunkers' might be an alternative as an image-highlighter or, as just another ruin-aesthetic theme explored through similar recycling practices.

THE BUNKER AS A FUNKY STAGE

This section considers unaffected space where the bunker functions as a funky stage and serves a metaphor for activities such as events, exhibitions, branding and role-playing. One example is the old subterranean air-base at Säve, Gothenburg, where an experience-based aviation centre, *Aeroseum* has been created. Here, visitors are able to look at and try out old aircraft and helicopters, both virtually and in reality. The air-base complex is a gigantic subterranean air-dock constructed during the Cold War and which was supposed to protect the Swedish Air Force against a nuclear attack. In addition to guided tours and other activities, *Aeroseum* offers possibilities for conferences and corporate events and its somewhat spectacular environment is increasingly being used for television and commercials, especially for cars. In 2010, the public broadcaster, Sveriges Television used the airbase as a setting for the concert of the week. Meanwhile, the world premiere of the new Saab 9-3 was held at *Aeroseum* in 2007. As seen in Figure 4.5, a whole range of Saabs were staged and exposed with elaborate lighting and video projections.

Suggestive bunker facilities like *Aeroseum* have the ability to appeal to the senses by their austere, dark grandeur. According to the museum's director, companies think that the bunker provides an exciting and extraordinary set for their events (interview with Eliasson). Hence, the subterranean air-dock works as a funky scenography in which to stage newness. Furthermore, the Cold War story constitutes a backdrop to the story that Saab wants to tell. The site and its intimate relationship with aerodynamics, plain functional design and the high speeds of airplanes, all become metaphors for what Saab – a company with roots in aeroplane technologies and design – has to offer. Two stories overlap and intertwine and thus, one could speak of a 'narrative convergence' that encourages mutual cooperation, a win-win situation of corporate symbiosis (Strömberg 2009: 230). The marketing event of Saab at *Aeroseum* exemplifies the 'catwalk economy' where brands are constantly looking for new spectacular environments and suitable technologies: choreographies of selling which appropriate unexpected contexts and unique scenographies (Löfgren 2005: 62).

Another example of a bunker serving as a stage for other narratives is the temporary exhibition of the Chinese terracotta army located in a Cold War bunker situated at Skeppsholmen, Stockholm. In corporation with the *Museum of Far Eastern Antiquities*, the Swedish National Property Board (SFV) developed an exhibition concept suitable for the figures of the Chinese Terracotta Army. These antiquities are displayed in the cavernous interior of the subterranean former headquarters of the Swedish Navy which, after being taken out of military service at the end of the Cold War, had its the entire interior demolished in the 1990s. According to Sanne Houby-Nielsen (the former head of the museum) the story of China's first emperor, Qin

4.5   Staging newness: Saab-event at Aeroseum staged by as systems GmbH.

4.6   The bunker as a stage: The Chinese terracotta army exhibition at Museum of Far Eastern Antiquities in Stockholm.

Shihuangdi, and his underground army, is one of a number of shows that cannot be depicted in an ordinary exhibition hall. She believes that the underground environment is particularly suited to enhance the experience of looking at archaeological objects and perhaps especially the martial qualities of the terracotta warriors whose creator, the emperor Shihuangdi, sought to extend of his practices of warfare through time and into the realm of the immortal: 'the cliff walls of the bunker down here were significant. The displayed items are specifically from a period of time when the Chinese burial customs changed to rock tombs' (Bäckstedt 2010).

THE BUNKER AS A CULTURAL PLAYGROUND

But what happens when the bunker becomes a 'funky' stage for potentially more controversial narratives? In 2007, the event company *Berget Event* arranged the fifth in a series of 'airsoft games' in the subterranean fortress of Hemsön, Sweden, dating from the Cold War. The event was called 'Berget 5' and attracted over a thousand participants. The plot of the game was based on a counterfactual scenario with a hypothesis of what would have happened if the Cold War had not finished: 'The year is 1992 and Finland has been occupied by Soviet forces – it is Sweden's turn now …'. The Berget games can be described as a live role-play with elements of military simulation, an enhanced participatory extension of the dramatized narratives which have become an increasingly popular way of communicating and experiencing history. Calling it a mix of 'scouting, role-playing, and military service', the event company made an agreement with the Swedish National Property Board (SFV) to rent parts of the fortress as a realistic scenographic backdrop, a support to the game's narrative (interview with *Berget Event*).[3] In the beginning, locals were sceptical and critical of the arrangements. One of the local politicians claimed that she would 'rather see peace activists in the town than people who play war' (Lundberg 2009). Airsoft games are provocative, not least because of the realism and their emotional closeness to contemporary conflicts. This gives rise to a number of ethical issues which problematize the boundary between perceived reality and the fiction being acted out. The airsoft game at the minor battery of Hemsö fortress is an example of a radical approach to built heritage. On the one hand, there exists a certain distance from historical context. The real threat and the nuclear fear are gone. What remains are the concrete bunker shells of the Cold War which can now be filled with new content. On the other hand, there is an existential proximity to history in the way the participants and organizers seek realism in the dramatization of a counterfactual story that may be perceived as more offensive than if, say, a medieval narrative was being enacted.

The spatial context, however, is critical for the credibility of the game as well as the acceptability of violent fiction. The bunker constitutes a spatial, social and narrative 'free zone' for acting out fictional conflicts. The underlying belief is that the context of the game accepts infringements. According to Mikhail Bakhtin, the carnival in history has had a dissolute quality which allowed people to cross social boundaries and embrace the grotesque, as a kind of social valve: 'While the carnival lasts, there is no life outside it. During carnival time life is subject only to its laws, that is, the laws of it own freedom' (Bahktin 1984: 7). In a similar manner, the airsoft game takes Hemsö fortress into temporary possession as a 'narrative free zone' for experiences and symbolic kicks.

4.7   Dramatized Soviet repression combined with dinner: A Soviet Bunker as a cultural playground.

In Nemenčinė outside Vilnius, Lithuania, there is another, perhaps more radical, example. A former subterranean television station from the Soviet era has evolved into a peculiar tourist attraction: *Soviet Bunker 1984 – The Underground Museum of Socialism*. Here, in dramatized guided tours you can experience Soviet-style repression, with dinner included. You will be drilled to stand in line, do push-ups and be insulted by people playing KGB officers. As a souvenir, you will receive a gift from the Soviet era and a certificate on completed basic disciplinary training. Although the bunker was never used by the KGB, it is a story of Soviet tyranny that unfolds here, a fictional version of a narrative of oppression existing on the verges of entertainment. To sum up, the underground world of bunkers thus offers a spectrum of associations which are useful in new contexts. The airsoft game, *Aeroseum* and the exhibition hall show that Cold War bunkers can make room for other stories whose assemblies converge with the historical and spatial context as a metaphor. These post-military spaces are generated by a range of practices of simultaneously exposing and mixing and managing the different historical layers of the building. In the words of Vivian Sobchack (1997), airsoft participants experience these different layers simultaneously as a kind a 'palimpsest of historical consciousness'. History and the post-military landscape become a 'cultural playground' (Mathiesen Hjemdal 2002).

SEMIOTIC GUERRILLA WARFARE

4.8   The 'first' readymade, a urinal. Marcel Duchamp: *Fountain*, 1917.

Art theory allows a deeper understanding of these examples of reuse. The manner in which bunker buildings, places and military spaces are reused, redesigned, re-enacted and remodelled for the purpose of tourism, cultural activities, leisure, shopping, and marketing can be see as analogous to the art practices of readymades and found objects with their connotations of mass production and surreal and subversive undertones. Readymades are ordinary manufactured objects with non-art functions that the artist selects and modifies. As exemplified by the first exhibited readymade – Marcel Duchamp's urinal – by simply choosing the object and repositioning or joining, tilting and signing it, the object becomes art.

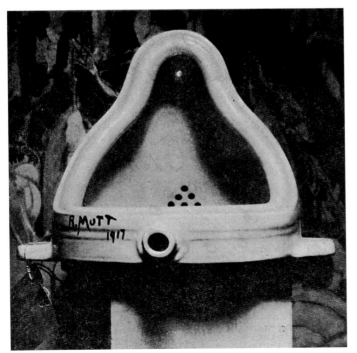

The earliest definition was formulated in the theorist André Breton's surrealist dictionary in 1938: 'an ordinary object elevated to the dignity of a work of art by the mere choice of an artist' (Breton 1938: 23). Breton also categorized the readymade as an *objet trouvé* (found object) which has become a more general term for techniques such as readymades, assemblages, collage and trash art. Furthermore, there are different types of readymades: 'un-altered' which are stripped of their real meaning when placed in a new context (like Duchamp's *Fountain*); or 'assisted' when they are elaborated with mixed objects (like Picasso's *Head of Bull*) (Duchamp 1961: 141–2). The first readymade art was a gesture designed to shock. From that point of view, they represented a negation of a work of art at the time, a subversive 'anti-art' with the capacity to shake the ideological foundations of the art institutions (Waldman 1992: 136).

The subversive undertone of readymades and found objects is similar to the notion of bricolage, a term which originates from the French word *bricoleur*: a person who makes creative and resourceful use of whatever materials are at hand regardless of their original purpose (Lévi-Strauss 1966: 16–17). Later, bricolage became a popular theoretical model in cultural studies to describe the processes by which people acquire objects from across social divisions to create new cultural identities. Like, for example, Dick Hebdige's book *Subculture: The Meaning of Style* which explores subcultural stylism and subversive self-expressions in punk. Hebdige's recurrent examples include the safety pin, one of the leading attributes in punk fashion, which became a form of provocative decoration in ears and noses. Its functional meaning was disrupted and reorganized as an act of bricolage by perturbation and deformation (1979: 106–7). In the words of the Dadaist Max Ernst, the 'bricoleur' juxtapose two apparently incompatible realities on an apparently unsuitable scale to produce an 'explosive junction' (Ernst 1948: 13, 21–2).

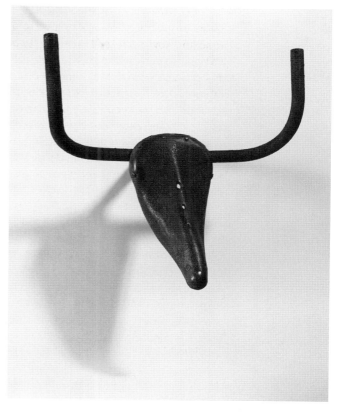

4.9 Semiotic guerrilla warfare by Picasso: A bicycle handlebar added to a saddle becomes a head of bull (1942).

These practices of appropriation are interrelated but formulated in different settings. The basic narrative is one of subversion against convention and dominance, a common form of 'semiotic guerrilla warfare', to borrow the melodramatic words of Umberto Eco (1972). In the cultural alchemy of spatial appropriation, the 'added value' in reusing bunkers as design hotels, for example, would be the potential of making a statement by using contrast as a strategy. Both the excitement for the user and profit for the creative industries lies within the intertextual, contradictory and somehow, promiscuous, playing with references and materials.

READYMADE SPACES ARE FOUND SPACES

The etymological leap from Duchamp's readymade to the notion of 'readymade space' is achieved by indicating their functional, aesthetic and cultural correspondences. What does a design hotel hosted in a former military bunker have in common with the exposed urinal of Duchamp or the safety pin in the punk's nose? Well, it is not only their potential of making a statement through re-contextualization but also the fact that they are mostly objects (or spaces) of mass production which are *found*, that is, they have been rediscovered and appropriated. In this point of view, readymade spaces are 'found spaces' in the same way as

André Breton once classified Duchamp's readymade as a found object. As Walter Benjamin states in his book *The Work of Art in the Age of Mechanical Reproduction*, the mechanical reproduction has changed the way we consider art. Today, the constantly changing notion of art has also had an impact on how we consider manufactured and mass-produced everyday objects or pieces of trash in aesthetic terms. On the basis of the bunker case studies, two categories of readymade spaces can be distinguished: firstly, buildings and spaces which are modified, comparable to Duchamp's 'assisted readymade': the readymade space as a makeover; and secondly, buildings and spaces which are preserved as they are but placed in a new context by making room for other narratives like 'the unaltered readymade' of Duchamp: the readymade space as a stage. Like the readymade object, readymade spaces are borne from mass-production and share attributes of seriality, prefabrication and standardization.

READYMADE SPACES AS COUNTER-BRICOLAGE

Re-contextualized buildings and spaces are able to communicate fresh meanings. The readymade space is a tool to communicate values of innovation and creativity. Many of these become materialized visions and symbols of renewal and regeneration in times of structural change in society and of the ever shifting articulation of taste and lifestyle. But these practices tend to originate in subcultures outside the business sphere of the cultural economy. *The Factory*, Andy Warhol's visionary studio, for example, was a sort of announcement for the on-going gentrification process of Manhattan. Meanwhile, Hamburg, Amsterdam and Copenhagen are all examples of cities with so-called alternative areas, the result of prevailing housing policies. Christiania, for instance, a former military base in Copenhagen, was occupied by squatters in 1971. The district has developed into an area with innovative housing and entrepreneurship based on creative reuse. Indeed, the connection between gentrification and new or alternative social movements is crucial. Often, for example, activist cultures (such as the Situationists, squatter movements, and environmentalists, etc.) play a critical role in the re-evaluation of potential areas for gentrification. In a European context, the new social movements have paved the way towards the creative reuse of factories for post-industrial purposes (Franzén 2005). Moreover, as Georgy Katsiaficas (1997/2006: 6) states, participants of such movements live in groups to 'negate the isolation of individuals imposed by consumerism', thus seeking to 'decolonize everyday life': practices of cultural bricolage.

Appropriation, however, is not always an oppositional practice. Re-use of readymade spaces in the cultural economy is more or less based on an appropriation of the creative tactics of marginalized and oppositional cultures and their re-introduction into mainstream culture. The subversive expression or the 'explosive junction' mentioned earlier, is normalized, commoditized and spatially converted into a stylistic contrast or a lifestyle statement: like the bunker hotel of Fårösund. This, therefore, is simply another face of the processes of aesthetization in society, a form of counter-bricolage that uses spatial appropriation, not as a subversive act, but as creative tactic in the pursuit of profit (Sturken and Cartwright 2001: 68–9). Literally speaking, the cultural alchemy of appropriation turns the materiality of bare concrete walls into new economic value.

CREATIVE DESTRUCTION OR DESTRUCTIVE CREATIVITY?

The case studies demonstrate the opportunities of former military bases as readymade spaces. By experimenting with their spatial, imaginative and historical potential, new activities have occurred in the wake of demilitarization. Military bases have gone from being a part of a national defence economy to play a significant role in the cultural economy of a post-military society. This corresponds with the theories of the economist Joseph Schumpeter who introduced the term 'creative destruction' to explain how declining industries and less relevant businesses are necessarily torn down and replaced with more viable ones. In view of this, there are several potential benefits in reusing the residual materiality of war and its constant preparations. Firstly, they can make room for new activities and new businesses which might generate new development in areas of economical decline. Or, they can at least function as a sign of economic regeneration. Creative reuse may also imply certain forms of preservation. New activities may actually prevent the built heritage from being destroyed.

But the practices of readymade spaces also entails complications and gives rise to ethical questions. Firstly, the radical reuse of buildings as makeovers and promiscuous re-appropriations might physically damage or trivialize the cultural heritage to the point it can lose its context and authority as a historical site. Secondly, there might also be emotional drawbacks when military sites, or other spaces with negative connotations or heritage, are reused for new purposes. The airsoft role-playing game in *Soviet Bunker 1984* is a rather provocative example of reuse which capitalizes on a historical situation of repression and the production of fear. Are the entrepreneurs going too far in search for spectacular experiences? Or – to twist the concept of Schumpeter – is it rather a matter of 'destructive creativity' whenever creative reuse is practiced at the expense of the cultural heritage, human dignity and memories of war?

In the case studies, the environments of the Cold War have become cultural playgrounds and fictitious, free zones. The given prerequisite is that 'Big Brother' – the militarism – is gone and that we have gained enough distance from the historical events. This process, however, is uneven. While some nationalities can afford to play with history and convert them into attractions and harmless relics, certain Baltic States because of their history of Soviet occupation have a completely different and more complex relationship to Cold War history. Here, few military bases have been declared as cultural heritage worthy preservation. Perhaps the Lithuanian example cited above primarily reflects the way people in this region process their history of occupation: to attempt to render the infected memories of Soviet era harmless and financially profitable simply by mocking and satirizing their unpleasantness? The way military bases and bunkers are turned into tourist attractions, how they are reused and how the story is re-told, also tells us a lot about each epoch and each country's way of dealing with the past. At the same time, readymade spaces are test sites for the boundaries of the heritage industry because they challenge institutionalized ways of relating to the spaces of history.

NOTES

1   The title of this paper is in fact an intentionally chosen analogy to Robert Willim's notion of 'industrial cool'. This is a theoretical notion which illustrates the distant and aesthetic approach of post-industrial factories (2008: 21–2). Hence, the purpose of this analogy is to elucidate the similarity between the post-societies. 'Funky' as well as 'cool' both have their etymological origin in Afro-American jazz-culture, meaning 'fashionable in a way that is unusual and shows a lot of imagination'

(McMillan Dictionary). The words both express a retained distance and a reflexive mode, which is exactly what appropriation practices of creative reuse are all about.

2   The costs were high and the company went bankrupt before completion. The SFV finished the works and subsequently rented the building to the Pontus group who run the hotel and restaurant.

3   Since their first role-play in 2002, *Berget Event* has gradually expanded to become the world's leading organizer of airsoft games turning over six million Swedish kronor a year.

REFERENCES

Bakhtin, M. 1984. *Rabelais and his World*. Bloomington, IN: Indiana University Press.

Bäckstedt, E. 2010. Bergrum blir ny kulturlokal. *Svenska Dagbladet*. Stockholm. 20 May.

Bell, D. 1973. *The Coming of the Post-Industrial Society: A Venture in Social Forecasting*. New York: Basic Books.

Benjamin, W. 2008. *The Work of Art in the Age of Mechanical Reproduction*. London: Penguin.

Berget Event 2009. (interview) 1 June.

Bourriaud, N. 2002. *Relational Aesthetics*. Dijon: Presses du reel.

Breton, A. (with Paul Éluard) 1938. *Dictionnaire abrégé du surréalisme*. Paris: Gallerie Beaux-Arts.

Breton, A. 1945. *Le surréalisme et la peinture*. New York: Brentano.

Castells, M. 1996. *The Information Age: Economy, Society and Culture. Vol. 1. The Rise of the Network Society*. Malden, MA: Blackwell.

Debord, G. and Wolman, G.J. 2006. A user's guide to détournement, in Knabb, K. (ed.) *Situationist International Anthology*. Berkeley, CA: Bureau of Public Secrets.

Debord, G. 1956. Mode d'emploi du détournement in *Les Lèvres Nues*. No 8.

Duchamp, M. 2009. Apropos of 'readymades', in Evans, D. (ed.) *Appropriation*. Cambridge, MA: MIT Press.

Eliasson, R. 2011. (interview) 25 August.

Ernst, M. 1948. *Beyond Painting and Other Writings by the Artist and his Friends*. New York: Ams Pr Inc.

Evans, D. 2009. *Appropriation*. Cambridge, MA: MIT Press.

Franzén, M. 2005. New social movements and gentrification in Hamburg and Stockholm: A comparative study. *Journal of Housing and the Built Environment*. Delft: Delft University Press, No. 20.

du Gay, P. and Pryke, M. 2002. *Cultural Economy: Cultural Analysis and Commercial Life*. London: Sage Publications.

Graham, S. 2010. *Cities Under Siege: The New Military Urbanism*. London: Verso.

Greenberg, R. 1996. The exhibited redistributed, in Greenberg, R., Ferguson, B.W. and Nairne, S. (eds) *Thinking about Exhibitions*. London: Routledge.

Göthe, S. 2003. *Ansökan om tillstånd att uppföra en konferensanläggning inom Fårösund fästning, Gotland*. Stockholm: Kulturmiljöavdelningen, Riksantikvarieämbetet.

Hall, S. 1993. Encoding, decoding, in During, S. (ed.) *The Cultural Studies Reader*. New York and London: Routledge.

Hammarstedt, J. 2010. (interview) 5 May.

Hebdige, D. 1979. *Subculture: The Meaning of Style*. London: Methuen.

Katsiaficas, G. 2006. *The Subversion of Politics: European Autonomous Social Movements and the Decolonization of Everyday Life*. Atlantic Highlands, NJ: Humanities Press.

Klein, N. 2000. *No Logo: No Space, No Choice, No Jobs, Taking Aim at the Brand Bullies*. London: Flamingo.

Lash, S. and Urry, J. 1994. *Economies of Signs and Space*. London: Sage Publications.

Lefebvre, H. 1992. *The Production of Space*. Oxford: Basil Blackwell.

Lévi-Strauss, C. 1966. *The Savage Mind*. Chicago, IL: University of Chicago Press.

Lundberg, L. 2009. Satsa inte på krigslekar, in *Allehanda*, 5 November.

Löfgren, O. 2005. Catwalking and coolhunting: The production of newness, in Löfgren, O. and Willim, R. (eds) *Magic, Culture and the New Economy*. New York: Berg.

Mathiesen Hjemdal, K. 2002. History as a cultural playground. *Ethnologia Europaea*, 32 (2), 105–24.

Papastergiadis, N. 2006. Modernism and Contemporary Art in *Theory, Culture & Society*, 23 (2–3), 466–9.

Prosjektgruppen Bunkerologi. 2006. Bunkerologi in *Byggekunst* No. 8.

Schneider, A. 2006. *Appropriation as Practice: Art and Identity in Argentina*. New York: Palgrave Macmillan.

Shaw, M. 1991. *Post-Military Society: Militarism, Demilitarization and War at the End of the Twentieth Century*. Cambridge: Polity.

Sobchack, V. 1997. The Insistent Fringe: Moving Images and Historical Consciousness. *History and Theory*, 36 (4), 4–20.

Strömberg, P. 2007. *Upplevelseindustrins turistmiljöer: visuella berättarstrategier i svenska turistanläggningar 1985–2005*. Uppsala: Konstvetenskapliga institutionen, Uppsala universitet.

Strömberg, P. 2009. Arctic Cool: Icehotel and the Branding of Nature, in Hansson H. and Norberg, C. (eds) *Cold Matters: Cultural Perceptions of Snow, Ice and Cold*. Umeå: Umeå University and the Royal Skyttean Society.

Strömberg, P. 2010. Swedish Military Bases of the Cold War: The Making of a New Cultural Heritage. *Culture Unbound. Journal of Current Cultural Research*, 2, 635–63.

Sturken, M. and Cartwright, L. 2001. *Practices of Looking: An Introduction to Visual Culture*. Oxford: Oxford University Press.

Waage, A. 2009. (interview) 14 September and 23 August.

Waage, A. 2010. (interview) 23 August.

Waldman, D. 1992. *Collage, Assemblage, and the Found Object*. London: Phaidon.

Welsch, W. 1996. Aestheticization Processes: Phenomena, Distinctions and Prospects in *Theory Culture Society*, 13 (1), 1–34.

Willim, R. 2008. *Industrial cool. Om postindustriella fabriker*. Lund: Humanistiska fakulteten, Lunds universitet.

Young, J.O. 2008. *Cultural Appropriation and the Arts*. Malden, MA: Blackwell.

Zukin, S. 1989. *Loft Living: Culture and Capital in Urban Change*. New Brunswick: Rutgers University Press.

Part II
The Invisible Front:
Domesticity and Defence

5

'Hiding the Assets': 'Self-concealing' Architecture and the British Landscape During the Second World War

James Robinson

INTRODUCTION

> *To-day it is a question of the aeroplane eye, of the mind with which the Bird's Eye View has endowed us; of that eye which now looks with alarm at the places where we live, the cities where it is our lot to be. And the spectacle is frightening, overwhelming. The airplane eye reveals a spectacle of collapse (Le Corbusier 1935: 5).*

These words, appearing in the preface of *Aircraft* (1935) written by renowned modernist architect, Le Corbusier, testify to the opening up of a new world of spatial interrogation, of the revealing of a new visual perspective from which to critique landscape traditions and architectural practices. Indeed, *Aircraft* is, in many ways, a celebration of the development of aviation technologies; comprised primarily of images of aeroplanes, their components, and photographs of the landscape taken from the air. The book casts the aeroplane as a technology of hope, of visual stimuli and craftsmanship, capable of inspiring the architect to adopt a fresh and harmonious approach to their work. While the aeroplane had, since its inception, instilled these feelings of excitement, optimism and promise, its ability to open up the landscape to fuller, clearer and critical interrogation had only just been realised during the First World War. Transformed into a technology of war and utilised for the purposes of aerial reconnaissance (as well as bombing), the vertical, downward looking perspectives of the aeroplane eye revealed features in the landscape which were visually concealed to the grounded observer. As Jay notes, 'the western front's interminable trench warfare created a bewildering landscape of indistinguishable, shadowy shapes, illuminated by lightning flashes of blinding intensity, and then obscured by phantasmagoric, often gas-induced haze' (1994: 212). On a battlefield where effective visual perception was hampered by these effects, and the soldier easily disorientated, the aeroplane eye offered the clearest view of the landscape. As Virilio observes, by this time, 'aviation was ceasing to be strictly a means of flying and breaking records … it was becoming one way, or perhaps even the ultimate way, of *seeing*' (1989: 17). The aeroplane, therefore, became a valuable asset; from the air, observers could easily locate and map enemy trench networks, artillery positions, and other military hardware, as well as record troop movements.

The expanded utilisation of vertical perspectives to comprehend the battlefield, inevitably, triggered a military and defensive response; to use Virilio's terminology, the extension of the military gaze from grounded, horizontal viewpoints, to downward-looking, aerial perspectives culminated in spaces of conflict becoming transformed and redefined by the 'aesthetics of disappearance' (1989: 2). Indeed, fears of the prying eye in the sky culminated in military institutions developing new deceptive technologies which would facilitate the concealment of one's assets. It was during this time period that the practice of camouflage, as a visual and military technology, began to surface; from the concealment of men and materials under nets, through to the painting of artillery and other hardware with contrasting colours of paint, camouflage emerged as a new weapon of modern warfare, utilised to preserve one's resources and to mask military intent.

With the end of the First World War in 1918, however, camouflage aesthetics disappeared into obscurity. Its conception as a predominantly military technology did not inspire much enthusiasm in a world shocked and stunned by the atrocities and destruction that the Great War had produced. On the other hand, the aeroplane continued to excite, captivate and fuel the popular imagination of peoples from around the globe (Wohl 2005). Indeed, the war seemingly redefined and expanded the potential roles that the aeroplane could play in civilian life. While surplus bombers and reconnaissance aircraft were converted into airliners to support an ever-increasing desire for air travel, wartime developments in aerial photography enabled new ways of interrogating and understanding everyday landscapes and architectural practices. Within inter-war Britain the proliferating field of aerial photography was being utilised by archaeologists to reveal the hidden landscapes of past societies, with features such as Iron Age hill forts being uncovered through the adoption of an aerial perspective (Hauser 2007, Stichelbaut et al. 2009). Furthermore, aviation and aerial photography were considered to provide a fresh opportunity to look at the built environment, to expose and critique the grotesque, the vulgar, the conspicuous and the un-harmonious. For architects such as Le Corbusier, it was contended that 'by means of the airplane, we now have proof, record on the photographic plate, of the rightness of our desire to alter methods of architecture and town-planning' (1935: 11). The presence of the aeroplane constituted a rallying call, an opportunity to critically engage with architectural aesthetics, and to correct the undisciplined and chaotic nature of the built environment.

Although such sentiments were held within the practice of modern architecture, no clearly defined agenda or method as to how this could be achieved was laid down. In the case of Britain, it was not until the re-emergence of camouflage in the name of civil defence that a new architectural style would be devised which would take the 'Bird's Eye View' as its starting point. Referred to as 'self-concealing' architecture by British civil camouflage practitioners, this novel approach to conceiving and planning buildings attempted to fuse together the military technology and techniques of camouflage with contemporary civil architectural aesthetics and knowledges. By inviting architects to consider and reflect upon three design components – Siting, Lay-out and Constructional Form – 'self-concealing' architecture would emerge as an extension, re-appropriation and critique of existing inter-war architectural trends, with modern sensibilities of order and harmony being evoked and transformed for the purposes of defence.

CLARITY VERSUS AMBIGUITY: ARCHITECTURAL TENSIONS IN BRITAIN'S INTERWAR LANDSCAPES

Throughout the 1930s, the British landscape had become increasingly dominated by the emergence of a modern architectural aesthetic. This was a particular style which set a precedent for a planned and organised landscape, composed of simple, geometrical and pale-coloured buildings (see Figure 5.1). Such a modern architectural tradition was nurtured through a variety of visual and literary forms; from exhibition spaces and displays of modern design, through to pictorial and written depictions in guidebooks, travel narratives and structural design journals such as the *Architectural Review* (Linehan 2003, Brace 2001, Gruffudd, Herbert and Piccini 2000, Gruffudd 1994, Hewitt 1992). Furthermore, certain organisational bodies had begun to materialize which encouraged the proliferation of this modern architectural philosophy. Organisations such as the Council for the Preservation of Rural England (C.P.R.E.), the Council for the Preservation of Rural Wales (C.P.R.W.) and the Design and Industries Association (D.I.A.), all sought to promote a discourse of planner-preservationism throughout the 1930s and 1940s (Matless 1990, 1998, Gruffudd 1995a, 1995b). This discourse held 'praise for a landscape of progress, of clarity, of function, of harmony, of permanence and of order' (Matless 1990: 205). Within these planner-preservationist movements, new landscapes of modernity which incorporated and embodied these elements were celebrated and applauded over what was felt to be the emergence of 'jazz-like', unplanned and haphazard building practices. The contemporary text, *The Face of the Land* (1930), co-edited by Harry Peach and Noel Carrington, represents one typical example of how contemporary planner-preservationists commended

5.1 'In peace-time, if factory shows up well from the air – so much the better. It makes free advertisement … but in war, advertisement may be fatal': Aerial photograph illustrating the planned, organised landscape of modern Britain in the 1930s.

clean building designs and practices, whilst condemning those considered to be untidy and chaotic.[1] Within this particular publication, photographic plates illustrating similar features were presented in pairs emphasising how, for instance, forms such as electricity pylons should and should not appear. Through these comparative appraisals, clear contrasts between unnatural and inorganic architectural styles and more natural looking ones were established and reinforced. What emerges from these accounts and critiques is the apparent encouragement of a supposedly harmonious yet progressive architectural aesthetic.

However, despite this shift towards a more fit for purpose architectural style, this modern aesthetic posed significant challenges when it came to the matter of concealment. Certainly, it was evident that the types of harmonious design styles which parties such as the planner-preservationists were encouraging, came into immediate tension with camouflage ideals, culminating in conflictual interpretations of what 'being in harmony' was understood to mean. Inevitably, when the British civil camouflage project was instigated in October 1936, there was an instant critiquing of many of the architectural practices which planner-preservationism had encouraged. In many ways, the calls for clarity of form, of regularity and of order were completely incompatible with the mentality of civil camoufleurs who were responsible for merging strategically important features into the landscape. It is important to highlight that these critiques aimed at Britain's modern landscapes were as a direct result of the different visualities through which appreciations of civil architecture were being conducted. As had been the case for their earlier military counterparts during the First World War, the critiques of Britain's 'Home Front' landscapes by civil camoufleurs were founded upon assessments of modern structural forms from the air.

Throughout the 1930s, political concerns about 'the bomber always getting through', echoing a speech made to the House of Commons by Prime Minister Stanley Baldwin on 10 November 1932, coupled with the destructive effects of aerial bombardment during the Spanish Civil War, and in particular the events of Guernica, had stimulated a great deal of anxiety about the potential effects that an aerial attack could have upon Britain's cities.[2] In response to this, pre-emptive civil defence measures were instigated on 9 July 1935, when the Home Office circulated its first set of proposals for Air Raid Precautions to local authorities and private employers. As part of these measures, it was decided that camouflage could be passively deployed as a strategy of aerial protection, aiding in the misguiding and baffling of the bomber pilot and/or the aerial observer as they sought their target.

Coinciding with this, it was contended that the civil camoufleurs had to adjust themselves to the new perspectives and 'vertical visualities' which the aeroplane enabled. Mirroring the earlier sentiments of Le Corbusier, civil camoufleurs became acutely aware that the aeroplane and its ability to extend visual critique vertically would unmask the modern landscape in new and unique ways to those of ground viewing. While appraisals of the landscape from the ground had come to dominate architectural critiques of building styles, the civil camoufleurs recognised that the aerial view opened up the ways in which buildings could be considered, provoking alternative ways of examining and understanding architecture. From this new viewpoint, civil camoufleurs, therefore, became immensely critical of a modernism which had emphasised clarity and which now rendered civil structures vulnerable when observed from the air. The publication *Notes on the Concealment of Buildings against Raiding Aircraft* provides an insight into the elements which were deemed to render a building conspicuous when viewed from this perspective; it is argued that it was a combination of 'a) large and regular plans, b) smoothness of upper surfaces and adjacent ground, c) contrast between roofings and surroundings, d) regular lay-out of a group of buildings and e) their adjacents such as roads, paths and railway sidings' which all contributed to the 'giving away' of man-made features such as factories when viewed from the air (Anon 1919). Furthermore, the aerial visual experience provided the camoufleurs with a unique opportunity to be critical of modern building materials such as concrete and glass which had been actively incorporated and utilised within many of the new features which had emerged within the British landscape. From the air, the smooth appearance and light colour of concrete was considered to be exceptionally outstanding when compared to the much darker tone of more natural features, whereas the reflection of sunlight upon a glass surface was seen to draw the attention of the aerial observer as they cast their attention over the landscape below. In order to mask all of these factors, it was contended that new architectural sensibilities needed to be developed and conceptions of harmony needed to be re-thought and re-appropriated to ensure the effective merging of conspicuous features into the landscape.

'PREVENTION IS BETTER THAN THE CURE': MOVING TOWARDS ARCHITECTURAL SOLUTIONS TO CONSPICUOUSNESS

Faced with the various challenges presented by modern architectural styling, the British camoufleurs were to devise new and novel techniques of concealment to combat the issues of conspicuousness. The principal treatment which was resorted to in order to camouflage prominent buildings and landmarks in the landscape was the application of a matt paint coating. Paint as a solution to the camouflage problem took two forms. Firstly, the simple method of toning down was utilised. In these cases, a paint colour would be selected which would share the same tonal value as that of the surroundings. Once applied to the building, the matching tones of the paint with the locality were seen to enable the 'fade-out' of the structure, particularly when viewed from the air. The second type of paint scheme to be applied was that of disruptive or imitative patterning. In disruptive patterning, a design was often selected which was based upon either artistic or biological knowledge. This was deployed in order to break up regularity and the structural form of the building. With regards to imitation, the mimicking of a feature in the surrounding landscape would be attempted; in urban areas, this involved reproducing or replicating residential areas, where large factory workshops were adorned with a pattern reminiscent of several rows of terraced housing.

5.2   A sketch produced by Oliver Bernard, illustrating his idea for the inclusion of structural additions to the roof of a building in order to 'distort' its regular outline.

Paint, however, was not the only solution to be adopted. Constructional methods were also embraced as alternative techniques of concealment. Strategies such as the use of netting or the addition of steel wool to the roofs of cylindrical features such as gasometers were frequently utilised in an attempt to either physically obscure features in the landscape or to mimic the textural appearance of the surrounding natural landscape. Alternative constructional methods were also suggested but never trialled. In a letter dated 17 March 1937, Oliver Bernard, an architect by trade, proposed a method he described:

> as "distortion", because as an architectural idea which has not been practiced before, it embodies structural eccentricity in buildings to preserve the normality of their situation, and also adds protective value to concealment by nature of concrete and other materials employed.

Bernard suggested that structural additions should be incorporated onto the top of buildings to break up their regular appearance, sharp lines and smooth surfaces; in the sketches he provided with this letter, these additions took the form of overlapping, wispy cloud shapes, which were suggested to give the appearance of deciduous woodland when viewed from the air (see Figure 5.2). Bernard envisaged that these could 'be applied to an existing building or form an inherent part of [future] construction'. However, the issue with all of these methods – painting, netting, and structural additions – was that they were very much a cure for pre-existing problems which, as the war progressed, many camoufleurs argued need not have necessarily existed in the first place. It was with this realisation that attention shifted to looking more at strategies and techniques of prevention.

   One solution to this was the encouragement of camouflage aesthetics within mainstream architectural practice. The value of this was something alluded to by Oliver Bernard. In his letter discussed above, he had argued that his method of 'distortion' would 'depend for its success on forethought in siting and designing [of] works'. However, Bernard failed to elaborate more upon this in his discussions, and the general neglect of his structural idea served to further ensure that the combination of camouflage and architectural aesthetics continued to be overlooked. It was only in October 1938 that further debates on the question of integrating camouflage aesthetics into architecture in order to counteract building measures that were producing exceptionally prominent industrial spaces were initiated. With the outbreak of the Munich Crisis, when tensions between Britain and Nazi Germany escalated, various attempts had been made by both governmental as well as unofficial bodies of camouflage to conceal important features within the landscape. In the case of unofficial bodies, this had culminated in a series of camouflage malpractices and what governmental camouflage experts had professed were the adoption of seemingly incorrect design principles, producing inappropriate and ineffective schemes. In light of this episode, Colonel Francis Wyatt, Director of the Air Ministry's Camouflage Branch based at Farnborough, had produce a memorandum on 'Deficiencies in Camouflage Organisation'. Interestingly, as part of this analysis, he argued that 'new buildings should be designed and sited if possible, so as to simplify camouflage: a great deal could be done in this way and cost no more. The architects involved should be placed in touch with this Department and, furthermore, the Royal Institute of British Architects (RIBA) should be invited to think out the problem from the point of view of design and materials' (Wyatt 1938). This proposal, in many ways, represented the first time that someone employed as a civil camoufleur had expressed the desire to merge camouflage and architectural design. Wyatt's suggestion, however, appeared to have been ignored; instead, attention was being directed towards using conventional methods of concealment, as well as consolidating camouflage organisation, which in the preceding months before the outbreak of war in September 1939 was in a state of immense disorder. It was not until 1940 that further discussion on architectural practice and camouflage sensibilities re-emerged. In a letter to the Ministry of Supply, Sir John Anderson, then Minister of Home Security, wrote that 'apart from the question of camouflaging existing factories, it has been suggested that more regular consideration should be given to the possibilities of easing the task of concealment of new vital factories by modification in external design, and possibly their siting. Such questions have recently been discussed occasionally between your Department and mine, but I think it would help both of us if the general problem were examined more systematically' (Anderson 1940).

Subsequent changes in camouflage policy and organisation which occurred throughout the winter of 1940–1941 also served to make self-concealing architecture more of a reality. In January 1941, the Camouflage Directorate, under Wing Commander T.R. Cave-Browne-Cave, was established in order to manage more effectively general camouflage practice. As part of this re-organisation of the operational structure of civil camouflage, Herbert Morrison, the new Minister of Home Security, argued that the newly-founded Camouflage Directorate should become more actively involved in the designing and development of new industrial buildings. He felt that 'much expense may be saved and more effective camouflage secured if the requirements of camouflage are taken into account in the design and lay-out of the building and treatment of the site. Effect will be given to this principle in regard to any buildings erected for the Ministry of Home Security which may have to be camouflaged'.[3] Morrison had even gone to the length of complying 'with a request by the Minister of Aircraft Production to lend a camouflage officer from the Civil Defence Camouflage Establishment to that Ministry so that the ultimate requirements of camouflage may be taken into account in regard to [their] plans for new buildings' (Morrison 1940).[4]

In attempting to account for this shift in mentality towards the construction of new buildings, it could be argued that this was part of broader criticisms which were being directed towards the more conventional methods of camouflage, and in particular an over-reliance upon artists. As a result of their camouflage work during the First World War, from dazzle-painted of navel vessels and artillery guns, artists had emerged as the expert in camouflage in the eyes of those co-ordinating civil defence efforts (Newark 2007, Williams 1989, 2001). However, throughout the Second World War, things were beginning to change and despite many of their inventive efforts, the privileged position of the artist within camouflage work was coming under scrutiny. Indeed, specialists from other trades were attempting to negotiate a position from themselves within camouflage work; biologists and chemists as well as film set makers, to name but a few examples, were all attempting to make their mark on camouflage. With the formation of the Camouflage Directorate, an attempt was being made by the British government to incorporate these different types of knowledges into camouflage practice, therefore enabling a greater variety of camouflage solutions to be devised which could then be adopted to conceal features in the landscape. As part of this process, engagements with structural engineers and architects were encouraged to foster new camouflage techniques. Lieutenant Colonel C.H.R. Chesney, in his 1941 book entitled *The Art of Camouflage*, was one such proponent of getting architects more involved in camouflage work. Certainly, he was immensely critical of the unique positioning of the artist within camouflage circles. He exclaimed, for instance, how 'paint is only an accessory to the crime, and seldom by itself constitutes satisfactory camouflage … Camouflage is not *primarily* the job of a painter artist! … The more trained and expert he is as a painter, the less desirable is it that he should be placed in the position of controller'. Instead, Chesney called for the more active involvement of architects in camouflage work. He contended that 'the best camouflage work upon an object is done before the object is sited or has even been designed' (103). Taking this into account, and reflecting the views of Morrison, Chesney argued that 'provision in first design will save the enormous costs involved in trying to correct the original absence of provision, besides being twice as effective' (116). By 1941, it was clear that there was a very real desire to include architects within camouflage work, and to therefore encourage the designing of buildings and structure which possessed self-concealing qualities. By promoting this self-concealing ethic, it was clear that this would facilitate the much easier merging of industrial features into the landscape, thereby removing their presence and enhancing their survivability in the event of aerial attack.

'CONCEALMENT OF NEW BUILDINGS': PROMOTING SELF-CONCEALING ARCHITECTURE

These developments in civil camouflage practice and the pro-active encouragement of architects to get involved in camouflage work set in motion the rise of the publication *Concealment of New Buildings*, which was developed throughout the remainder of 1941 and printed at the start of 1942 as part of the Camouflage Directorate's Camouflage Memoranda Series (see Figure 5.3). In putting together this manual, it was argued that this particular booklet should act not only as an authoritative, instructive piece generated by an official civil camouflage body, but should

5.3   The front cover of *Concealment of New Buildings*, produced by the Camouflage Directorate, 1942.

also adopt illustrative strategies. It was maintained that images and diagrams should form the heart of this booklet. This was simply not because civil camouflage was considered to be a wholly visual technology, but it was also felt that this would be a useful approach to adopt 'in order to catch the eye of the architect who finds his desk inundated with official papers as well as to give those without flying experience a better idea of some aspects of the problem' (Darwin 1941). What is evident here is that the representatives of the Camouflage Directorate clearly wanted to ensure that architects fully appreciated the problems which they faced when designing buildings.

In terms of the structure of the booklet, this was arranged into three sections, each of which called attention to the characteristics which rendered a building conspicuous when viewed by the bomb aimer or aerial observer, and which architects should therefore consider in the production of their design. The booklet contended that 'to achieve satisfactory concealment, three principal factors must be considered: – Siting, Layout and Constructional Form' (Camouflage Committee 1942: 7). Consideration of each of these elements could therefore produce a self-concealing building; it is noted that 'absence of such forethought may produce buildings which will be far more difficult and costly to camouflage' (4). Certainly, it is argued that an ignorance of these factors in peace-time had produced the situation that the camoufleurs were currently attempting to deal with; 'in peace-time, if a factory shows up well from the air – so much the better. It makes a free advertisement … but in war, advertisement may be fatal' (5–6) (see Figure 5.1).

Siting

One of the central themes which runs throughout *Concealment of New Buildings* is the pertinence of the aerial view. The importance of this is perhaps most greatly accentuated in the first section on Siting, in which aerial awareness and an understanding of the vertical interpretation of the landscape is most acute. In this opening chapter, it is noted how 'the navigation of the attacking bomber is checked and assisted throughout its journey by the recognition of well-defined landmarks and the final recognition of the target is greatly helped if it lies close to some feature which is easy to recognise from the air' (9). In order to illustrate this, a combination of cartographic material as well as aerial images highlighting prominent landmarks are utilised here.

At the same time, the booklet also encourages the architect to make examinations from the air themselves, and from this, to identify spaces which are best suited for locating a new building. It is argued that only thorough experiencing vertical visualities and aerial sensations that full appreciation of the problem can be comprehended and ideal sites for new construction be ascertained; 'by air observation alone can assurance be obtained as to its freedom from objectionable landmarks'. Furthermore, the booklet highlights that the prominence of certain topographical features when viewed from the air may have a direct impact on which sites could be used for development; such natural landmarks, it is argued, 'will usually make concealment impossible despite anything which may be done by subsequent camouflage of the buildings. Once the landmark has been seen and recognised, the position of the target, even if hidden, will be fixed; and the position once fixed, recognition will usually be possible' (9). In particular, the booklet highlights how 'the intersection of rivers, main roads, railways or canals, and well-defined loops in any of these are dangerous. You might welcome a site like this for its good rail and road services, but the enemy would welcome it more as an easy target' (11) (see Figure

5.4   'The intersection of rivers, main roads, railways or canals, and well-defined loops in any of these are dangerous. You might welcome a site like this for its good rail and road services, but the enemy would welcome it more as an easy target'.

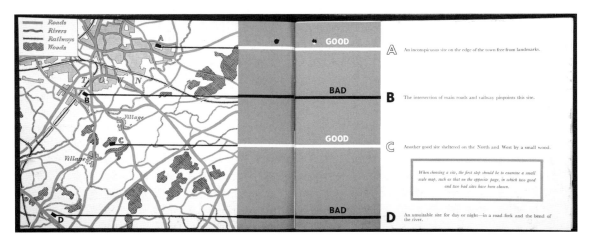

5.5   An illustration from *Concealment of New Buildings*, demonstrating 'good' and 'bad' locations for the siting of a new factory.

5.4). It is here that a critique of Britain's modern landscapes also emerges; the booklet notes how 'modern town planning often makes conspicuous and characteristic patterns. A site near these is dangerous' (13). In order to isolate ideal sites, the booklet makes use of a cartographic representation of a fictional urban area on which good and bad spots for new factories are identified. In Figure 5.5, Sites A is described as 'an inconspicuous site on the edge of town free from landmark … Buildings on this site could easily be made to look like an extension to existing housing', whereas at Site B 'the intersection of main roads and railway pinpoints this site' and therefore such a location should be disregarded (18–19)(see Figure 5.5).

Lay-out

Following on from Siting, the next issue which is examined is that of Layout. What is interesting here is how 'fitness for purpose', functionality and order, all of which were promoted by planner-preservationists, are seemingly re-interpreted for the purposes of camouflage. For the civil camoufleurs, suitability of form becomes more about selecting an architectural lay-out which would facilitate the easier merging of the superstructure into the landscape. Indeed, it is argued that the general lay-out that a building should take be 'controlled by the type of Camouflage to be employed' (21). In the booklet, two forms of camouflage are outlined and deemed to be the most important when considering the ways in which man-made features could be blurred when viewed against the surrounding landscape. These were 'Camouflage for Concealment, in which it is sought to hide the object' and 'Camouflage for Disguise where hiding is not attempted but rather a change in appearance from that of a vital target to one of little importance' (23). It was argued that 'concealment is the ideal of Camouflage, but circumstances often make Disguise the more desirable method, whilst with large buildings or groups of buildings a combination of the two methods is usually most successful' (23). The booklet makes it quite clear that the surrounding geography has a direct effect on which approach is

5.6 An illustration from *Concealment of New Buildings*, demonstrating 'bad' and 'good' layouts.

taken, or indeed, whether a mixture of the two is applied. In the case of urban environments, both concealment and disguise are encouraged. It is highlighted how a 'normal layout would isolate the factory from its surroundings, service roads and car parks and tend to outline the buildings. But if suitably planned, the lay-out can continue existing development and the usual tell-tale service roads and car parks may be eliminated or screened' (26) (see Figure 5.6). For rural areas, where civil camoufleurs argued that irregularity dominated the landscape and where the challenges were somewhat different, the tactic of concealment alone is advocated; 'concealment is … more suitable than disguise as houses. A normal layout … is obviously undesirable, as it is easily seen by its regularity and the light frame of its roads. A better situation [would be] … where full use is made of the adjacent wood and where roads are no longer obvious and cars may be hidden in the trees' (26).

Debates surrounding lay-out were not solely confined to locating and designing new factories and workspaces but were also extended to include the temporary huts which were to provide accommodation for construction workers and their families. In part, this was due to anxieties that aerial attacks were being extended to target worker populations themselves. It was argued the arrangement of workers' lodgings could, therefore, aid the enemy bomber in not only locating their objectives, but could also serve to render them as a target. *Concealment of New Buildings* argues that 'huts scattered as if shaken from a dice box are sure to attract attention' (35). Elsewhere, geometrical ground patterns are labelled as 'a bulls eye'; 'hutted camps are often noticeable from the air because their lay-out is either geometrical or grid-like or dispersed over a large area with an aimless irregularity. They have usually no orderly lay-out of the kind common to domestic buildings, neither have they garden plots which are such a noticeable feature of housing estates when seen from the air' (31). What is evident here is an extension of some of the debates of the planner-preservationists, where irregular, scattered development is frowned upon. For workers lodgings, the strategy of disguise is encouraged, with the merging of these features into existing patterns of development. *Concealment of New Buildings* suggests that 'disguise may take the form of a suburban village or farm lay-out. New roads must be laid out to link up with existing roads and the huts sited so that the plan is in character with its environment' (27). To complete the effect, architects are also instructed to pay attention to other natural and artificial ground patterns to complete the illusion. False hedges, crops, cultivation, tracks and roads are all encouraged to distract attention from the hutments themselves; 'to the air view the treatment of the ground round a hutment is of more importance than the disguise of the huts themselves' (29).

Constructional Form

In the final section of the booklet, an evaluation of the process of Construction is undertaken, and it is here that relationships and communication networks between the architect and the camoufleur are encouraged. Indeed, the booklet highlights how:

> if proper consideration is to be given to a suitable form of construction giving improved concealment, the earliest consultation between Architect and Camouflage Expert is essential (42).

It is with this issue of Constructional Form that accountability for the civil camouflage problem is perhaps most significant; the booklet discusses how:

> the difficulty and costliness of camouflage for buildings has in the past been largely due to their external shape. This has been dictated by the requirements of production or function and by convenience in erection (42).

Despite the fact that this is considered to be the most significant issue that architects needed to contend with in order to produce self-concealment, surprisingly only one suggestion is proposed to deal with this aspect. The booklet advocates a building design which can be physically integrated into the landscape (see Figure 5.7); the ideal, it is argued:

5.7   Illustrations showing the appearance of a semi-buried factory.

> is no doubt the buried or semi-buried factory, but short of this, one with a flat roof surrounded by banks which slope gently into the surrounding ground can be very effectively hidden (42).

Although the argument is made that 'for many reasons such construction may not always be possible', the booklet maintains that 'the cost of building these types is often not much higher than for normal construction, whilst the amount of applied camouflage necessary to provide any given level of concealment is considerably less' (42). Furthermore, such a design, it is argued, 'gives complete disguise from the air whilst vital work goes on uninterrupted in the spacious factory below' (51). What is interesting about this final section is that it would seem inevitable that the camouflage of new buildings could only be affected through the locating of them in a subterranean space, and I would argue that this official publication seemingly ignores alternative architectural options that were being proposed at the time. For instance, *The Art of Camouflage* advocates several alternative constructional features which could be incorporated to achieve self-concealing architecture. Chesney suggests, for instance, that the incorporation of glass should be avoided; 'if it must be provided then the orthodox glassed face towards the northern sector is the best arrangement possible. Reflection is thus reduced to the minimum' (Chesney 1941: 117). Moreover, Chesney suggests making buildings as low as possible; 'many factories … are built unnecessarily high. Every inch of height that is not essential should be cut out' (117). Finally, he encourages architects to think about including trees to disrupt the shadows cast by buildings; 'instead of cutting out all those in the immediate neighbourhood of the building as is the usual

Factory Type H.

custom, they can be left when advantageous for camouflage purposes, and more planted to that end' (117). All these mundane and yet rather simple constructional elements are ostensibly disregarded in the Directorate's publication, and this would suggest a regulation of camouflage knowledge and practice by official camouflage bodies.

CONCLUDING REMARKS: CAMOUFLAGE AESTHETICS IN THE PRESENT

Throughout history, warfare has acted as an endless catalyst for technological development and ideological progress. More often than not, these developments have had profound implications upon the perceptions and appearance of particular spaces and places, both military and civilian. Indeed, in modern warfare, a continuous stream of technological advances have undoubtedly transformed the battlefield, resulting in the destruction or modification of existing features, or the production of new offensive or defensive spaces. As this chapter has illustrated, the emergence of the aeroplane in the early twentieth century as both a modern technology and war machine had profound implications upon the imagining, experiencing and transforming of conflict spaces. As well as extending warfare to the civilian population, its production and enabling of new ways of seeing and engaging with the built environment very much prompted and inspired architects to appraise and re-think ways of producing buildings which would facilitate their merging and harmonising into the landscape. While an attentiveness to siting, lay-out and constructional form was encouraged in the name of defence for industrial sites and locations, the emergence of a self-concealing architectural aesthetic during the Second World War represents an attempt to redefine conceptions and the production of a harmonious style as part of an everyday architectural style.

Positioning this period of architectural design within a much broader history of camouflage aesthetics throughout the twentieth and into the twenty-first century, it is clear that the technologies of modern warfare, and of camouflage, have and continue to leave their imprint upon the performance and practice of both civil and military architecture in the British landscape since 1945. Tactically important military features constructed since the Second World War have actively sought to integrate camouflage ideas and principles into their design; from secret, subterranean Cold War bunkers (e.g. Kelvedon Hatch, Cheshire), through to the 'turfing over' of contemporary airfield dispersal points and weapons storage facilities (e.g. Defence Munitions site at Kineton, Warwickshire). At the same time, the adoption of camouflage aesthetics has also been extended beyond the spaces of defence and the military, and has become translated into everyday, public spaces. From the Tours Aillaud in the Parisian suburb of Nanterre, completed in 1977 by the architect Émile Aillaud, to present-day attempts to render invisible telecommunications infrastructure by means of fibreglass cactuses, boulders and the mimicking of trees, civilian architecture continues to be driven by a desire to integrate what was once a technology of war into the everyday performances of architecture (Blechman and Newman 2004: 397). It would, therefore, not be unfair, nor be unreasonable, to declare that camouflage aesthetics and notions of self-concealing architecture have seemingly permeated and are ever present in every avenue of contemporary architectural thinking; writing in 2006, architectural theorists Neil Leach has suggested that now 'human beings are governed by a chameleon-like urge to blend in with our surroundings – to "camouflage" ourselves within our environment. We need to feel at home and to find our place in the world' (2006: ix). This affectual and emotional impulse to fit our buildings harmoniously into the everyday landscape shows no sign of dissipating as the demands for camouflage continue to evolve. Indeed, in today's society, where the discourses of environmentalism and sustainability are prevalent, the need to conceal has extended beyond the visual; as Newark writes, 'it is not only the visible language of plant-covered roofs and turf walls that is being quoted; these new buildings must also perform in an invisible world by reducing carbon emissions' (2007: 188). Combined with a desire to render buildings invisible by moderating artificial light pollution, heat loss, and excessive power consumption, camouflage has become more than a visual aesthetic conceived during wartime; it has become a part of everyday life. It is, perhaps, from the spaces and technologies produced by warfare and military conflict that solutions may be derived to these new challenges pressed upon contemporary landscape and architectural design.

NOTES

1   For other examples of contemporary planner-preservationist critiques of the British landscape, see also Williams-Ellis (1928, 1937).

2   The bombing raid on Guernica, taking place on the 26 April 1937, represents the first mass aerial attack upon a civilian population. Carried out by the German Luftwaffe's 'Condor Legion' during the Spanish Civil War.

3   Morrison had assumed the responsibilities of Minister of Home Security from John Anderson on the 3 October 1940.

4   The Civil Defence Camouflage Establishment (C.D.C.E.) was established in the wake of the Munich Crisis, and operated as the principal government institution for civil camouflage. In February 1939, it commenced the systematic camouflaging of important civil features, using a roller-skating rink in Leamington Spa as its base for the designing of such schemes.

REFERENCES

Anderson, Sir J. 1940. Draft Correspondence: To the First Lord of the Admiralty, the Secretary of State for War and Minister of Supply. February. The National Archives (hereafter TNA), HO186/395.

Anon. 1919. Notes on the Concealment of Buildings against Raiding Aircraft. TNA, CAB16/170.

Bernard, O. 1937. Correspondence: To the Minister for Co-ordination of Defence. 17 March. TNA, CAB16/170.

Blechman, H. and Newman, A. 2004. *DPM – Disruptive Pattern Material: An Encyclopedia of Camouflage: Nature, Military, Culture*. London: DPM.

Brace, C. 2001. Publishers and publishing: Towards a historical geography of countryside writing, c.1930–1950. *Area*, 33(3), 287–96.

Camouflage Committee. 1942. Concealment of New Buildings: Camouflage Committee Memorandum. TNA. n.d. HO217/2.

Chesney, C.H.R. 1941. *The Art of Camouflage*. London: Robert Hale Ltd.

Darwin, R.V. 1941. Correspondence: To G. Bristow, Ministry of Works and Buildings. 13 October. TNA, HO186/1343.

Gruffudd, P. 1994. Selling the Countryside: Representations of Rural Britain. J. Gold and S.V. Ward (eds), *Place Promotion: The Use of Publicity and Marketing to Sell Towns and Regions*. Chichester: Wiley, 247–63.

Gruffudd, P. 1995a. 'Propaganda for seamliness': Clough Williams-Ellis and Portmeirion, 1918–1950. *Ecumene*, 2(4), 399–422.

Gruffudd, P. 1995b. Remaking Wales: Nation building and the geographical imagination, 1925–1950. *Political Geography*, 14(3), 219–39.

Gruffudd, P., Herbert, D.T. and Piccini, A. 2000. In search of Wales: Travel writing and narratives of difference, 1918–50. *Journal of Historical Geography*, 26(4), 589–604.

Hauser, K. 2007. *Shadow Sites: Photography, Archaeology and the British Landscape 1927–1951*. Oxford: Oxford University Press.

Hewitt, J. 1992. The 'nature' and 'art' of Shell advertising in the early 1930s. *Journal of Design History*, 5(2), 121–39.

Jay, M. 1994. *Downcast Eyes: The Denigration of Vision in Twentieth-century French Thought*. Berkeley, CA: University of California Press.

Le Corbusier 1935/1987. *Aircraft*. London: Trefoil.

Leach, N. 2006. *Camouflage*. Cambridge, MA: MIT Press.

Linehan, D. 2003. A new England: Landscape, exhibition and remaking industrial space in the 1930s. D. Gilbert, D. Matless and B. Short (eds), *Geographies of British Modernity*. Oxford: Blackwell, 132–50.

Kelvedon Hatch. n.d. The Kelvedon Hatch: Secret Nuclear Bunker. Available at: www.secretnuclearbunker. com [accessed 14 October 2011].

Matless, D. 1990. Ages of English design: Preservation, modernism and tales of their history, 1926–1939. *Journal of Design History*, 3(4), 203–12.

Matless, D. 1998. *Landscapes of Englishness*. London: Reaktion.

McCamley, N.J. 2007. *Cold War Secret Nuclear Bunkers: The Passive Defence of the Western World during the Cold War*. Barnsley: Pen and Sword.

Morrison, H. 1940. Memorandum by the Minister of Home Security on the recommendations of the Fourteenth Report from the Select Committee on National Expenditure. December. TNA, HO186/975.

Newark, T. 2007. *Camouflage*. London: Thames and Hudson.

Peach, H.H. and Carrington, N. (eds) 1930. *The Face of the Land*. London: George Allen and Unwin.

Stichelbaut, B., Bourgeois, J., Saunders, N. and Chielens, P. (eds) 2009. *Images of Conflict: Military Aerial Photography and Archaeology*. Newcastle: Cambridge Scholars.

Virilio, P. 1989. *War and Cinema: The Logistics of Perception*. London: Verso.

Williams, D. 1989. *Liners in Battledress: Wartime Camouflage and Colour Schemes for Passenger Ships*. London: Conway Maritime.

Williams, D. 2001. *Naval Camouflage 1914–1945: A Complete Visual Reference*. London: Chatham.

Williams-Ellis, C. 1928. *England and the Octopus*. London: Geoffrey Bles/CPRE.

Williams-Ellis, C. (ed) 1937. *Britain and the Beast*. London: J.M. Dent and Sons.

Wohl, R. 2005. *The Spectacle of Flight: Aviation and the Western Imagination, 1920–1950*. London: Yale University Press.

Wyatt, Col. F.J.C. 1938. Notes on Deficiencies in Camouflage Organisation – October 1938. 4 November. TNA, HO186/390.

6

Home Base: Militarization of the American Home in the Second World War

Rebecca Lyn Cooper

INTRODUCTION

In recent decades, a great deal of scholarly attention has been devoted to examining the impact of the Second World War on changing ideas about the proper role and capabilities of women. Scholars have often noted that the lack of men available for wartime production due to combat mobilization made it possible, if not mandatory in many cases, for women to take up many of men's traditional roles, and in the process, to demonstrate the potential capabilities of women in the workforce. Thanks in great part to potent and durable symbols like 'Rosie the Riveter', the participation of women in wartime industry has been relatively easy to visualize and therefore readily available for analysis. Comparatively little has been written of the domestic life of women and its relation to the war effort, and virtually nothing about the mobilization of the space of the house itself. This oversight is especially puzzling given that the overwhelming majority of women did not participate in either military service or wartime industries, remaining at home to care for their families and serve the nation through their otherwise typical domestic roles and tasks.

In this particular form of 'domestic service' no space was as vital and important as the kitchen. Perhaps no other space in the American home has received as much attention, inspired as much controversy (or as intense a nostalgia), or witnessed more radical transformation in response to pressures of modernity. The kitchen can seen as a microcosm of both the house itself and – by an extension of thought common to many thinkers of the nineteenth and twentieth century (Walker 2000: 66) – of the nation as a whole (O'Neill 1995: 130). An investigation of its development up to the start of the Second World War and its repurposing in support of the American war effort during the first half of the 1940s, can help to illuminate many of the changes wrought on the lives of Americans by the development of the United States into a modern industrialized nation. From 1840 to 1940, the kitchen underwent an intense spatial and technological transformation, from a space and a set of procedures that were essentially medieval to something completely modern, partaking of all the best that science, technology, and industrialization had to offer. From 1940 to 1945, this newly modernized space was then made available for conscription by the United States

Good Soldier #1....

With our nation at war, public morale assumes an importance of the first magnitude. And the responsibility of maintaining that morale rests chiefly on the shoulders of America's women—a responsibility to make their homes havens of confidence and calm.

It is not always easy, particularly in these trying times, to keep a stiff upper lip. But from our day-to-day experience with over a million families from coast to coast, we find that not only are America's women good soldiers but *their* steadfastness reflects itself in the spirit of the entire family.

One of the greatest challenges to peace of mind in America's homes is financial worry. It is usually the woman's job to solve such problems, since, although, the man may be the breadwinner, the wife is usually the *Treasurer* of the family. While in some homes increased income has made possible the filling of many long-felt needs, in other homes incomes haven't yet caught up with increased living costs. In some of these cases an accumulation of old debts that piled up in less fortunate times, or through emergencies, continues to challenge the morale of the home.

Actually, the means are at hand to meet this challenge. One of America's best known financial organizations — *Personal* Finance Company — is offering a service that has been designed to help families meet financial obligations and free their minds for important work.

Personal Finance Company believes that no one should borrow when there is some other commonsense way to solve a financial problem. But when a cash loan is the answer, more than 400 *Personal* offices from coast to coast stand ready to serve.

In addition to its regular service, *Personal* is filling the special needs of the moment: Cash loans are being made to people who want to buy tools for their new defense jobs ... to people who need uniforms ... to people who want specialized training ... to people who must move to be nearer their new-found work ... to people who want to clean up old bills so they can give 'all-out' concentration to their daily jobs.

Never before has the flexibility of *Personal's* service been more dramatically demonstrated. Whether you're living where you always have, or just moved to a new community, getting a loan at *Personal* Finance Company is no more difficult for any credit-worthy family than opening a charge account at a store. The main requirement is just your ability to make reasonable monthly repayments.

If you have need for a cash loan of $25 to $250 or more, you will find the address of a *Personal* Finance Company office listed in your local telephone directory. If one is not listed, write to 1300 Market Street, Wilmington, Delaware for the address of the office nearest you.

Need cash for your
INCOME TAX?
Personal Finance Company is offering Tax-Loans which provide a lump sum of cash immediately, repayable in modern are monthly instalments. Also available, a 'Simplified Work Sheet For Income Tax Payers'—a convenient form for accumulating and arranging the necessary figures before making out your Income Tax Return. You can get this Work Sheet, free, at your local *Personal* office. No obligation—it's a *Personal* service.

6.1   With the massive mobilization required to enable the United States entry into Second World War, the entire population had to be drafted into the war effort.

government and brought into service as a site for a series of important reorganizations of domestic activity peculiar to the Second World War. First, it is the site on which the marks of the wartime drive to remake American society as more regimented, organized, rational and efficient can most easily be discerned as they affect the smallest gestures and choices of average citizens. It is also the site where the majority of auxiliary work that enabled the massive wartime mobilization of the American population was most crucially settled. For every soldier in the field, for every worker in the factory, there were many more women in homes across the country who coped with higher prices and scarcity, who acquiesced in complex rationing schemes and spurned the black market, and who supported the war effort directly by feeding and clothing their families and keeping their houses amidst conditions universally more difficult than had been faced by any previous generation. This study traces the development of the modern American kitchen and the way its new form was then 'drafted' for use in support of the American entrance to the Second World War.

AMERICAN WOMEN IN A WORLD AT WAR

What makes the Second World War significant and unique is the manner in which, under the doctrine of total war, military mobilization spread throughout every aspect of American society. Accordingly, even women in their homes were reminded continuously that they were 'in the Army now' and expected to behave appropriately.

The war effort pervaded every aspect of American society, crossing colours, religions, classes, and even genders, with the government's call to mobilize drifting down onto the most personal of decisions and activities (Weatherford 1990: 201). Women served the war effort, as did men, either directly, through military or auxiliary service, or indirectly, by taking jobs in wartime industries. Yet, as stated above, as important as these roles were, they account for only a small portion of American women at the time. In all branches of military service, there were perhaps only as many as a half-million women enlisted and serving over the course of the war. Meanwhile perhaps just over five million women, or roughly 15 per cent of the female population (Campbell 1984: 167; Hesse-Biber and Carter 2000: 38), served on the Third Front in some production capacity. The rest, of the women, participated in the war effort every bit as fully as those who sought work in the military or industry but did so in the space of their own homes. These women who toiled on the home front served the war effort by keeping America running smoothly, serving simply as W-I-V-E-S or W-A-Hs (women at home).

6.2   Military rhetoric invaded every aspect of culture after the United States entered the war.

The service of these 'soldiers in housedresses' was mostly invisible, though the success of the war effort rested in no small part on their shoulders and required their full and active participation. One reason for the obscurity surrounding the efforts of America's 'kitchen commandos' was that these efforts, as crucial as they were to larger issues of production, troop training, equipment and mobilization and the delivery of food and material aid to allies, were all accomplished within the space of the home, a space which, according to Scott (1988: 42) has been long considered abject and unworthy as a site for cultural or academic enquiry due to its associations with women and the unpaid work of home-keeping (Cowan 1983: 18).

THE KITCHEN REVOLUTION

Within the house, the network of meanings surrounding the space of the kitchen was extremely complex. On the one hand it has historically served as the heart of the house, both in terms of spatial arrangement but also, and more importantly for some, as the place where the wife and mother performs her daily duties of care

KITCHEN COMMANDOS

There's one offensive always in progress — the lady-of-the-house *versus* dirt and disorder — and as for mopping up, she's been at it for years! Special demands are made on any work dress. In Good Housekeeping Textile Laboratory we've checked the dresses on these three pages for fading and shrinkage (cottons, not more than 3%). The girls in the Institute laboratories actually wore them at work, to check on proper fit, working comfort, washability, and serviceability. Fresh for the foray is this one-piece, peg-topped, cotton-chambray and checked gingham. Red, blue, or brown. Sizes 10 to 18. About $8

GOOD HOUSEKEEPING FASHIONS • EDITED BY MARTHA STOUT

6.3   In addition to its role as the 'heart of the home' the modern American kitchen had to feed an army of home front and production workers, tasks which advertisers elevated through connection to similar tasks undertaken on the 'fighting front'.

for the inhabitants. On the other hand the kitchen was also a place of damp, dirt, drudgery, danger, and bad smells (Snodgrass 2004: 309). The activities which took place within the kitchen were also largely primal, involving mastering the elements in order to address the most basic physical need of the human body. In many cases, the kitchen suffered the taint of this contact with the body and the primal need for food, and until fairly late in the nineteenth century the kitchen was viewed with suspicion and contempt as an atavistic relic, a dangerous space to be navigated with caution while, at the same time, it served most families as the primary space of dwelling within the house (Ierley 1999). This connection with the primal and the traditional spheres of women's work accounts for much of the weight behind the view of the kitchen as the least modern aspect of a space already understood to have been left behind by the advance of technology and modernity.

From 1840 to 1940, however, the forces of innovation, industrialization and modernization brought profound change to the kitchen, altering its nature and its form forever. An individual somehow plucked from any previous period of world history and placed into a typical kitchen in 1840, would still find it relatively contiguous with such spaces of the past and would be able to grasp the purpose and function of the space and its equipment fairly quickly. So sweeping was the wave of change which washed through the kitchen in that hundred years that the same individual, brought into an American kitchen in 1940, would find the space incomprehensibly alien, its surfaces blank and inscrutable. Certainly this is a result of the introduction of technology in the form of manufactured materials and appliances, but is due as well to the change in the basic morphology of the house, from a room loosely organized around a fireplace which was its primary fixture, to a room of abstract equipment and continuous smooth surfaces where all hints of use are hidden behind discretely closed cabinet doors. This is the space that served as the setting for the efforts of the American housewife in 1940, fully modernized by the application of the latest technology, inspired by the best practices of housekeeping now understood as domestic science, rather than a home art, and furnished with a wide array of industrially produced items, from the appliances and cabinets which furnished it, to the implements used to produce meals, and even to the food itself. This streamlined, efficient workspace of glass and enamel-coated steel was delivered complete into the heart of the American home right at the moment when the country most needed all of its citizens to be as efficient and effective as any factory worker, and as well trained and motivated as any soldier.

HEART OF THE HOME FRONT

The needs of wartime mobilization required that the vast production capability of the United States, unleashed after years of Depression, be funnelled almost completely into gearing up for the war (Campbell 1984: 165). It was largely through women's effort in their kitchens that the 'free labour' of the home could be mobilized to meet the need for increased industrial production and to replace the domestic servants who left household service in droves for jobs in the military or in war related industries (Campbell 1984: 173). It was by virtue of women's acquiescence and participation in the rationing programme and their efforts as meal planners that the best use was made of scarce and controlled commodities. And it was through women's tireless efforts to learn new cooking methods and recipes, their willingness to try new products to stretch rationed foodstuffs, and their conversion of yards and flowerbeds into victory gardens that the American family was able to make it through the scarcity of the war years with a diet that actually improved in food quality and healthiness (Campbell 1979: 94).

   Though they did not work outside the home, these women nonetheless worked very much at the direction of the US Government which, through the efforts of the Magazine Bureau of the Office of War Information, sought to provide them with motivation, training and a variety of practical and useful tools that the average housewife could put to immediate use in her home. Magazines such as *Women's Home Companion*, *Ladies' Home Journal*, *House Beautiful*, *American Home*, and *Good Housekeeping* all worked closely with the Bureau, and with the business community through the War Advertising Council (Walker 2000: 15), to keep women informed about the needs of their country and the best practices to meet those needs. And overwhelmingly, it was the kitchen that these practices were meant to address in answer to the government call for reorganizing and mobilizing the home into a rear-guard supply depot. Through articles, pamphlets and advertisements, women were encouraged to apply military logic and discipline to reorganize their families in support of the nation's build-up to battle.

MOBILIZING FOR HOME FRONT SERVICE

First among the duties required of these household soldiers in the run-up to war was a basic reorganization of the home front.

   In order to free men, and sometimes women, to put in as much time as possible at work and in volunteer service, Mother had to take responsibility for reconfiguring the home to most efficiently prepare meals, coordinate the day's housekeeping and maintain household

SOLDIERS IN HOUSEDRESSES
—you're helping to win !

Pequot is proud to serve both you and our armed services

THE ALARM CLOCK is your bugle, Mrs. Housewife—the housedress your uniform. And we'd like to pay a tribute to your military virtues. Your *courage* in accepting the harsh necessities of war. Your *obedience* to ration regulations. Your *sacrifice* of comfort—walking and carrying bundles when it's cold, canning your garden surplus when it's hot.

Maybe they don't sound sublime, these war tasks of yours. But they happen to be *your* job, the job you're trained for, and you're doing it mighty well.

You know what Pequot's special skill is—making sturdy fabrics. Night and day

Pequot Mills roar on, to turn out sheets and special war fabrics for military use.

So great is this new production record, that some Pequot Sheets can still be made for homefolks. They're genuine Pequots, you can be sure. The same superior, long-wearing quality that made you vote Pequot your favorite sheet in nation-wide polls.

If you need sheets, you need Pequots more than ever. Never in your housekeeping life has thrift been so essential. Pequot Mills, Salem, Massachusetts.

BUY ONLY NECESSITIES— and the first and the greatest necessity to invest in, for our future safety, is— WAR BONDS.

PEQUOT SHEETS
PEQUOT SHEETS AND PILLOW CASES

6.4   Despite the need for women to contribute to the military effort and the production line, women's highest service was still understood to be in the home.

goods (Paddleford 1942: 63). The ideal presented in pamphlets and posters produced by the government, and in the editorials, articles and advertisements offered by the War Advertising Council was that of the patriotic mothers and wives of America standing up in support of democracy, willing to devote their entire efforts to defend their way of life (Banning 1942: 124). By constantly reiterating the goals to be set and steps necessary to achieve them, women at home could be brought together into a singularity of purpose and focus no less potent than that produced in the average soldier through his indoctrination in boot camp. For the housewives of America, the discipline and regimentation necessary could be enforced by a combination of carrot and stick; magazines and government pamphlets offered concrete advice and directions to provide a virtuous example, and added the subtle fear of negative reinforcement through peer pressure and the social shame of deviation from the norm. Though women were free to ignore the call to reduce waste and organize the family into an efficient and smoothly running machine, to do so risked the contempt of others; slovenliness, failure to comply with government directives, and hoarding or waste would be noticed by the neighbours and delivery boys and revealed through the careless talk of children, resulting in scorn heaped onto the offending family.

Magazines of the period certainly presented women in their role as caretakers and home keepers, willing to do anything to fulfil their obligations to their family and the nation, but they also focused again and again on the efforts of children and other family members (though not often on husbands). Women were encouraged to see themselves as generals or sergeants in the home, manning their 'battle stations' at the oven and the kitchen sink and supervising their 'troops', and viewing their children as potential sources of labour in a scheme of total mobilization, members of her 'squad' of household helpers, not simply as individuals requiring care. Children of all ages, from young 'pigtailers' to teenagers, were warned not to be 'a deserter' but to pitch in and do their part to help Mother around the house. Advertisements presenting children as a source of potential household labour, and articles which gave moms practical solutions for how to mobilize these auxiliary troops (Hindman 1941: 46) not only communicated to the children themselves that such help was required of them – that doing their job in the home was both their patriotic duty and a way to ease the burden on Mom – it also served to help women see their children as resources to be relied upon, a useful labour pool if carefully organized and properly supervised.

Such planning and organization was critically necessary in this period as wartime necessities and scarcity made even simple tasks like buying groceries into time consuming and complicated ordeals. Though the majority of women did not enter the workforce, two thirds of the female population served in a volunteer capacity for the Red Cross, Office of Civil Defense or other local organizations (Hartmann 1982: 22), while many of their men worked multiple shifts in offices or factories. Even those women who did not work outside the home had to

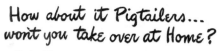

carefully schedule their time in order to accommodate the demands of the school timetable and the punch clock. Mealtimes had to be coordinated as meticulously as battlefield assaults, with every step and action carefully scripted.

Menus and time sheets posted in the kitchen helped Mother to plan ahead to make the most of scarce time and to lessen the work for minds and bodies tired from a day full of labour. Magazines of the period continued to offer recipes and meal plans as they had before, but there was a new emphasis on structure and regimentation, and on the provision of new tools to aid women in their meal preparation tasks. Articles gave women practical advice in full page spreads, encouraging them to view time as a scarce commodity that needed to be managed as carefully as any stick of butter or sack of sugar, and to plan her day to the very minute.

The logic of the factory production line migrated into the kitchen in the form of assembly line preparation of meal components that could be stored in the refrigerator or icebox until they were needed and then mobilized to feed the family quickly with a minimum of

6.5 Magazine features and advertisements iterated to children (primarily girls and teens) the message of home-front help for mother as a patriotic duty.

fuss. Meals prepared ahead of time reduced the amount of work later in the day when Mother was already tired from her duties, and also made it possible for children, or even the occasional husband, to pitch in and lend a hand. The pages of *Better Homes and Gardens* and *Good Housekeeping* especially exhorted women to make the best use of their counters and refrigerators, including charts and lists which could be cut out of the magazine and mounted on the inside of cabinet doors or posted on the refrigerator, offering instructions on how to rationalize tasks from the assembly of a salad dressing to the precise timing for all the elements of a meal to move through the oven. Magazines often included elaborate guides and diagrams for how to best pack the refrigerator to make the most efficient use of cooling and to load the oven to cook make the most of scarce heating fuel. Effective use of the limited space inside of the refrigerator seems to have been a particular concern of the staff of the *Good Housekeeping* Institute and meal plans often included instructions and even photographs to illustrate the efficient stacking of cookware.

6.6 Magazine features and advertisements iterated to children (primarily girls and teens) the message of home-front help for mother as a patriotic duty.

MANAGING SCARCITY

Shopping was a major challenge, one of the most difficult tasks to face wartime consumers, a task which fell mostly on the shoulders of women (Hartmann 1982: 22). Not only did shortages make finding all the necessary items difficult at best, but even if the shopper was able to find all the goods she was looking for, the rationing system put in place beginning in 1942 made figuring out which of those goods she was entitled to purchase an even greater challenge. Sugar was the first commodity to be rationed followed quickly by coffee (Weatherford 1990: 202). Rationing schemes for these items were relatively simple. Every family received a specific number of ration coupons for items like sugar and coffee, with each coupon equivalent to one pound of the commodity in question. A pound of sugar from one retailer was equal to a pound purchased at any other, though the shopper had to be sure of the current 'ceiling price' for a given item, so that she would not undermine the war effort by participating in the black market (Weatherford 1990: 214). The rationing system for items like vegetables and especially meats, however, was dramatically more complex.

Certain cuts of meat or more desirable vegetables would be assigned a higher point value depending on their relative scarcity, or on the expected future demand for that particular item, while the quality of the particular item was also factored into the number of points it might be assigned (Fisher 1943: 157). Point levels and ceiling prices were set by the Office of Price Administration, and were subject to constant changes based on shifting production conditions, military needs and scarcity due to black market trading (Campbell 1979: 66). Women needed to carefully prepare their shopping lists, tracking current point values for their desired items, managing their ration coupon allotment, while anticipating potential changes in point values and prices resulting from shifts in the fortunes of the war. In order to make the best use of their ration books and to ensure an adequate diet for their families, wartime women had to plan their family diet with intense tactical skill. *Good Housekeeping*, from the earliest days of

If someone said you were not feeding your family well, you'd be prompt to make a vigorous denial. The hours you spend in your kitchen! The laurels you've garnered for your delicious cooking! But could you honestly answer yes if someone asked whether you always combined sound dietetics with your tasty dishes? Are you successful in making your menus supply the food values necessary for the good health of your family and making them like it?

AMERICA IS NOT WELL FED. Studies of American eating habits show that not many women could answer yes to these questions. It may shock you to think of your family's diet as deficient. But it is a fact that dietary deficiencies are found in many American homes. I am not speaking of poor homes—that is another problem entirely—but of the average, comfortable homes that have never known what it is to miss a meal.

A FULL STOMACH ISN'T EVERYTHING. Being well-fed is not a matter simply of having enough to eat, but of having enough of the right kind of food—the foods that supply the vitamins, minerals, and other nutritional factors each of us needs in the daily diet if we are to enjoy buoyant health and keep our bubbling energy.

The lack of these factors, even to a mild degree, is a constant sap on vitality. Although that lack may not incapacitate the individual, his health is kept below par. It lowers resistance to infectious diseases, particularly colds, and may be the cause of extreme nervousness and irritability. In women it contributes to the complications occurring in pregnancy, reducing their chances of bearing healthy children with safety. Often it is the reason for children's slow progress in their growth or in school. Adults suffer from that tired feeling, sometimes to the point where they become shiftless and lazy, because they have been deprived of the vitality and the will to do. Many a failure in life might be traced to the dining-room table.

America
expects every cook to do her duty
says
HELEN S. MITCHELL, PH.D.
Director of Nutrition on the Staff of the Coordinator of Health, Welfare, and Related Defense Activities

NUTRITION AND NATIONAL DEFENSE. Up to now there has been a wide gap between scientific knowledge of nutrition and its practical application to everyday meal planning. But the gap is being closed. Nutrition has been made a part of the National Defense Program. A world at war threatening our way of life has jolted us into the realization that we cannot be a strong nation unless we are a healthy nation. And health begins with the food we eat. Tanks, guns, battleships, and planes may be of little avail unless the nation behind them is able to find within itself the stamina and courage to face unflinchingly an uncertain future.

THE PART YOU MUST PLAY. Every homemaker is being asked to do her share by adding to her cooking lore a working knowledge of sound dietetics. This simply means learning how to plan and prepare meals that will keep your family feeling fit. It may mean learning a new method or two, so that food values will not be destroyed or wasted in cooking. It should not increase your food budget, if you learn to buy well and wisely. Many of the cheaper foods are among the most nutritious.

In short, we are not asking you to add to your meal-planning activities, but to alter your menus a bit and perhaps persuade your family to cultivate a few new likes. This is where your culinary skill comes in. Superb cooking and good nutrition go hand in hand.

HOW TO LEARN YOUR PART. You should not have to go beyond your home town to get the information you will need to help you plan more nutritious meals. Under the guidance of State Nutrition Committees, many local agencies are prepared to aid you, such as Health Departments, Public Health Nurses, the American Red Cross, Home Economics Departments of schools and colleges, and county extension workers. Your public library should be able to supply books and pamphlets. If not, a recommended (*Continued on page 175*)

wartime rationing, published charts and articles explaining the rationing point system and the basis for pricing schemes, advising women to devote a corner of their kitchen to strategic planning, with carefully prepared meal plans, lists of ingredients required for favourite recipes, current foodstuffs inventory and, most importantly, 'Uncle Sam's Food Rules' posted in clear view to enable the regimentation and rationalization of family meal preparation.

Logical planning and organization for efficiency was the key in women's home front battle to care for their families. Women were encouraged to plan meals meticulously up to a week or so in advance, to efficiently provide the best nutrition for their home front warriors Under their 'U.S. needs US strong' programme, the Office of Defense Health and Welfare produced elaborate charts of dietary requirements and, for the first time, pushed for laws that required that foods like milk and bread be enriched with extra vitamins to contribute to the overall health of the nation (Campbell 1979: 87). The advice offered by these charts often relied on the presence

6.7 Prompted by the discovery that American men called up for military service were surprisingly underweight and undernourished, popular magazines developed a re-education campaign for women.

"I will take good care of the things I have"

Kalamazoo tells you how to make your cooking and heating equipment *last longer*

Gas Burners and Electric Burners work best when clean. Don't let food boil over. Free clogged gasburners by running pipe cleaner or hat pin through holes. Electric coils can be kept clean by brushing after coils have cooled but don't use a wire brush or any tool that may chip unit and require replacement.

Tops are porcelain enamel. Don't put hot foods or ice cold liquids directly on them. Wait until after range has cooled before cleaning—then wipe with soapy water and dry cloth. To avoid stains, remove acid such as lemon juice or vinegar immediately before it has a chance to dry and spot.

Broilers. Clean after every use. Grease heated a second time not only permeates food but discolors broiler. Trim excessive fats off meat before broiling, and avoid spatter. Use mild cleanser in removing burned food.

Ovens. Wipe after every use. If racks should tend to rust, clean well and rub with salad oil. Rusting in ovens can be decreased by opening door a few minutes before actual use to let steam escape. Repeat after use to prevent condensation inside.

Heaters. Over-heating of your unit is often responsible for cracking and warping of cast iron parts. Don't let clinkers accumulate in grate. Remove ashes frequently—otherwise heater efficiency is reduced.

Furnace Rules: ⅛" of soot in radiator may cut heating efficiency 10%. A burned out smoke pipe is a fire hazard. Always take clinkers out from the top. Don't allow ashes to accumulate in ash pit. Fluctuating temperatures waste fuel.

KALAMAZOO STOVE & FURNACE COMPANY, KALAMAZOO, MICHIGAN

MILLIONS of women have taken this pledge

Three cheers for you, Mrs. America, and all the things you're doing at home to help win the war. You're Betsy Ross, Barbara Fritchie and Molly Pitcher, reborn. You're a real fighting American.

Without bugle or roll of drums you're in stride with the march to victory—you're setting the thermostat at 65°, saving money to buy bonds, serving less meat, keeping the children well, turning off lights and radios, defrosting the refrigerator, doing Red Cross work, saving metal, taking First Aid, sharing cars, writing letters — anything, everything to win.

Yes, America is tied to your apron strings—and proud of it.

QUALITY   LEADERS   SINCE   1901

6.8 Since all civilian production was reduced and even eliminated during the war years, housewives were encouraged to take the necessary steps to preserve the appliances they had.

of a refrigerator in the kitchen, with writers stressing the extra nutritional benefits provided by having foods stored in a cooler environment, and charts noting the extended lifespan of various food items when stored in the freezer or refrigerator. For a population of American cooks already busy from their duties in the home and as a volunteer, the refrigerator, by enabling the cook to go many more days between shopping trips, was a critical tool. An average day already bursting at the seams with other tasks was made much more difficult by wartime shortages and rationing, which could make a simple shopping trip stretch indeterminately with the need to go from place to place looking for particular goods and finding only empty shelves (Campbell 1984: 180). This was made even more troublesome and time consuming by the strict rationing of gasoline and tires, and the fact that women's driving was often seen as discretionary and restricted as being unnecessary to the war effort (Weatherford 1990: 210). Unable to rely on the family car to shop whenever they happened to need something, women had to plan ever more carefully, as any forgotten item could require hours of making the rounds of stores in an all-too-often

fruitless search for scarce items. The ability to shop less often and, aided by the family car and the refrigerator, to obtain more of the family's needs at one time and keep them fresh until they were ready to be eaten, was crucial to allowing women at home to provide the nutritious meals the nation was demanding for American families.

As shipping difficulties and material shortages left American companies spending more advertising space explaining why they could not freely provide their products to American consumers than actually promoting those products, food packaging companies like Del Monte Foods also sought to meet consumer demand with free meal planning charts and advice on how to best ensure that families received all the necessary nutrition. Del Monte's 'Buy-For-A-Week' programme enlisted housewives to participate in rational meal planning, providing charts and mix and match systems designed to make the best use of rationed and difficult to find goods. Such charts and the regimentation of mealtime tasks made shopping, preparation and cooking more efficient, allowing women to keep their 'housewife's pledge' to be efficient and reduce waste in their kitchens.

This pledge was most often connected to the effort to preserve existing appliances so that material and manufacturing capacity could be devoted to the production of planes, tanks and munitions, but articles and advertisements also extended the message to stress the need to preserve food and scarce cooking fuel. Instructions and recipes published in popular magazines as well as cookbooks and household guides for women encouraged them to make use of every inch of their kitchen space, efficiently arranging their counters and refrigerators, but also to make best use of the full area of the oven. Readers were reminded that when cooking or baking, they should never cook only one thing at a time. In an echo of the contemporaneous poster cautioning drivers that 'When you ride ALONE, you ride with Hitler!' home cooks were offered meal plans and instructions to fill every inch of their ovens, preparing cakes and casseroles with residual heat that could be eaten cold or simply warmed up later. As discussed above, prepared-ahead dishes also allowed for the task of meal preparation to be streamlined and simplified in much the same way as tasks on the assembly line, to enable any family member to participate in bringing a meal to the table.

MANAGING HOME FRONT PRODUCTION

In addition to rational meal preparation and the conservation and efficient use of appliances, women were expected to turn their homes into another engine of the production front, with the space of the kitchen again taking centre stage in the struggle. Beyond simply organizing and planning more efficiently for success, women at home were expected to actively participate in production by putting crucial goods back into production, both by using less of scarce items and by producing replacement foods and items which could allow material to be sent overseas for American troops and Allies (Coles 1943: 44). All across America women signed pledges to buy only necessities, and to take good care of the items they had, working to make do with less, and make what they did have stretch a bit farther. Government pamphlets, newspaper advertisements, magazine articles and even popular Disney cartoons exhorted women to save their tin and steel cans for recycling and to save their cooking fats to be converted into glycerine for use in the making of artillery shells. Wartime women used their kitchens as collection centres as they carefully gathered every scrap of usable material to be turned over to local coordinators and funnelled into the production of armaments and munitions.

American housewives were encouraged to produce *more*, primarily through conservation of what was available to them on the home front (Coles 1943: 47). The quest to do more with less spread throughout the house, but it was in the kitchen that the housewife could achieve the most savings, and it was the kitchen where most government agencies and popular media focused their attention. Judging by the amount of ink devoted to the topic, how to make decent meals under wartime conditions and how to make ration points and scarce items stretch farther was foremost in the minds of American homemakers. Cookbooks offered recipes for using novel food items like eggplant and squash, while many magazines offered guides for how to cook unfamiliar items, suggestions and recipes for making rations items spread farther, and instruction in how to evaluate unfamiliar cuts of meat and various meat products (Campbell 1984: 187). From 1943 on, few issues of *Good Housekeeping* were without at least one or two articles offering recipes for 'meatless' and 'wheatless' days, as well as guides for altering

GOOD HOUSEKEEPING INSTITUTE • KATHARINE FISHER, DIRECTOR

Ben Prins

Serve by salvaging

OLD RUBBER

We know you "gave your all" in support of President Roosevelt's Scrap-Rubber Campaign last June. But it isn't enough. The only way we can lick the rubber shortage is to keep a steady stream of old rubber flowing into our rubber factories.

Fine-tooth-comb your house again, and let not even the smallest scrap escape. Uncle Sam needs every ounce of rubber you can give him.

Look for such things as discarded overshoes, boots, tennis and bathing shoes; kitchen aprons made of rubber; bathing suits and caps; rubber-covered dish drainers; faucet and shower sprays; rubber spatulas and dish scrapers; soap dishes; sponges; hot-water bottles; syringe bulbs; ice bags; tennis and golf balls; crib pads, bibs, toys; tricycle tires; dress shields; elastic tape; old tires and tubes. *Not wanted are hard-rubber things*, such as combs and storage-battery cases.

FATS

Don't throw away kitchen fats you have no use for. They are needed urgently to make nitroglycerin for explosives and other essential war products.

Our chief prewar source of industrial fats and oils—coconut oil—is in Japanese hands. Luckily kitchen fats do about as well, and there's no dearth of them. We've been throwing into our garbage cans about two billion pounds yearly.

Your job is to help salvage this surplus, by saving any animal or vegetable oils or fats you don't want—drippings from roasts and broiled meats, contents of deep-fat kettles, bacon grease, etc. Melt them, strain, store in tin cans or other containers—*except glass*—and keep in a cool place. When you have accumulated several pounds, take them to your meat market or frozen-food storage-locker plant, where you will be paid the prevailing price per pound.

TIN CANS

Start saving tin cans, too, if you live in one of the following areas, where collection programs are being set up to keep detinning plants humming. Wash cans clean; remove tops, bottoms, and labels; squash with foot until about ¼" separates the sides; place top and bottom inside.

Albany-Schenectady, N. Y.; Atlanta, Ga.; Baltimore; Birmingham, Ala.; Boston; Buffalo, N. Y.; Chicago; Cincinnati; Cleveland; Columbus, O.; Denver; Detroit; Hartford-New Britain, Conn.; Indianapolis; Louisville, Ky.; Lowell-Lawrence, Mass.; Milwaukee; St. Paul, Minn.; New Orleans; New York City; northern New Jersey; Philadelphia; Pittsburgh; Portland, Ore.; Providence, R. I.; Rochester, N. Y.; St. Louis, Mo.; San Francisco; Scranton-Wilkes-Barre, Pa.; Seattle, Wash.; Springfield-Holyoke, Mass.; Troy, N. Y.; Washington, D. C.; Youngstown, Ohio.

6.9 Magazines of the war period constantly stressed the virtues of thrift in service to the war effort.

existing recipes to use less of rationed commodities like sugar and butter. In addition to the usual potboiler stories and essays, the February 1943 issue of the magazine included two full-page spreads on guidelines to ensure proper nutrition, tips on how to get the most coffee from a pound, over a dozen recipes for using up leftovers and making small amounts of high-point-value foods stretch even further, rules for substituting corn syrup, molasses, and honey for sugar in common recipes, and a double page spread on how to prepare such exotic foodstuffs as liver, heart, tongue and sweetbreads. Moving beyond editorial content, the pages were also full of advertisements for replacement food items such as powdered soup mixes offered to replace canned soups made scarce by the lack of tin, margarine to replace scarce butter, and pre-packaged foods like Kraft Dinners – easy to make and cheap enough that any family could afford to keep a few boxes in the pantry for the end of the ration period when supplies were getting hard to come by.

Last, but certainly not least, the American kitchen was a place of actual production for many families as mothers signed up to serve as Garden Soldiers, growing their own food in backyards and community gardens.

All across the country, each man, woman and child received the same number of ration coupons; rationing plans and allocation of ration books did not take into consideration geography or climate, or any other factor of locality (Campbell 1984: 166), leaving many families who lived far from higher production areas to search stores without much hope for scarce vegetables and fruits. It was up to these families, and hence to the woman at home, to make use of any outdoor space, no matter how small, as a garden to help provide additional food. By 1943, two thirds of American households had Victory Gardens, while in fully three quarters of those households, women were preserving their own vegetables (Campbell 1984: 181) to replace canned produce no longer available either because of metal restrictions or food shipments to the fronts and to Allied countries. The kitchen was crucial in the Victory Garden effort, as all the abundance that the American housewife could coax from her flowerbeds and lawns would go to waste within weeks of harvest if not for home preservation and canning. The US Department of Agriculture produced a number of informative pamphlets intended for housewives giving practical information on home canning, preserving and drying of foods. These publications were augmented by the efforts of magazines like *Women's Home Journal*, *Ladies' Home Companion* and *Good Housekeeping*, among others. *Good Housekeeping*'s Katherine Fisher, director of the Good Housekeeping Institute, regularly wrote articles with practical advice on preserving a range of food items from fruit to vegetables and even meats, along with storage guidelines and instructions for preparing preserved foods at mealtime. Here too, efficiency was critical, as American housewives were instructed on how to make the most of every food item, learning how to use novel food items or products they might have discarded before the war. Enabled by the precise control of cooking temperatures offered by the modern range top and by the plentiful supply of clean hot water supplied to American kitchens at the turn of a tap, women were able to take up water-bath canning to an unprecedented level, using charts produced by the government as well as instructions tested and verified in kitchens like those at the *Good Housekeeping* Institute to preserve a wealth of fruits and vegetables to augment those available commercially.

THE AMERICAN HOUSE GOES TO WAR

The American home was a space as important as any other in the Second World War effort. As noted above, changes in the doctrine of war and the scale of mobilization necessary for war preparedness required that the totality of a society be involved in war planning. During the Second World War as never before, civilians were drawn into the war effort, both as unfortunate targets and victims, and as active participants in the battle from the rear. Crucial to this participation on the part of the United States were the efforts of average American housewives, who kept their homes running and their families healthy while at the same time contributing to the war effort by making what was available to them stretch farther, by collecting and reclaiming valuable scrap which would otherwise have been lost, and by producing their own food. But these activities in no way exhausts the many ways that American homes, 'manned' by 'soldiers' in housedresses and aprons, were mobilized to serve the war effort. American houses also served as centres of education and community as women organized groups to share knowledge and strategies for coping with the many wartime deprivations they experienced. In many cases, homes had to serve as hospitals for children and family members who fell ill in any number of disease waves that always come along in wartime, from the measles peak in 1941, through typhus, cholera, influenza, and mumps, to the scarlet fever epidemic in 1944, with doubling and even tripling cases of serious polio throughout the war period. Millions of women also used their homes to support their volunteer work for organizations like the Red Cross, meeting to produce baked goods and knitted items to be sent overseas, providing both homey cheer and much needed products for soldiers on the front lines as well as prisoners in war camps. Women and girls organized letter writing drives in their homes, challenging each other to write to servicemen so that no soldier would go a week without a friendly message from 'back home'.

Much of this effort, though so crucial at the time, has been obscured in recent years by relative invisibility of its site. Though much work has been done to investigate the role that wartime production played in the construction of houses and production of household appliances, especially in the post war period, comparatively little has been written from the perspective of the impact of militarization on the use of domestic spaces during the build-up and wartime years. Most research has tended to focus on the home as a product and commodity, while role of the space of the house itself as a site of production and as a venue for the preparation of wartime commodities has largely gone unremarked. And yet the space of the American home of the 1940s, and especially its kitchen, represents as potent a weapon as any other developed for the war effort 'over there'. Equipped with technologies such as the stove and the refrigerator, as modern as the bombers which replaced them on the production lines, organized with the best techniques for efficient use developed by experts from government scientists to the staff of the *Good Housekeeping* Institute, and staffed by the American housewife at the head of her auxiliary army of children and family members, the American kitchen of the early 1940s served as important a role in securing victory as any bomber or battleship.

REFERENCES

Banning, M.C. 1942. *Women for Defense*. New York: Duell, Sloan and Pearce.

Brown, P.M. 1943. My New Plans for Rationing and Prices. *American Magazine*, May, 21–23.

Campbell, D.M. 1979. Wives, Workers and Womanhood: America During World War II (Ph.D. diss.). Chapel Hill: University of North Carolina at Chapel Hill.

Campbell, D.M. 1984. *Women at War with America: Private Lives in a Patriotic Era*. Cambridge: Harvard University Press.

Coles, J.V. 1943. *Consumers Can Help Win The War*. Berkeley: University of California Press.

Cowan, R.S. 1983. *More Work For Mother: The Ironies of Household Technology from the Open Hearth to the Microwave*. New York: Basic Books.

Fisher, K. 1943. What You Should Know About the New Point System of Rationing. *Good Housekeeping*, February, 157–59.

Hartmann, S.M. 1982. *The Home Front and Beyond: American Women in the 1940s*. Boston: Twayne Publishers.

Hayes. J.L. 2000. *Grandma's Wartime Kitchen: World War II and the Way We Cooked*. New York: St. Martin's Press.

Hesse-Biber, S. and Carter, G.L. 2000. *Working Women in America: Split Dreams*. New York: Oxford University Press.

Hindman, J. 1941. Kitchen's Drafted, Too. *American Home Magazine*. December.

Ierley, M. 1999. *The Comforts of Home: The American House and the Evolution of Modern Convenience*. New York: Clarkson Potter.

Marsh, D. 1943. I've got my first job – and I still get the meals. *Good Housekeeping*, February, 84–5.

O'Neill, W.L. 1995. *A Democracy at War: America's Fight at Home and Abroad in World War II*. Cambridge: Harvard University Press.

Out of the Frying Pan and Into the Firing Line (dir. Ben Sharpsteen, 1942).

Paddleford, C. 1942. What War Has Done to Life in the Kitchen. *House Beautiful*. September, 63.

Scott, J.W. 1988. *Gender and the Politics of History*. New York: Columbia University Press.

Snodgrass, M.E. 2004. *Encyclopedia of Kitchen History*. New York: Taylor & Francis Books.

Walker, N.A. 2000. *Shaping Our Mother's World: American Women's Magazines*. Jackson: University Press of Mississippi.

Weatherford, D. 1990. *American Women and World War II*. New York: Facts on File, Inc.

7

The Art and Science of Invisible Landscapes: Camouflage for War and Peace

Sonja Duempelmann

INTRODUCTION

In 1917 the American architect Andre Smith noted, 'it is the aeroplane that has given to modern warfare a new weapon of defence and protection – camouflage … It is the garment of invisibility that is capable of not only protecting the individual soldier and the furniture of war, but of screening the movements of an entire army' (Smith 1917: 469). Already during the First World War, camouflage – which offered protection from ground and air views – had become a vital necessity in warfare. Progress in aviation and aerial photography during the interwar years meant that by the Second World War concealment from the aerial view in particular not only had to be more sophisticated but that it also had to be practiced on much larger scales than ever before. To prevent structures and buildings on the ground from being visible and easily identifiable various measures were used for their horizontal and vertical concealment and for deception. They included the structures' unobtrusive integration into the respective environment by means of carefully selecting their site, form, colour and texture, by preserving existing vegetation and planting new trees and shrubs on site, and by using artificial camouflage like netting, smoke and decoys.

The design of war landscapes using diverse means of camouflage became an important and integral part of tactical and strategic military planning. As American architecture professor Richard Belcher pointed out in 1942, precautionary camouflage took 'the form of regional planning' (Anon. 1942a). For camouflage to be successful more than individual targets needed to be disguised. The airplane had not only introduced a new perspective from which the enemy could be observed and attacked, it had also changed the dimensions of time and space. It took only minutes to fly over large stretches of land. If enemy bombers were to be disoriented and deceived to prevent aerial attack, camouflage projects for entire regions had to be developed. Camouflage needed to be carried out in environments with different land use patterns – in cities as well as in rural areas – and, as the American painter Harper Goff pointed out in 1943, the camoufleur had to 'observe from the air the organic structure in the earth which weaves itself like a tapestry across the map' (Goff 1943: 27). This article concentrates on selected examples of land camouflage in rural areas. It shows why and how landscape architects in England, the United States and Germany contributed to camouflage projects during the Second World

(a) STEEL WOOL AND WIRE ON PIPE FRAME.

Fig. 50—Dummy trees.

(b) CLOTH STRIPS AND CHICKEN WIRE ON WOOD FRAME.

7.1   Fake trees for camouflage.

War and how the methods used to layout camouflaged landscapes of war were in turn employed in the post-war years to devise what landscape architects in Britain called 'landscapes of power'.

Outside of cities, industrial plants and airfields were amongst the most vulnerable potential targets to be concealed. As the American architect Konrad Wittmann remarked in 1942, '[u]ntil now, we designed a factory with ground-plan and elevation, but it is no longer unimportant how it looks from the sky' (Wittmann 1942). Furthermore, industrial plants were no longer to be seen as contrasting with nature, or even as 'a design of dreary industrialization hostile to nature'. Instead, factory buildings were to become 'part of the landscape' (Wittmann 1942: 30). A variety of measures were used to blend war production plants into the landscape. Factories were to be situated along the contour lines preferably with the widest façade oriented east-west to reduce shadows. Façade patterns, colours and textures that easily merged with the surrounding landscape were to be chosen. The siting of industrial plants in woods or on the edge of woodland was considered particularly suitable due to the absorption of shadows by the trees. Roads leading to the factory buildings should follow the contours and only be one-way to make them as inconspicuous as possible. Parking areas also needed to be dispersed and protected from view by irregularly spaced groups of trees (Wittmann 1942: 33, 40). Fake and live tree and shrub plantings surrounding the buildings were proposed to distort the form and shadow of the buildings.

Building forms could also be distorted and shadows prevented in the first place by covering the roofs with camouflage nets that expanded to the ground at an angle at the side of the buildings and whose texture resembled that of the surrounding land. While a fitting texture could be achieved using rubbish, excelsior, wood-shavings, dry shrubs, hardy bushes, pine branches and southern moss (common heather, *calluna vulgaris*, was used in Europe), it was found that roofs could also be planted with live grass and shrubs. Finally it was discovered that the grading of the adjacent terrain at an angle of ten degrees could also eliminate shadows (Wittmann 1942: 44–7, 67, 81). When large areas needed to be concealed with camouflage nets, it was advised that a decoy landscape be constructed on top (Breckenridge 1942: 195). A British series of drawings illustrated the procedure for an entire supply camp.

SHEET Nº

TYPICAL METHOD OF PLANTING TO ABSORB CAST SHADOWS

7.2   Method of planting to absorb cast shadows.

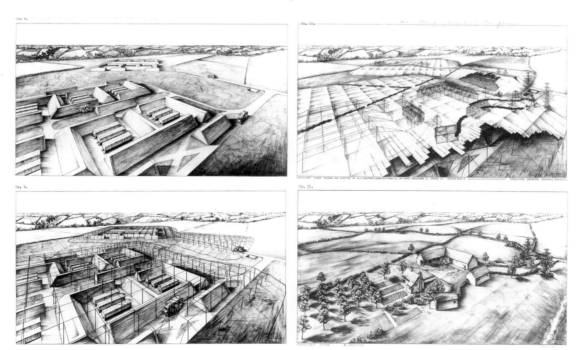

7.3   Suggested camouflage for a supply camp.

The camp was covered with a net and plank construction that provided the 'ground' for an ensemble consisting of a dummy cottage, barn, kitchen garden, orchard and dummy hedges delineating fake fields. Two of the most impressive schemes of this type in the United States were carried out on the West Coast in the spring of 1942 when the United States was anticipating Japanese air attacks as a result of the events in the Pacific theatre of war. Both, the Lockheed and the Douglas aircraft factories in Burbank and Santa Monica were assumed to be likely Japanese bombing targets. In the months between April and September 1942, painters, set designers, illustrators and other staff from the Hollywood studios disguised the aircraft production plants as suburban neighbourhoods. In addition, a decoy replica of the Douglas plant was constructed in open fields near the actual factory (Stanley II 1998: 171–5, Reit 1978: 88–9, Goff 1943: 27).[1]

Besides industrial areas, airfields belonged to the more extensive grounds that needed to be concealed at least well enough to confuse bomber pilots, if not deceive them entirely. Airfields posed a double challenge to the camoufleur: while they were to be rendered invisible to the enemy, they needed to be recognizable to their own army pilots. When the American CBS correspondent William Shirer was flown into Ghent in a German Army Transport Plane in August 1940 he noted the camouflage that almost prevented the pilot from finding his landing field: 'From the air … it looked just like any other place in the landscape, with paths cutting across it irregularly as though it were farm land'. Once on the ground, Shirer could observe the 'mats plastered with grass' that hid the planes and other aircraft that were hidden underneath the trees in the woods nearby (Shirer 1941: 469).

Concealing concrete runways and blending existing airfields into the landscape proved to be a big challenge, requiring a number of strategies that involved the invention of several artificial surface coatings and the colouring and chemical treatment of vegetation. To blend airfields into adjacent field patterns, mobile hedges were used in Britain. These hedges on wheels consisted of dry brush and branches. They were positioned on the runways to complement the surrounding field pattern and could be temporarily removed whenever a plane needed to land or take-off. Merrill E. De Longe reported that Germany had perfected the creation of mobile landscapes on and near its airfields, and had 'even gone so far as to have smoke coming out of the chimneys of these make-believe houses, which are lined up along runways, with trees growing in front of them, much as they would appear in a typical town'. All structures were mounted on slides or rollers, so that they could be pulled off the runways when planes needed to land or take off (De Longe 1943: 134).

In the United States, the Corps of Engineers had from 1940 onwards pressed for the camouflage of airfields in critical areas on the East and West coasts. Due to the events of war, by the end of 1942 some 15 to 20 airfields located within 300 miles of the United States coastlines had finally been camouflaged (Hartcup 1980: 58–9). The first existing airfield to be camouflaged was Bradley Field near Windsor Locks (today Bradley International Airport). The 1,600-acre field had been acquired by the State of Connecticut as an airport in 1940 and was leased to the US Government for Army use shortly thereafter. In 1941 plans were drawn up to render Bradley Field 'invisible' from the aerial view. As with all such schemes Bradley Field's camouflage was based on the idea of blending the airfield into the surrounding countryside. The airfield was located in a rural area characterized by a closely-knit field pattern and orchards. To simulate the land use pattern with its orchards, plowed and strip-planted fields, different hardy grasses and other crops were planted adjacent to the runways.

Creating the effect of orchards on fields was achieved through outlining the circa 25 feet perimeters of the tree crowns on the ground with lime. The circular areas representing the tree

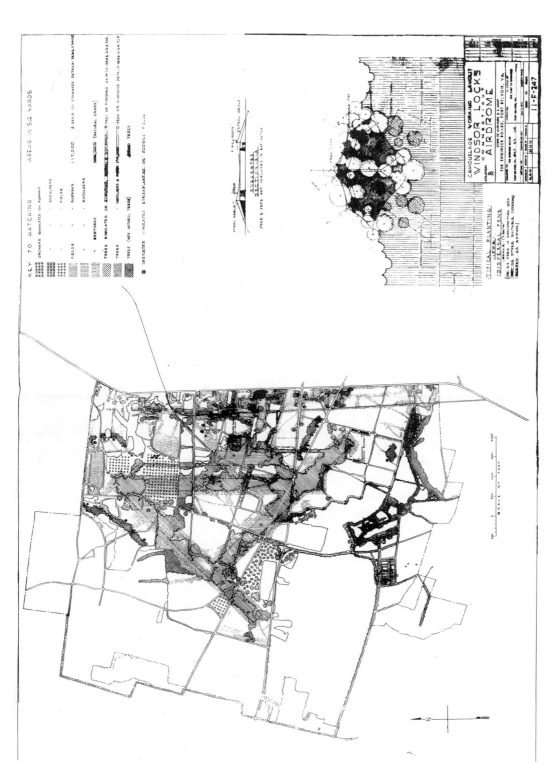

7.4   Plan for the camouflage of Bradley Field, Connecticut, 1941.
       Note that the three landing strips are barely visible.

crowns were treated with a grass killing solution consisting of sodium chlorate and water. The fake horizontal tree crowns were then covered with brush piles that were burnt and the fire extinguished as soon as the brush was charred. Smaller brush piles were placed south of the charred tree areas and spray-painted green. The grass was kept short, and the brush piles were spray-painted at regular intervals until midsummer after which time the paint was allowed to fade until into the winter months, thus merging more easily with the seasonal changes of the vegetation. While the same general technique was employed for simulating hedgerows, the field pattern was continued across the runways by applying asphalt that had been treated with wood chips, slag or high-pressure steam cinders and aggregate (Anon. 1941b). Ploughed fields and strip-planted fields required additional treatment with brush that was first laid out in strips two feet wide and two feet apart and then charred to stain it black. The strips between the brush that aligned with the charred strips on adjacent simulated field areas were spray-painted with a black bituminous emulsion. Existing farm buildings in the area were converted into the necessary facilities and additional new buildings were dispersed around the airfield (Anon. 1941a, Reit 1978: 67–9).

CAMOUFLAGE AS 'ART-SCIENCE' AND 'COOPERATION WITH NATURE'

By the Second World War both artistic and scientific endeavours resulted in landscapes being created with the help of natural and artificial camouflage. Invented by the French artist Lucien-Victor Guirand de Scevola during the First World War, camouflage had in all countries initially attracted artists who were considered 'the painters of a new brand of scenery' (Saint-Gaudens 1919: 322). De Scevola was not a cubist painter, but he admitted to using cubist techniques in his camouflage work. Cubist painters and camoufleurs both used the breaking up and disruption of forms and contours, albeit for different purposes. While the cubist painters strove to offer new perspectives and readings of their objects, the camoufleurs aimed at preventing their objects from being observed in a new perspective and attempted to shield them from view entirely (Kahn 1984: 19). In 1918, the writer Lida Rose McCabe observed that the camouflaged navy stationed in New York Harbour was 'a veritable floating salon of Cubist, Futurist and Vorticist colour-feats significantly emphasizing the passage of the one time derided culturists from theoretic into actual warfare!' (McCabe 1918: 316) It seems that warfare might indeed have contributed to a wider acceptance of these new directions in art and of what Paul Virilio (1994: 48–9), following Guillaume Apollinaire, has called an 'aesthetic of disappearance'.

Warfare, however, not only provided modernist patterns to be perceived from the water and land as in New York Harbour. While the camoufleurs were struggling to use cubist methods and techniques to break up forms and make the naval battle ships merge with sea and sky, and artillery and guns with varying landscapes, their colleagues in the air were being trained to differentiate between landscape patterns coded fittingly as 'cubist country' and 'futurist country'. As art historian and critic John Welchman (1988: 19) has observed, these terms used in a 1918 photo atlas prepared by the Royal Air Force to describe 'irregularly shaped and dispersed … unbounded fields' in the first and irregular 'abstract-seeming … field patches broken up by occasional roads' in the second case, clearly associated the 'aerial photograph … with … Modernism'. In the same sense the English composer and musicologist Norman Demuth had compared 'the crossing and re-crossing of paths' appearing in aerial photographs with 'a spidery drawing by Paul Klee', and had claimed that 'a certain "Composition" by Fernand Leger

THE ART AND SCIENCE OF INVISIBLE LANDSCAPES: CAMOUFLAGE FOR WAR AND PEACE

is an excellent reproduction of a mid-European ground plan!' (Demuth 1942: 43) While Edward Steichen argued that only his knowledge of the Impressionists and Cubists enabled him to carry out his aerial reconnaissance mission, Ernest Hemingway claimed to begin 'to understand cubist painting' after his first flight in 1922 (Virilio 1994: 48–9, Welchman 1988: 19).

Besides being influenced by modernist art, camoufleurs were also drawn to science. In fact, camouflage and mimicry in the animal world, as illustrated in American painter Abbott H. Thayer's 1909 book *Concealing Coloration in the Animal Kingdom* had had significant impact on the early development of camouflage patterns and schemes (Friedmann 1942, Behrens 1997: 99). Principles that belonged to the camoufleur's 'ABC', like counter-shading, colour harmony, mimicry, disruptive design, and changes of colour to match changing surroundings, could be gleaned from nature directly. Fittingly, the camoufleur was described in a 1917 *New York Times* article as the 'military nature faker' (Anon. 1917a, Anon. 1917b). It was only a short step for US cavalry officers to suggest in the interwar years that camouflage principles should be used to protect moving animal targets as well: They proposed that light-coloured horses – a security threat since time immemorial and still at the time considered necessary for warfare – should be dyed 'against low-flying aviation attacks' (Anon. 1927). Thus, research into the scientific fundamentals of camouflage during the interwar years showed that protective concealment required both artistic and scientific expertise. While cubism provided an example of how forms and contours could be disrupted, research into the physical properties of visual phenomena and into the psychology of their perception furthered the understanding of optical illusion. By the Second World War camouflage had therefore come to be seen as what the British architect and officer in the Air Ministry's Camouflage Branch Hugh Casson called an 'art-science' (Casson 1944: 66).

'Cooperating with nature' was considered one of the fundamentals of this 'art-science'. As one *New York Times* journalist put it:

> … in the year 1941 camouflage, whether industrial or strictly military, goes with marked singleness of purpose 'back to nature'. … Broadly phrased it may be said that the camoufleur paints a picture. … it is a matter of covering areas that are often enormous. It is three-dimensional (Jewell 1941).

It is no wonder then, that camouflage during Second World War increasingly provided occupation for gardeners, horticulturists and landscape architects. Landscape architects in particular were trained in a way that could facilitate camouflage measures on small and large scales. Not only were they experts in site analysis and design, they were also trained to read aerial survey maps and visualize landscapes from the air and from the ground (Root 1942: 17). They could develop designs and plans for various scales ranging from small garden plots to regional landscapes, including planting designs. Their material was nature and its landscape. As the British architect and camouflage officer Hugh Casson suggested, camouflage could remind the landscape gardener 'of Price, and Sir William Temple's "Sharawaggi"' (Casson 1944: 68).[2] In fact, imitation and deception, methods used in eighteenth- and nineteenth-century picturesque garden landscapes promoted by Uvedale Price and William Temple in Britain figured prominently in twentieth-century camouflage work. While the ideology underlying eighteenth-century picturesque landscape gardens was obviously different from that of twentieth-century camouflage schemes, the aesthetic intent was the same. Artificial landscapes were to look as natural as possible and in their imitation of nature and human settlements they were to deceive the viewer. It is therefore not surprising that Robert P. Breckenridge's 1942 thumbnail illustration of a suggested camouflage planting scheme resembled an early nineteenth-century image

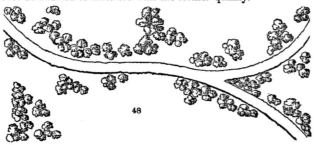

LAYING OUT AND PLANTING.   165

having the margins definite and smooth, while the picturesque
walk has the edge indefinite and rough.   Utility requires that
the gravel, in both styles of walk, should be smooth, firm, and
dry; for it must always be borne in mind, that, as landscape-gar-
dening is a useful as well as an agreeable art, no beauty must
ever be allowed to interfere with the former quality.

In laying out grounds, or in criticising such as are already
formed by eminent artists, it is necessary always to bear in mind
the difference between the gardenesque and the picturesque;
that is, between a plantation made merely for picturesque effect,
and another made for gardenesque effect.   Gardenesque effect
in plantations is far too little attended to for the beauty of the
trees and shrubs, whether individually or collectively; and picturesque effect is not generally understood by gardeners: so that
the scenery of suburban residences is often neutralised in character
by the ignorance of professional landscape-gardeners of the gardenesque, and of professional horticulturists and nurserymen
of the picturesque.   To make the most of any place however
small, all the styles of art ought to be familiar to the artist; because there are few places in which, though one style prevails,
some traits of other styles may not be advantageously introduced.
· M S

7.5   John Claudius Loudon, sketches illustrating the 'gardenesque [top] and picturesque [bottom] way of planting trees'.

provided by John Claudius Loudon to illustrate the picturesque way of planting trees.

By the end of the eighteenth century it had already become a generally accepted notion that landscape gardening belonged to the arts. It was considered an art to turn a piece of land into a landscape garden that imitated nature. This artful imitation of nature, like the artful imitation of objects in a still life painting, could provide pleasure. In his 1757 *Philosophical Enquiry* Edmund Burke described imitation as 'the second passion belonging to society' (Burke 1757: 28–30). According to Burke, for an artwork to produce a pleasurable effect it needed to offer the viewer opportunities to complement the picture with his own imagination. Burke was already expressing the basics of an idea that Gestalt psychologists like Max Wertheimer Rudolf Arnheim, and Wolfgang Köhler would describe more than 150 years later as the process of 'unit forming' and 'visual thinking' that was central to camouflage. According to Burke, deception lay at the heart of all art; and perhaps more implicitly than in any other, deception was a means used in the art of landscape gardening.

This observation was further elaborated on by Burke's contemporary Thomas Whately. Writing on gardening Whately argued that in the creation of artificial ruins, lakes and rivers, an 'overanxious solicitude to disguise the fallacy is often the means of exposing it; too many points of likeness sometimes hurt the deception; they seem studied and forced; and the affectation of resemblance destroys the supposition of a reality …' (Whately 1770). Many years later, Whately's observation reverberated in one of the central principles of camouflage, described in a publication issued by the US Office of Civilian Defense like this: 'plants wrongly used, in a camouflage installation, may be as dangerous a tell-tale as any misuse of paint' (1943: 20). Plants played an important role in many camouflage schemes, and landscape architects were trained to design with them on small and large scales.

LIVING CAMOUFLAGE

Confronted with an increasingly tight economy, many landscape architects began to offer their services to the military. In Germany, they began to work for Nazi programmes like *Schönheit*

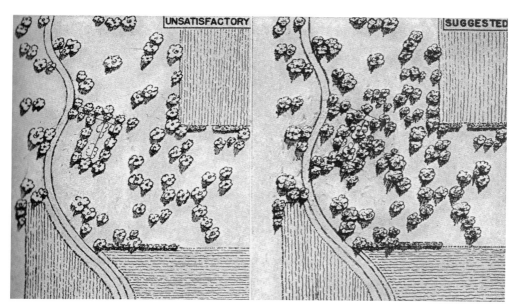

7.6 The camouflage planting on the right was considered more effective. Note the irregular groups of trees mask the rectangular building near the left edge of the illustration.

der Arbeit and *Kraft durch Freude*, initiatives that besides lifting public morale and spirits were intended to 'camouflage' camouflage measures.[3] Landscape architects like Hermann Mattern were commissioned with designs for factories as part of the nationwide programme 'Schönheit der Arbeit' for the beautification and improvement of work places and environments. While intended to provide landscape architects and contractors with work, factory workers with healthy, uplifting spaces for their work breaks that instilled in them a feeling for the nature of their homeland, the greening of industry had an equally, if not more important, side effect: air raid protection. Tree plantings were supposed to hide industrial buildings and blend them into the surrounding countryside both because of their unseemly architecture and because of their vulnerability to aerial observation and attack. While dumps and heaps of rubble were to be 'greened' to beautify the factory premises, their planting also protected the factories from easy detection from the air – after all, untreated spoil not only looked 'untidy' but had also facilitated the identification of enemy positions in the First World War (Mappes 1942, Gunder 1942, Kolbrand 1942).

Influenced by intelligence reports on the German treatment of industrial plants, British military officers turned to landscape architects and horticulturists for their expertise in what they called 'living camouflage'. The biggest advantages of live plant material were considered its 'more convincing' nature, its permanency, its improvement and development from camouflage to concealment over time and its seasonal change that blended the ground patterns into the surrounding countryside.

The English garden architect James Lever designed planting plans for 'living camouflage belts' that would be inconspicuous from the air. Following German examples, Lever aimed at enclosing industrial grounds with forested areas – living camouflage belts – that could provide the nursery stock for future camouflage measures in other locations. Lever based his planting design on the aerial view of 'a typical English wood of long standing [that] shows up from the air as a blackish brown mass, due to the great density of – to coin a word – twigage [sic]'. He recommended the use of native plants because they had smaller leaves and produced 'that dense mass of black brown twiggage [sic]' that provided better concealment throughout the entire year.[4]

Although landscape architects and horticulturists played important roles in all war-faring countries, the US military found these professionals and their method – camouflage with planting – of special importance. 'The knowledge of the basic fundamentals of landscape architecture and its habitual use of site planning technique is very helpful to the camoufleur' (Doliva 1942), one lecturer pointed out, and another regarded the landscape architect as being in the advantageous position 'to play a double role, on the one hand contributing to the cause of obscuration, and on the other, bringing aesthetic improvement to many a bleak spot' (Anon. 1942b, Creville Rickard 1942). Plants were the most suitable materials to camouflage extensive military and industrial areas, common in the United States where land was in abundance. In 1943 the Office of Civilian Defense finally attested that the modern landscape architect's 'training is excellent preparation for the understanding of camouflage in terms of handling terrain' and that 'a qualified landscape architect should have charge of the designing of planting' (United States Office of Civilian Defense 1943). Landscape architects themselves noted that camouflage could even be considered landscape architecture. Like landscape architecture, Armistead Fitzhugh argued, camouflage required 'a balanced artistic and scientific approach' (Fitzhugh 1943: 119).

The heightened interest in camouflage planting went hand in hand with an increasing awareness in the nursery industry. The American Association of Nurserymen and the Camouflage Section of the Engineer Board at Fort Belvoir, Virginia, developed an annual manual that categorized and listed available plant materials for camouflage in each of the different corps areas of the United States. Botanists at Harvard University's Arnold Arboretum conducted research into surface-covering water plants for the disguise of harbours and large water surfaces, and they worked on the development of a spray that could prevent cut plant materials from wilting and losing colour. Due to their importance for air raid protection, shade trees along roadsides were to be protected from insect pests. Various authors therefore argued that insecticides needed to be used on shade trees rather than on food crops. After all, Cynthia Westcott insinuated, healthy 'shade trees may save more lives than wormless apples' (Westcott 1942). The immediate concern for survival was very strong and concern for the larger environment and the effects that the extensive chemical treatment of plants and wide stretches of land only became topics in the post-war years. Thus, different types of fertilizers, sodium arsenate that killed grass tops, ammonium thyocyanate that turned grass brown and then white, and iron sulphate and tannic acid solutions that turned ground cover black were indiscriminately used on extensive areas to simulate different field patterns and shadows.

LANDSCAPE OF POWER

A motivation for camouflage research during the war years was the assumption of many professionals that camouflage would prove useful in peacetime as well. Hugh Casson argued in 1944 that camouflage principles could be used in peacetime to site factories in a way that would make them inconspicuous. Indeed, many methods used for camouflage were employed when the landscapes of war were turned into what Sylvia Crowe in Britain called a 'landscape of power' – characterized by power stations, power lines, transformers, telegraph poles and wires, radio masts and airfields. Although Crowe (1958: 99) embraced the 'new shapes' caused by transportation and industry, she – like many of her colleagues – approached her post-war commissions for the British forestry commission and the Central Electricity Generating Board in a similar way to that of a camouflage officer. Having served as an ambulance driver in France and in the Auxiliary Territorial Service on the English South coast and later in Gravesend during the Second World War, it appears likely that Crowe would have had occasion to witness land camouflage projects. But regardless of whether she and her colleagues had witnessed or were involved in camouflage projects, many landscape architects were fascinated by this war work, as a photograph by Susan Jellicoe, wife of acclaimed British landscape architect Geoffrey Jellicoe attests. The photograph of an airfield in Gloucestershire shows an aircraft hangar covered in camouflage nets including shrubs to blend it into the surrounding agricultural land when viewed from above. In a number of ways horizontal and vertical land camouflage resonated with landscape architects' work in peacetime. Landscape architects – like camoufleurs in wartime – had to anticipate change and the ephemeral quality of their design and materials. Much of their work had to do with veiling and screening on the one hand and unveiling and rendering visible on the other. As discussed above, some of the major landscape architectural works in the eighteenth century can be read as artful works of concealment and deception involving the management of visual experience through earth movement, elaborate plantings and the construction of staffage. These design strategies that had resulted from an artful, aesthetic, albeit politically and philosophically motivated intent in the eighteenth century. After having been transformed into a vital necessity during the war years, by the post-war years had become to be seen as a modern necessity.

Thus, in keeping with the 1957 Electricity Act that held the Central Electricity Generating Board, the Electricity Council and the Minister responsible for the preservation of amenities, Sylvia Crowe's agenda was determined by the idea that the buildings and structures of the new nuclear power, communication and transportation industries needed to be assimilated into the landscape by preserving and redesigning, where necessary, 'the entire surface-cover of the land into one flowing comprehensive pattern' (Crowe 1958: 110, Central Electricity Generating Board 1971: 22). Several of her drawings illustrate how power and transformer stations could be integrated unobtrusively into the existing landscape pattern, demonstrating the principles used in industrial camouflage during the Second World War.

Like the early camoufleurs and military officials during the First World War who had noted parallels between camouflage work, landscape patterns and modern abstract art, Crowe compared the patterns of the 'landscape of power' with Paul Klee's composition of arrows and interpenetrating lines. The interlocking shapes and lines of abstract art had so far only been translated into garden designs, e.g. by Thomas Church in California. Crowe aimed at using 'patterns of interlocking shape' to transform entire landscapes (Crowe 1958: 24). She found confirmation for her preoccupation with landscape pattern in Gyorgy Kepes's 1956 publication *The New Landscape in Art and Science* (Crowe 1958: 20). Based on an exhibition at MIT the book highlighted patterns in aerial, telescopic and microscopic views including driving patterns in a ploughed field, strip cropping and contour cultivation, a Nebula, the moon, the Alaskan coastline, the ocean, part of a deer tongue, stamina hairs of plants, and the dendritic structure of white cast iron. This 'new vision' realized through the optical techniques offered by the telescope and the microscope and by the new perspectives provided by airplanes and rockets could, according to Kepes, inspire artists, architects and designers to envision a 'new landscape' understood as a balance where technology was to be 'brought into harmony with the rhythms of the seasons, the breadth of the sky, the resources of the land' (Kepes 1956: 74). Kepes, like his teacher László Moholy-Nagy, had also been involved in camouflage work during

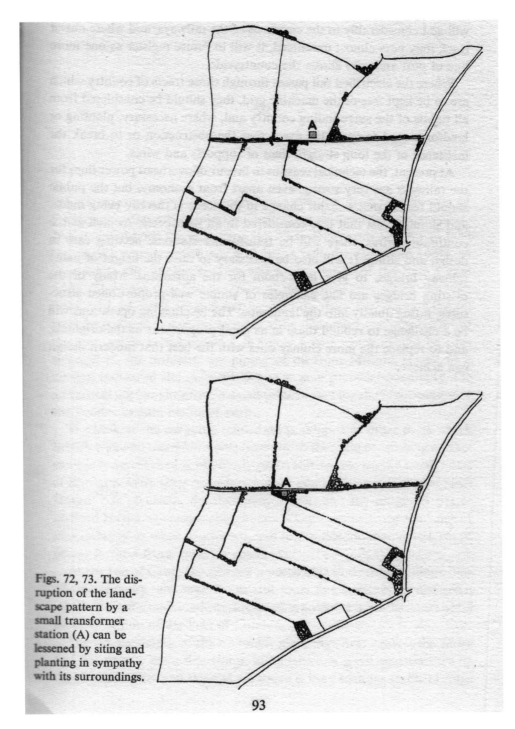

Figs. 72, 73. The disruption of the landscape pattern by a small transformer station (A) can be lessened by siting and planting in sympathy with its surroundings.

93

7.7   Sylvia Crowe, example of the unobtrusive integration of a transformer station into the landscape pattern.

the Second World War. Like Moholy-Nagy he sought to elevate scientific microscopic and aerial photographs to art by revealing their abstract qualities and patterns and by presenting them as a disembodied and detached 'new vision'.

For the creation of 'new landscape', or a 'landscape of power', explored by landscape architects like Sylvia Crowe, not only its pattern from the air was important. Building masses and forms also had to blend into the landscape from the ground view. Planting, siting and excavating could be used to 'camouflage' and screen transformer stations and make them appear as if they 'sprung from the earth' (Crowe 1958: 87–8). True to the British landscape, Crowe promoted the adoption of the eighteenth-century ha-ha to blend buildings with the landscape contours: 'This is', she argued, 'a useful device when the building requires the appearance of rising cleanly from the open ground, with the landscape sweeping up to it, without planting or walls' (Crowe 1958: 50–51). Amongst the camouflage principles Crowe embraced in her post-war work were the disruption and breaking-up of clear edges, forms and silhouettes of large buildings through plantings and landforms, the use of colours that matched buildings to their surroundings, and roads and fences running parallel to contour lines. According to her, the 'organic pattern' of the rural surroundings should impose itself on the industrial plant (Crowe 1958: 36; 1960: 4, 6).

The nuclear power station Trawsfynydd in Merionethshire, Welsh Snowdonia, was one of the sites where Crowe strove to achieve 'a direct union between the main buildings and the surrounding Welsh mountain landscape' by carrying the 'wild landscape … right up to the structures'.

Trawsfynydd was the fourth nuclear power station of Britain's 1955 nuclear power programme devised to respond to the increased demand for electricity in the post-war years. Construction was begun in 1959 on the shore of Trawsfynydd Lake, a large reservoir that had been built three decades before for the Maentwrog Hydroelectric power station and that would provide the nuclear power station with the necessary cooling water. The pump house was sunk below ground level, the approach road was unlit, uncurbed and laid out along the contours, the substation was sited on low ground and its surface partly sown with dwarf clover 'to break up the great expanse of hard surface as seen from higher viewpoints'. Ground modelling was used to merge the buildings with the surrounding landforms. The ground between the Turbine House and the substation was modelled so as to appear as a spur of the surrounding hills. At the northeast corner of the substation tree-planted mounds were built to conceal parts of the power station from the road.

Furthermore, the reactor buildings were designed so that they would not tower above the outline of Craig Gyfyns and the concrete building façades were coloured grey to match the rock in the immediate environment (Central Electricity Generating Board 1961, Crowe 1960: 6). The principles put forward by Crowe and some of her landscape architecture colleagues were also exemplified by Geoffrey Jellicoe's design for the landscape treatment surrounding the nuclear power station at Oldbury located on the River Severn between Gloucester and Bristol that was commissioned in 1963 and opened in 1967. The power station was positioned on a platform made from dredged soil.

Jellicoe had already expressed his conceptual ideas regarding the landscape treatment of power stations in a 1945 article published in the *Architectural Review*. He considered the 'wildest' landscape and sites located furthest away from human habitation as the most ideal locations. Thus, in his conceptualization, powerful energy found a metaphorical equivalent in powerful nature. The power station and its environment were to be conceived as one landscape design. The flat open Oldbury site fit his ideas well, since he had also posited, that

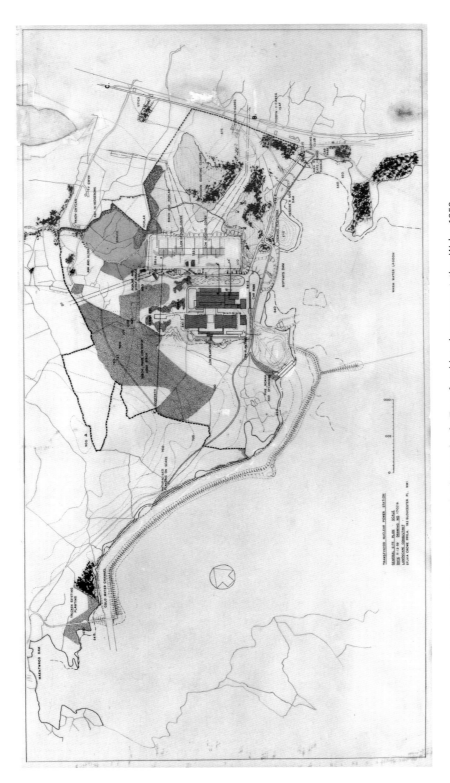

7.8   Sylvia Crowe, landscape plan for Trawsfynydd nuclear power station, Wales, 1959.

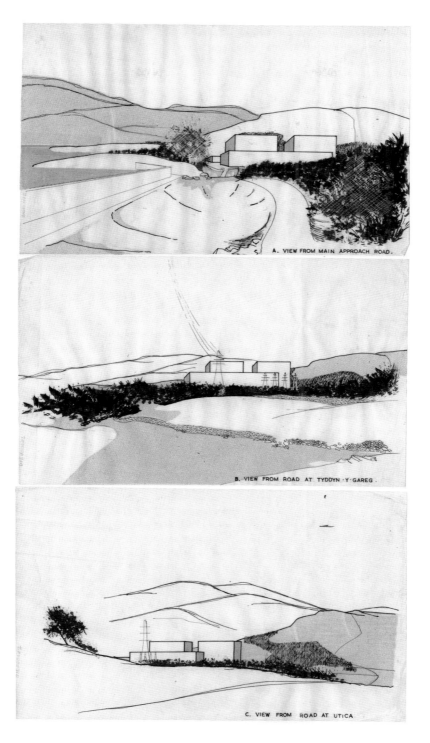

A. VIEW FROM MAIN APPROACH ROAD.

B. VIEW FROM ROAD AT TYDDYN·Y·GAREG.

C. VIEW FROM ROAD AT UTICA

7.9   Sketches illustrating views from roads approaching and
passing Trawsfynydd nuclear power station, Wales.

'the ideal location for industrial buildings beyond human scale is an open landscape' (Jellicoe 1945). Jellicoe designed an abstract field pattern for the terraces surrounding the station's platform. Structured by hedges and cultivated with different crops and orchards, the designed landscape was connected to the historically grown, more intricate and irregular field pattern of the surrounding countryside by a ring of pasture land (Thirkettle 1961: 14). Jellicoe wanted his rectangular field terraces to mediate between the small-scale irregular field pattern of the environs and the monumental clear shapes and forms of the power station (Jellicoe 1966: 9–11). While it was hardly possible to conceal a nuclear power station in the flat landscape of a river estuary from the horizontal view, the field pattern and associated colours Jellicoe used for his design aimed at blending the station's structures into the existing landscape pattern when seen from the air.

The concern that guided Sylvia Crowe and many of her British colleagues at the time was the 'breach between the artist and the scientist' (Crowe 1958: 41). The British

7.10   Susan Jellicoe, aerial perspectives showing model of Geoffrey Jellicoe's landscape design for Oldbury nuclear power station on the River Severn.

landscape architects – a new group of experts that had attained public recognition since the 1951 Festival of Britain where they had been responsible for much of the design of open space – joined the discussion that was dominating much of the intellectual culture and the media. In 1946 the BBC had 'called the division between scientific and humanistic thought "the challenge of our time"' (cit. in Ortolano 2009: 5). The British physicist and novelist Charles Percy Snow had begun to elaborate on 'The Two Cultures' in the *New Statesman* in 1956 (and more famously in his subsequent 1959 Rede Lecture at Cambridge University) thereby bringing an old discussion about the relationship between the arts and the sciences to a new highpoint and sparking what has become known as the 'two cultures' controversy. Criticizing the intolerance and the chronic – and in part – wanton misunderstandings between scientists and artists, Snow demanded that communication and interaction between the two groups was vital and necessary, not least for tackling and overcoming world problems like the 'H-bomb war, over-population, the gap between the rich and the poor' (Snow 1959: 48–9). Even if they were concerned more with local, regional and national issues, some landscape architects at the time realized that they could contribute to re-establishing the lost connections between art and science and attempt to reconcile scientific and artistic endeavours. Crowe mused that 'It may be that it is the role of landscape design to bridge this gap, for landscape architecture is rooted equally in art and science, and has as its aim the reconciliation of artifice to nature, and of art to science' (Crowe 1958: 41). This had also been landscape architecture's call in camouflage work.

Landscapes of war and power were seen by landscape architects in all countries as providing new opportunities and perspectives enabling them to further emancipate themselves and promote their young profession. Through their ability to read maps, plans and aerial photographs, to imagine landscapes and design plantings, landscape architects were well-equipped for some tasks of military camouflage. Through their use during the Second World War, many methods and design principles to site and blend buildings into the landscape became paradigms that continued to shape landscape design approaches in the post-war years. Landscape architects' direct and indirect wartime experience likely helped to refocus their attention on planning and design issues regarding the larger landscape in the post-war years. Camouflage techniques that built upon civilian landscape traditions in the first place were used in the post-war years to weave together again the landscape – described by Crowe as having 'lost its continuous web of pattern' and having 'disintegrated like an exploding atom'. With the help of camouflage techniques landscape architects in the post-war period tried to turn landscape 'sometimes into a variation of the old pattern, sometimes into a completely new one' (Crowe 1957: 4).

NOTES

1   Already in the First World War 65 professionals from Hollywood, including assistant directors and scenic painters were reported to have been drafted into the first American Camouflage Section organized by the theatre director Homer Saint-Gaudens besides a number of artists who were considered especially adapted to the job. (See 'Progress of Camouflage in the US Army during World War I'. Edward Farmer Papers, Box 1, Hoover Institution Archives, Stanford University. Also see Hartcup 1980: 28–9.) While artists continued to play an important role in the camouflage units of the Second World War – with Edward Seago and Julian Trevelyan in Britain, Ellsworth Kelly, Laszlo Moholy-Nagy in the US, and Oskar Schlemmer in Germany – men and women from related disciplines also became involved. In Britain these included the magician Jasper Maskelyne, the film producer Peter Proud and the theater set designer Oliver Messel. In the US, the theater, set and fashion designers Jo Mielziner – who would go on to design the sets for *A Streetcar Named Desire*, *Death of a Salesman*, *The King and I*, *South Pacific*, *Cat on a Hot Tin Roof* amongst others and won five Tony awards – Harper Goff and Bill Blass, and animation artists and draftsmen from the World Disney Studio and Warner Bros signed up for camouflage work. Architects, like Hugh Casson in Britain, John C. Phillips, Jr. in the US, and landscape architects, like the Americans Armistead Fitzhugh, Perry H. Wheeler, George L. Nason, the Germans Ernst Hagemann, Hermann Mattern, Heinrich Wiepking-Jürgensmann, and horticulturists like Leslie Watson in Britain also played an important role in the respective nation's camouflage efforts.

2   The term 'sharawadgi' first appeared in print in William Temple's *Upon the Gardens of Epicurus; or, Of Gardening, in the Year 1685* (1690) where he used the word to describe the irregular way of planting in Chinese gardens. Rather than originating in the Chinese language, however, it appears that the term might derive from the Japanese word *sorowaji* describing asymmetry (see Murray 1998).

3   The Nazi program *Schönheit der Arbeit* was begun in 1934 under the supervision of Albert Speer. It encouraged the beautification of the working environment and therefore led factory owners to commission landscape architects with the design of parks and gardens adjacent to their factories.

4   It seems that Lever coined the term 'twiggage', that after his use appeared in American camouflage literature and was used for example by the Head of the School of Horticulture at the State Institute of Agriculture in Farmingdale on Long Island, Carl Wedell, who as a graduate of the Fort Belvoir Civilian Camouflage Course taught in the 1943 course in 'Protective Obscurement' at Columbia

University (Wedell 1943: 49). For Lever and the adoption of living camouflage by the British Forces see Major D A J Pavitt, 86/05/2, Department of Documents at the Imperial War Museum and Major D A J Pavitt, 86/50/3, Department of Documents at the Imperial War Museum.

REFERENCES

Anon. 1917. Wants camouflage force. 1917. *The New York Times*, 30 August, 13.

Anon. 1917. Call for 'fakers' to fool Germans. *The New York Times*, 4 September, 7.

Anon. 1927. Urge dyeing horses as war camouflage. *The New York Times*, 8 September, 20.

Anon. 1941a. Work begins on first camouflaged airfield. *Engineering News-Record* 126, 1 May, 1.

Anon. 1941b. Report on Camouflage for Windsor Locks Airbase Connecticut. 24 November. Camouflage Section The Engineer Board, Fort Belvoir, Virginia. Edward Farmer Papers, Box 1, Hoover Institution Archives, Stanford University.

Anon. 1942a. Cooper Union Starts Camouflage Course. *The New York Times*, 18 November, 29.

Anon. 1942b. Informational Memorandum. Issued by the Office of Civilian Defense Washington, DC, 21 May.

Anon. 1943. *Precautionary Camouflage: Planning for Low Visibility without Reliance upon Artificial Coverings*. United States Office of Civilian Defense. United States Government Printing Office: Washington, DC.

Behrens, R. 1997. Iowa's contribution to camouflage. *Iowa Heritage Illustrated*, 78(322), 98–109.

Breckenridge, R.P. 1942. *Modern Camouflage: The New Science of Protective Concealment*. New York, Toronto: Farrar & Rinehart.

Burke, E. 1757. *A Philosophical Enquiry into the Origin of our Ideas of the Sublime and Beautiful*. London: R. and J. Dodsley.

Central Electricity Generating Board. 1961. *Trawsfynydd Nuclear Power Station*. London: Pulman & Sons.

Central Electricity Generating Board. 1971. *Modern Power Station Practice, Vol. 1: Planning and Layout*. Oxford: Pergamon Press.

Casson, H. 1944. The aesthetics of camouflage. *The Architectural Review*, 96(9), 62–8.

Creville, R. 1942. Paper delivered to the Conference on Aerial Bombardment Protection. Sponsored by Harvard University, Massachusetts Institute of Technology and Northeastern University at Boston, Massachusetts, 19 April: 7. Edward Farmer Papers, Box 1, Hoover Institution Archives, Stanford University.

Crowe, S. 1957. Presidential Address. *Journal of the Institute of Landscape Architects*, 40(November), 3–5: 20

Crowe, S. 1958. *The Landscape of Power*. London: The Architectural Press.

Crowe, S. 1960. Power and the Landscape. *Journal of the Institute of Landscape Architects*, 52 (November), 3–7.

De Longe, M.E. 1943. *Modern Airfield Planning and Concealment*. New York and Chicago: Pitman Publishing Corporation.

Demuth, N. 1942. *Practical Camouflage or The Art of Guile*. Bognor Regis: John Crowther.

Doliva, J.K. 1942. The Assembly of Reference, Source Material and Data in Camouflage Design. Lecture held on 2 February. Edward Farmer Papers, Box 1, Hoover Institution Archives, Stanford University.

Fitzhugh, A. 1943. Camouflage: adaptation of basic principles of landscape architecture. *Landscape Architecture*, 33(4), 119–24.

Friedmann, H. 1942. *The Natural-History Background of Camouflage* (Smithsonian Institution War Background Studies 5). Washington, Smithsonian Institution: The Lord Baltimore Press.

Goff, H. 1943. Camouflage in America is more than a science: It is an art with a definite technique. *Architect and Engineer*, 152(1), 26–36.

Gunder, G. 1942. Soziale Grünanlagen. *Gartenkunst*, 55(11), 151–3.

Hartcup, G. 1980. *Camouflage: A History of Concealment and Deception in War*. New York: Charles Scribner's Sons.

Jellicoe, G.A. 1945. Power stations in the landscape. *Architectural Review*, 97(4), 116.

Jellicoe, G.A. 1966. *Studies in Landscape Design, Vol. II*. New York, Toronto: Oxford University Press.

Jewell, E.A. 1941. Art in a practical service to war. *The New York Times*. 14 December, X11.

Kahn, E.L. 1984. *The Neglected Majority: 'Les Camoufleurs', Art History, and World War I*. Lanham, New York, London: University Press of America.

Kepes, G. 1956. *The New Landscape in Art and Science*. Chicago, IL: Paul Theobald.

Kolbrand, F. Grün und Blumen im Fabrikgelände. *Gartenkunst*, 55(11), 153–62.

Loudon, J.C. 1838. *The Suburban Gardener and Villa Companion*. London: The Author.

Mappes. 1942. Schönheit der Arbeit. *Gartenkunst*, 55(11), 149–52.

McCabe, L.R. 1918. Camouflage, war's handmaid. *Art World*, 3(3), 313–18.

Murray, C. 1998. Sharawadgi resolved. *Garden History*, 26(2), 208–13.

Ortolano, G. 2009. *The Two Cultures Controversy: Science, Literature and Cultural Politics in Postwar Britain*. New York: Cambridge University Press.

Reit, S. 1978. *Masquerade: The Amazing Camouflage Deceptions of World War II*. New York: Hawthorne Books, Inc.

Root, R.R. *Camouflage with Planting*. Chicago, IL: Ralph Fletcher Seymour.

Saint-Gaudens, H. 1919. Camouflage and art. *The American Magazine of Art*, 10(9), 319–22.

Shirer, W.L. 1941. *Berlin Diary: The Journal of Foreign Correspondent*. New York: Alfred A. Knopf.

Smith, A. 1917. Notes on camouflage. *The Architectural Record*, 17(5), 468–77.

Snow, C.P. 1959. *The Two Cultures and the Scientific Revolution*. New York: Cambridge University Press.

Stanley II, R.M. 1998. *To Fool a Glass Eye*. Washington, DC: Smithsonian Institution Press.

Thirkettle, D. 1961. Ground modelling. *Journal of the Institute of Landscape Architects*, 53(2), 11–15.

Temple, W. 1685 (1690). *Upon the Gardens of Epicurus; or, Of Gardening, in the Year*.

Virilio, P. 1994. *The Vision Machine*. Bloomington and Indianapolis, IN: Indiana University Press.

Wedell, C. 1943. Camouflage Materials: Natural (Protective Obscurement. Notes from classes in Protective Obscurement). New York: School of Architecture, Columbia University, 47–51.

Welchman, J. 1988. Here, there and otherwise. *Artforum*, 27(9), 19.

Westcott, C. 1942. Protection of our shade trees is urged as a defense measure. *The New York Times*, 24 May, D9.

Whately, T. 1770. *Observations on Modern Gardening*. London: T. Payne.

Wittmann, K.F. 1942. *Industrial Camouflage Manual*. New York: Reinhold Publishing Corporation.

Part III
War in the Landscape: Infrastructures and Topology

8

The *Atlantikwall*: From a Forgotten Military Space Towards Places of Collective Remembrance

Rose Tzalmona

INTRODUCTION

> *What is dangerous is not technology. There is no demonry of technology, but rather there is the mystery of its essence. The essence of technology, as a destining of revealing, is the danger …*
> *The threat to man does not come in the first instance from the potentially lethal machines and apparatus of technology. The actual threat has already affected man in his essence.*

> Martin Heidegger, *The Question Concerning Technology*

In 1953 Martin Heidegger delivered his famous lecture 'The Question Concerning Technology', where technology was defined by using the Greek concept of *Technē* as a fundamental human activity (as well as the instrumentality) of a bringing forth, a revealing of what is hidden and a revealing of an ordering, as the essence of truth. Behind this definition of modern technology lies an epistemology of religious magnitude that includes not only that claim to truth but also, indirectly, the notions of good and evil and humanity's very essence. To Heidegger the danger lay when technology becomes determinant of its own truth and in the subsequent enslavement to the objects of technique, while its 'saving power' lay in reflection and in technology's so called essence as art, as a fundamental human activity (Heidegger 1977). It becomes much easier to call his dialectic into question when placing it within the context of Nazi ideology which, 20 years prior to delivering this paper, he so ardently advocated. Within the context of the war, the real danger of technology lies not as a determinant of its own truth, but when it brings forth a hidden presumed truth in the form of an ideology embedded in an unquestionable faith that attempts to contest and destroy fundamental human rights. Furthermore, what Heidegger claimed as technology's saving power, redemption through art and the act of dwelling, may also be questioned upon examining the consequences of a military space that embodied an architecture created as a means of representing an ideology that was founded upon racial theories, and which had made a claim to truth.

Architecture has always been an act that embodies artistic ideas, a structural logic as well as the prevalent social values of its time. The *Atlantikwall* would prove no exception to this notion as it represented the act of defending Third Reich ideology that had manifested itself physically in *Lebensraum* (where the racially superior would resettle in what later became known as the

Greater Reich's conquered territories). The Second World War in Europe represents a pivotal point in the cultural and architectural evolution of military space that may be approached from several opposing perspectives: the German military, the Allied forces, and the civilian populations who had experienced its consequences.

Building a colossal defence line that stretched along the coastlines of seven countries (from southern France through to the British Channel Islands, Belgium, Netherlands, Germany, Denmark to northern Norway), expressed the need to defend 'Greater Germany' from an impending Allied invasion. The *Atlantikwall* unified the western European coastline into a single military space, thus not only legitimising an ideology that stood in sharp contrast to modern western democratic values such as liberty, equality, state sovereignty and justice, but whose erection gave way to war crimes committed in the name of a way of revealing racial 'truth'.

The processes required to manifest this military space demanded a powerful centralised organisation that would be able to understand not only the geographical conditions of the Western European coastline, its cities and inhabitants, but also be able to translate this knowledge into a relentless plan for occupying those annexed territories. Conversely, in order to break the physical (and virtual) barrier created by the *Atlantikwall*, the Allied forces relied not only on sophisticated counter surveillance techniques, but also on local resistance movements who gathered intelligence pertaining to fortification building. The most complex processes to comprehend, however, are offered by the inhabitants of those occupied coastal regions who experienced this military space during the war and who often attempted to erase its traces in subsequent years. This included the removal of these iconographical symbols from the public realm, thereby allowing narratives to disappear, leaving but few symbolic traces for future generations. With the passing of 67 years since the liberation of Europe, however, this former military space that was transformed into a territory of collective amnesia, is slowly being rediscovered. As societies begin to search for remnants of their buried collective history, a process begins that could ultimately help transform these places into sites of collective remembrance.

BETWEEN DEFENSIVE AND OFFENSIVE ARCHITECTURE

In preparation for *Operation Sea Lion*, the invasion of the British coastline in the summer of 1940 issued War Directive 16 (16 July 1940). This stated that the Straits of Dover were to be sealed off with mine fields on both flanks and that the navy would build four heavy coastal batteries and radar installations not for defensive purposes, but to contribute to the attack. The failure of this operation which was followed by a second defeat along the Eastern Front (*Operation Barbarossa*, 22 June 1941), as well as an Allied attempt at landing on the Norwegian coast (*Operation Claymore*, 4 March 1941), resulted in a complete change in strategy from a policy of offence to defence. Faced with the possible, or even probable, loss of his conquered territories, ultimate defeat in the war and the jeopardy of his racial ideological principles and their inherent 'truth', Hitler issued a War Directive (20 October 1941) which decreed the building of defensive works on the British Channel Islands followed by another (14 December 1941) to fortify Norway. It appears, however, that several feasibility studies for defending the entire western coastline (as well as constructing U-boat bunkers) were already well underway as a result of the Allies' operation in Norway (Anon. 1942a). Such studies were usually conducted *a priori* not only to all policy making, but also as a prerequisite to what later would become Hitler's famous Directive 40 (23 March 1942) – addressed to the 'Supreme Command of the

German Armed Forces' (*Oberkommando der Wehrmacht*, OKW) – which prophetically predicted an Allied invasion and simultaneously gave rise to the *Neu Westwall: the Atlantikwall* (Trevor-Roper 1964: 110–16). Coastal defences would no longer be imposed upon individual coastlines, but addressed as a totality.

Already experienced in erecting fortifications in the *Westwall* (also known as the Siegfried Line) military architects and engineers of *Organisation Todt* (OT) were assigned by Hitler to supervise and execute the building of the *Atlantikwall*. This was to be the largest project ever constructed in reinforced concrete, comprising of 15,000 (of which 12,000 were erected) bunkers and an entire infrastructure incorporating not only road-works and railway lines but also anti-tank walls, channels, trenches, minefields and other obstacles, while deploying more than one million international (forced) labourers to build it.

Organisation Todt was a Wehrmacht auxiliary charged with construction works ranging from the tactical to the strategic. In the 1930s and early 1940s, under the initial leadership of the engineer Fritz Todt, the famous *Autobahn* highway system and the *Westwall* had been executed. In 1942, after his sudden death, *Organisation Todt* was taken over by the architect Albert Speer. He merged it with his own construction unit *Baustab Speer* which had previously been entrusted with designing *Neu Berlin* (*Germania*) the project to transform the Reich's capital into a city whose ruins, in a thousand years, would outshine those of ancient Greece or Rome. Merging with *Organisation Todt* effectively brought their civic plans to a halt. By 1945 the two organisations were part of the Ministry for Armaments and War Production (*Reichsministerium für Rüstung und Kriegsproduktion*) the sole agency for the entire war production programme, assigned with the primary task of foreseeing the construction of *Festung Europa* (Fortress Europe) whose major defence line was the *Atlantikwall*.

Once decreed, the *Atlantikwall* would be used not only as the means to an end, but become an end in itself. This defence line would be employed in a manner similar to other iconographic artworks from the period: as a subservient tool in psychological warfare. In this particular case, the various forms of representing it included propaganda films that presented the viewers with the apparently unlimited human and material resources involved in building the colossal coastal batteries and photomontages – in posters, newspaper articles and magazines – which sought not only to exaggerate the power of such an endeavour but also to link it back to German cultural history (Anon. 1943).

From the very beginning aesthetics and construction were entwined with Third Reich politics as a call to mobilise the masses. Propaganda with respect to this building project would therefore illustrate Walter Benjamin's (1936/2008) prophetic premise that mobilising all mechanically reproduced artistic resources (in this case film and mass-produced architecture), harnessed in the name of political ideology, would culminate in a new war. Technology, here, to place it against Heidegger's definition, would indeed reveal a hidden ugly truth as envisioned by the Third Reich: instead of the redemption so hoped for through art, technology would make use of it as a contrivance of enslavement.

CREATING A MILITARISED SPACE AS AN ACT OF ORDERING THE LANDSCAPE

The *Atlantikwall* may be understood in Heideggerian terms as an 'act of ordering', one that transformed the western European coastline into a single military space. Two methods were employed to establish this dominion over the landscape – surveyance (cartography and ordinance) and construction (armour and ordnance). As in all standard practice, surveying and site analysis form a prerequisite to design and construction. Nonetheless, twentieth century technology had given rise to a practice that was previously unknown – designing buildings as 'ready-made' entities, mass-produced standardised types which, theoretically, could be sited in any given location.

In the case of the *Atlantikwall*, surveyance and construction were initially independent processes. The ability to anticipate where the impending landing would take place lay at the core of developing an overarching defence strategy. The greatest advantage of defending a 5000km long coastline for the occupier is the knowledge that the potential *invader* cannot permit himself to spread his forces too thinly. The greatest weakness in managing a territory of this scope lay paradoxically, in the *occupier* spreading out his own forces too thinly. Accordingly, gathering the necessary cartographic material and aerial reconnaissance to determine possible landing sites proved strategically essential. Geographical borders appeared to have been as relevant as national ones, as each country was subdivided into manageable coastal units (KVAs) (Rolf 1982). Here regional differences inherent to cultural landscapes were taken into account as well as more detailed analysis and additional understanding of harbours and urban settlements.

By contrast, the actual building process focused on optimising local conditions for laying out coastal batteries and individual bunkers. Bunker typology was originally designed for the *Westwall* (1935–1940) and used as a basis for developing stronger and more complex types that would withstand the rapidly changing nature of artillery. Building the *Atlantikwall* required, therefore, both ingenuity and resourcefulness on behalf of its field architects and engineers

8.1   Northern France, Calais, *Atlantikwall* – Coastal artillery with camouflage nets and soldiers on patrol, April–July 1943.

who attempted to apply the design of those universal types onto various landscapes while simultaneously assembling strategic strongholds and coastal batteries. An ensemble for a standardised stronghold (*Stützpunktgruppe*) was laid out as follows: a centrally placed search light for an observation and command post, flanked on both sides by two artillery gun emplacements and a flanking artillery bunker. Due to the necessary artillery these bunkers were either fully visible or partially nestled in the land, but most certainly camouflaged. The second row of bunkers was mostly submerged (and therefore undetectable) and comprised of personnel accommodation, facilities and storage bunkers. Smaller structures were placed along the edges of each battery such as open artillery emplacements and equipment. The distance between the bunkers was determined by multiple overlapping shooting ranges of 120 degrees, which was initially determined by the surveyors in Berlin (Forty 2002, Harff and Harff 2002, Rolf and Saal 1986). The most important design criteria for the assembly of a stronghold was how ordnance could be transported and implemented, while individual bunkers required to be shell-proofed, camouflaged and fire resistant.

Technological advancements in building emerged as an aftermath of the Great War which, due to housing shortages, had led to standardisation in materials, construction, regulations and norms. Influential avant-garde experiments were conducted by the two Bauhaus architects Walter Gropius and Ernst Neufert, whose work in the 1920s formed the basis for Neufert's first architectural building standards the *Bauentwurfslehre* (1936). In 1943 a modified extended edition, the *Bauordnungslehre* was written, edited and introduced by no other than Minister for Armaments and War Production and new head of *Organisation Todt*, Albert Speer. This particular edition focused on creating a set of construction norms and building standards for mass-produced industrial buildings for a new Reich, ranging from factories to workers' housing, simultaneously constructing a subtle narrative suggesting that minimum standards and material production were seamlessly derived over the centuries from Vitruvian ordering principles and classical proportions (Neufert and Speer 1943).

Structured as a strict military organisation, the OT was to execute strategic policies decided on by the Supreme Command of the Armed Forces (OKW). Speer, his colleague Xaver Dorsch (Chief Engineer of *Organisation Todt*), and their staff concentrated on applying Neufert's building standards (minimum ceiling heights and room widths; uniformity of concrete; mass-produced formworks; pre-fabricated uniform steel beams; reinforcement bars; doors, frameworks and furnishings; heating and ventilation units; equipment and ammunition), methods and specifications which permitted accurate cost and material estimates per project. At OT headquarters in Berlin, plans were drafted for standardised bunker types that were then entrusted to the OKW's Commander, General Field Marshal von Rundstedt, who was responsible for carrying out his chief engineer's, *Oberbauinspector* Weiss, building plans. Weiss, stationed in Paris, had his own team and a special liaison staff of Army Fortress Engineers (*Festung Pionier-Stab*) who drafted plans that were then sent back to Berlin for routine approval. After the blueprints had been drafted and estimated costs of required materials calculated and work schedules derived, the responsibility for the actual construction was divided amongst the *Oberbauleitungen* (OBLs) who were in charge of a subdivided, geographical defensive coastal region.

Organisation Todt wisely allowed for latitude when local engineers and architects were contracted as they were better acquainted with local geographical conditions. Examples of differences between building in swampy, sandy, or bedrock formations, which at times

8.2   France, *Atlantikwall*, Mouth of the Gironde – Soldiers leaning over a map during a meeting at an inner court of a bunker.

required more material than originally allotted for a particular type, can be cited from each *Einsatzgruppe*. Following OT's approval, a Fortification Engineer Staff was charged with supervising the completion of a particular project. Documents reveal that most revisions (foreseen or unforeseen) during the peak construction periods of 1943 and 1944 did not go through this bureaucratic chain of command. In most cases, Army Engineers would 'borrow' OT supplies and manpower, 'request' them from local manufacturers, or simply hire their own local labourers to erect bunkers without any OT supervision (SHAEF 1945).

It was inevitable that, with such a powerful centralised chain of command (co-operating with *Wehrmacht*, Navy and Air force high commands), differences in opinion would occur and ambition, combined with a lust for power, would make it impossible to follow one coherent strategy. Hitler undoubtedly noticed that what was good for one army branch may not have been good for the war and had, therefore, requested his most trustworthy General Field Marshal Rommel, to objectively inspect the *Atlantikwall's* progress in its entirety and report his findings directly to him. Rommel made two such inspections in 1943 and 1944 (Sakkers 1993). He recommended that only the buildings that were already under construction should be completed and that attention should, instead, be diverted to focus on expanding landscape-based interventions such as laying underwater mines, digging anti-tank trenches, erecting concrete retaining walls, placing anti-tank obstacles on the shores and underwater mines (Harrison 1951). But no strategic tactical approach would have been capable of preventing the Allied forces from penetrating the *Atlantikwall* at its weakest link – Normandy.

FROM COUNTER INTELLIGENCE TO INVASION – (DE)CONSTRUCTING THE *ATLANTIKWALL*

While the Germans were preparing for an invasion the Allied forces in Britain were relying on the *Ordnance Survey* mapping agency to produce coherent up-to-date cartographic maps of Western Europe and of its coastline in this constant state of flux (Seymour 1980: 274–85).

8.3   France, Lorient – General Field Marshal Erwin Rommel by the *Atlantikwall* inspecting an OT work place.

The SHAEF (Supreme Headquarters Allied Expeditionary Force) office for Counter-Intelligence also relied on material gathered by local resistance groups about the location and nature of bunkers and other anti-tank obstacles, which were either reproduced in microfilm format or reconstructed from memory upon the informants' arrival in London. A special branch, for example, belonging to the Dutch intelligence stationed in London produced maps and sketches indicating the location and type of bunkers and obstacles, telephone and telegraph wiring between batteries, locations of V2 long range missile launching sites, storage facilities and the locations of Nazi headquarters including OT offices (Anon. 1940–45). Similar ground reports were also produced during interrogation of German POWs in France in the course of 1944.

Since intelligence reports could never be entirely comprehensive, employing tactical reconnaissance became vital to winning the war. This was brought under the control of the 1st Canadian Army, whose failed landing at Dieppe in August 1942, had had the effect of giving them the vital experience necessary for gathering reconnaissance in combined operations. In fact, complete corporation between all armed services was required and, between July 1943 and May 1945, the Royal Air Force (RAF) had distributed a staff member to each army group. While they were utilising the most updated versions of plotted maps and intelligence, extra

8.4   Operation Overlord, D-Day invasion aerial photograph showing Normandy beaches.

geographical information was needed of Normandy's cliffs that could only be obtained from very low angles. Oblique photographic techniques were thus further developed in order to observe changes made to the coastal strips (Anon. 1945).

Nevertheless, and despite this extraordinary organisation, local expertise was also provided by the French Resistance who announced a fake photo competition of Normandy's beaches to the local villagers, which in addition to valuable topographical information had also uplifted civilian moral.

But it wasn't only the RAF and military strategists who were able to use this intelligence material. Artists and designers (as experts in camouflage techniques) employed by the Allied forces, used the data gathered on anti-tank water channels and other obstacles to produce: mobile bridges for tanks that could bear a 60 ton load when set in position over an anti-tank channel; a 'Crab' flail attachment to a tank that could beat its way into minefields protective sheets that would allow tanks to blast their way through concrete tetrahedral; long-range flame-throwers for use against bunkers; and even decoy inflatable tanks and bunkers for camouflage purposes (Topham 2002). The greatest act of deception, however, lay in making preparations for an allied landing in Normandy, while attempting to deceive the Germans into thinking that the main attack would come either in Pas-de-Calais or Norway.

A TRULY 'COLLABORATIVE' EFFORT: EXPANDING MILITARY SPACE

How local inhabitants of these numerous settlements experienced this military space was largely dependant on the 'racial' and political relationship between Germany and those conquered nations. The notional differences between a militarised regime and a protectorate were only apparent during the initial war years. From late 1942 onwards all the beaches, and certain urbanised spaces, were defined as militarised zones. These *Sperrgebiete* – prohibited zones for civilians – were physically bounded by barbed wire, anti-tank ditches and Czech hedgehogs. Access was only possible through a few, guarded check-points with a special *Ausweis* (travel identity card) issued to 'indispensable' residents. The OT's and *Wehrmacht's* greatest challenge was to ensure that their militarised space would perform to its full potential without the presence of civilians who would either stand in artillery ranges or attempt to sabotage their operations. As Hitler decreed, complex processes of civilian evacuation would soon follow as building activity increased. Villages were easily evacuated, but the challenge remained in larger urban fabrics where the collaboration of local municipal planning authorities was required. In the case of The Hague – the only coastal city that held a *Rijkskommissariaat* (Protectorate) for the Occupied Territories – special measures were taken to 'fortify' it (Bosma 2006 and Sakkers 2004: 21–8). Meticulously organised evacuations were executed over the course of a year and a half, which resulted in displacing 135,000 people (a quarter of its population) to the eastern part of the Netherlands (Ambachtsheer 1995). Given that the evacuees needed a 'moving permit', a permit to hire a vehicle, and a limit was set that to property removed from their premises, it became apparent that plundering, looting and destruction of property was a foreseeable, yet uncontrollable inevitability (Anon 1942b).

Early in 1943, another municipal planning body was also keeping busy with defining and redefining the *Atlantikwall's* exact border conditions and determining which buildings in the

8.5   Digging an antitank channel as part of the border condition of the *Sperrgebiet* in The Hague.

Figure 8.6   The result of demolition works of entire urban quarters in The Hague. Shown here is the desolated street Goudsbloemlaan.

Hague would be designated for demolition. They first divided the *Sperrgebiet* into two zones (Anon 1942c and Ambachtsheer 1995) and classified who may actually remain and in each. The city was further divided into a series of *afdelingen* (departments). Each department was carefully drawn, and each quarter designated for demolition was numbered and defined. Exceptions were made to buildings and houses of those who were allowed to remain in the *Sperrgebiet* (such as OT employees or families with members of the Dutch National Socialist Party, the NSB). Several attempts were made to save examples of architectural or cultural heritage. While occasionally these succeeded, in most cases contractual agreements were drafted, labourers hired and demolition permits issued and churches, schools, hospitals and bridges were indiscriminately torn down (Schut 1946). The entire operation was flawlessly executed and resulted in the approximate demolition of one third of The Hague for the sole purpose of expanding the *Atlantikwall's* military space.

As a result of two exceptionally cold winters, 1944 and 1945 – where energy shortages (resulting in illegal tree-cutting from public spaces) were only exceeded by food shortages – plundering, looting and additional damage was inflicted on remaining properties. These acts were not carried out by the Germans or those in their service but by the local population. And, despite threats and sanctions, it appeared that the municipality was unable to control those desperate measures (Anon. 1945).

Additional civilian evacuations from places considered probable for an Allied invasion took place in: Finnmark, Narvik region near Bergen, Hammerfest's villages, Stavanger, and Trondheim in Norway; Hanstholm's villages in Denmark; IJmuiden, Zandvoort aan Zee, Katwijk, Hook of Holland and Walcheren's villages in the Netherlands; Ostend and Zeebrugge in Belgium; and Dieppe, Cherbourg, Le Havre, Lorient, and Saint-Nazaire in France.[1] Confiscation of private and public properties, depletion of natural resources, and the destruction of coastal regions, built-up areas and cultural patrimonies may, therefore, be added to the list of Nazi war crimes as a direct result of building the *Atlantikwall*.

In Albert Speer's (1970) post-war account of this building process he stated that the *Atlantikwall* made unrealistic demands on the total war industry, while there weren't even enough soldiers to inhabit all those bunkers. More than 13 million cubic meters of concrete was used as well as over a million tons of iron – which could have been deployed by the armament industry – was cast instead as concrete reinforcement bars costing almost four billion Reichsmarks. Considering that the *Atlantikwall* was rendered obsolete only two weeks after D-Day invasion, Speer concluded that this building project was the greatest waste of resources of the entire war. Simultaneously, however, Speer continued to paint a mythological image of the Führer who occupied himself late at night with designing bunker types out of sheer compassion for his *Frontsoldaten*. It goes without saying that, despite Speer's 'great moral responsibility', he expressed little remorse and no compassion for employing more than one million slave labourers ranging from Russian, Ukrainian and Polish POWs; those civilians from occupied countries (Norwegians, Danes, Dutch, Belgian and French) (Schumann 1943 and Seidler 1987) recruited under Fritz Saukel's *Arbeitseinsatz Programm* (Homze 1967); or the

Algerians and Tunisians from the French colonies – all of those who lived in the most appalling conditions in concentration and labour camps along the coast (Forty 2002) for the sole purpose of erecting 'wasteful' fortifications (Speer 1970). As a result of the Nuremberg Trials, this may be justifiably be recognised as a human rights violation and a crime against humanity. Ironically enough, Speer did succeed in becoming the builder of ruins, not in grandiose public projects that would compete with the empirical archaeological remnants of the ancient world, but in an equally megalomaniac project: a defensive line of 12,000 modern concrete structures, now found in a ruinous state, but promising to endure this millennium in its entirety.

8.7   France, Blanc Nez, *Atlantikwall* – Labourers building Coastal Battery 'Lindmann'.

POST-WAR EUROPE OR, RECOVERY THROUGH FORGETTING

> *Wo aber Gefahr ist, wächst*
> *Das Rettende auch.*
> *(But where the danger is found*
> *The saving power also.)*

> Friedrich Hölderlin, Patmos, 1803 (translated by, and cited in Heidegger 1977).

After the liberation, western-Europeans were left with clearing up the rubble; removing mines and obstacles; repairing damages done to the fragile dunes, beaches, ridges and cliffs during bunker construction; housing thousands of returning residents; and with rebuilding

8.8 Demolishing (antitank) obstacles from the German occupied beach of Scheveningen (The Hague).

demolished urban fabrics. In this period recovery was equated with forgetting and the restoration of the life one had prior to the war. In a process equally complex to their erection, bunker demolition took more than ten years, due to financial shortages and the overwhelming strength of the structures. Numerous tangible traces of the occupation (i.e. bunkers) were demolished and the remainder buried (under dunes or mounds) and forgotten, leaving but few symbolic traces behind for future generations.

In the process of tracing this form of 'collective amnesia', three periods may be identified. The first, which took place between 1945 and 1955, presented an initial form of recovery through illustrated books, comics, cartoons, films and poetry-bundles and memoires that commemorated the ravages left behind as a result of building the *Atlantikwall* (evacuation, demolition and plundering) as well as the bunkers themselves. In this particular form of recovery humour was often used as a common denominator due to its effectiveness and immediacy in providing solace to grieving communities. The second period (mid 1950s to late 1960s) was by far a more complex one as the apparent elated optimism of the 1950s induced a process of 'forgetting' – where recalling the war was not only avoided, but also the actual physical remnants were either, no longer present to evoke the retelling of these stories, or had been re-appropriated as vacation houses, or claimed by adventurous youths as playing grounds. Faced with the threat of nuclear war, a new generation of artists raised questions regarding the true nature of trauma and recovery, seeking to break the silence surrounding the Second World War as an heroic attempt at resisting this form of 'collective amnesia'. Nevertheless, the *Atlantikwall* remained marginalised as its own creation-story remained untold.

A similar process may also be seen in former West Germany which, was not only limited to visual arts, but extended beyond it to include literature. It was not till Günter Grass' novel *The Tin Drum* (1959) that the symbolic and spatial significance of the *Atlantikwall* (culturally, historically as well as architecturally) would receive a place within German cultural memory. Grass's description foretells a future, as it references a statement once made by Speer, 'Hitler wanted temporal effects and permanent witnesses. Should his empire fall after centuries, he said, "The ruins of our buildings will bare witness to the strength of our will and the magnitude of our faith"' (Speer 1970). It is laden with irony – instead of monumental ruins of great public buildings that, in a thousand years, would tell the story of a glorified Reich, Hitler would end by telling a less glorified tale in bunker remnants. These as Grass formulated, in a thousand years' time, would reveal the truly gruesome nature of the twentieth century.

The third period may have been signified by artworks by several German artists such as Anselm Kiefer (1969), Joseph Beuys (1971) and Markus Lüpertz (1969–70) who, in an attempt to deal with their national guilt, accountability and remembrance, created works which addressed the symbolic significance of the *Atlantikwall* for their generation. Yet it was not until Paul Virilio's photographic journey along the French coastline and its subsequent exhibition at the Centre Pompidou in Paris, followed by its publication as *Bunker Archaeology* (1975), that attention was drawn to bunker remnants as architecture – simultaneously objects, ruins, and symbols. Virilio's journey is a phenomenological interpretive exploration – conducted by a philosopher and architect and not by a historian – where (military) space and (war) architecture are regarded as iconographical, experiential and even poetic. Indeed, the poetic expression inherent in the photographs was accompanied by existential poems written by Rainer Maria Rilke and Friedrich Hölderlin. One specific stanza, *'Wo aber Gefahr ist, wächst / Das Rettende auch.'*, was quoted from Hölderlin's Patmos to accompany the chapter entitled 'War Landscape'. These exact lines, coincidentally or not, were previously used in Heidegger's essay on technology, to what appears to be similar reasoning: to illustrate how the inherent danger in technology and its appropriation in *Totaler Krieg* (Total War) that very *'Gefahr'* (danger) so succinctly identified by Hölderlin – also contained its own unfathomable *'Das Rettende'* (salvation). For Heidegger and Virilio – who both came from religious backgrounds – art and dwelling (architecture) and, in this case, the kind associated with the danger inherent in *Technē* (the *Atlantikwall*) also holds within it 'that which saves'. Here, the bunker is described as the 'ark that saves' (*Wehrmacht*) soldiers from perilous (Allied) bombings. 'War Landscape' refers, therefore, to the place where 'the saving power' resides. Virilio and the architect Claude Parent took bunker aesthetics a step further when designing the Church of St. Bernadette at Nevers, France in the late 1960s. It is important to pose the question of whether or not it is possible or appropriate to absolve the bunker of its crimes prior to grasping its full historical and symbolic significance and, if redeeming it in the process by transforming it into a sacred space is even desirable. Ultimately, such gestures may even undermine the *Atlantikwall's* significance as future 'sites of collective remembrance'.

TOPOLOGY OF REMEMBRANCE – TOWARDS *LIEUX DES MÉMOIRE*

> A state of peace among men who live side by side is not a natural state, which is rather to be described as a state of war … Thus the state of peace must be established. Between states … no punitive war is thinkable because between them a relation of superior and inferior does not exist. Whence it follows that a war of extermination, where the process of annihilation would strike both parties at once … would bring out perpetual peace only in the great graveyard of the human race' (Immanuel Kant, Perpetual Peace in Kant 1795/2005).

It is quite possible to speak now of a fourth period which has symbolically begun with the fiftieth anniversary of the liberation, a period which marks the transition of the Second World War from a remembered experience to a historical event. It delineates the quest for unravelling remnants of a buried history, a growing interest in preserving war remnants, and in narrating an inaccessible past to younger generations. Guided tours are currently being offered by numerous localised bunker groups who attempt to recreate and re-enact its former militarised presence. Yet despite this gradually increasing appreciation for the bunkers as war heritage, the *Atlantikwall* remains an anomaly to both municipal authorities and the general public. In his essay 'Echoes of war: Battlefield Tourism', Bruce Prideaux (2007) describes the significance of visiting former battlefield sites and lists several ingredients required to transform such places into tourist attractions (better known as 'dark tourism'). In more recent years a growing trend has emerged to include 'battleless battlefields', sites that hold former strategic fortifications and other military structures as indicative of an occupation that had anticipated combat, but where the latter simply did not take place. According to Prideaux, these sites achieve the same results as if physical battle did occur, only without the damages left behind. Applying his premise to the *Atlantikwall* shows that Normandy and Dieppe – as sites where combat did take place –

8.9   Former U-Boat bunker 'Hornisse' in Bremen Germany. Note, the bunker was converted in 1980 into a roof-top car park while simultaneously serving as the foundations for a boat-like office building. A small memorial plaque that was placed on the eastern elevation. For the full inscription, see the List of Figures.

may no longer be regarded as the only relevant sites of mourning, but that the *Atlantikwall* in its entirety can be redefined as a battleless battlefield. Considerable physical damages were inflicted upon coastal landscapes, cities and villages, and the scars left upon them still bear witness to those war crimes. Through the tangible physical traces we can bring out the hidden traces of human suffering (i.e. slavery and displacement of civilians) and unresolved traumas as forgotten narratives and historical truths.

Since 1995 numerous projects have been created for the conversion of individual bunkers. Although wide in scope, these projects may be characterised by their scale, use, location and the manner by which the notion of collective memory is either dealt with or ignored. Large-scale projects have been initiated by local municipalities who are faced with massive bunkers which cannot easily be demolished. These include the conversion of air-raid shelters and *Luftwaffe* Flak towers to apartment blocks and of air-raid shelters to cultural facilities and green energy stations, concentrated mostly in Germany. Meanwhile in France, the conversion of U-boat bunkers into cultural facilities have gained popularity and even include master plans for their surrounding areas (St. Nazaire, Bordeaux, and Lorient).

Medium-scale projects tend to embody the notion of collective remembrance as they incorporate cultural landscapes and architectural remains into new museums and visitor centres, yet remain highly problematic when staging pseudo-historical narratives. Small-scale projects may be classified as permanent and temporary interventions that range from very site specific permanent monuments such as land-art projects, sculptures, and architectural interventions; temporary land-art installations and artistic ways of exposing bunkers; performances and art

exhibits in or around bunkers; and video/light projections commemorating the *Atlantikwall* (Kimpel 2006: 100–119).

Despite this wide range of projects marking a change in attitude towards bunker remnants, the majority of these works have failed to demonstrate a greater urgency towards creating projects that simultaneously address the *Atlantikwall's* 'guilt-ridden' history as well as this defence-line in its entirety. It remains important, therefore, to critically evaluate architectural interventions not only for their contribution to urban life, but also for their power to narrate the biographical story of a place. Seventy years after the first plans were drafted to erect these fortifications, modern western society persists in its refusal to acknowledge the symbolic significance of these traumatic traces. Instead, a desire to ignore the sufferings of the collective 'others' whose traces have entirely been obliterated (i.e. slave labour camps) endures and this is evident in the sophisticated 'camouflage techniques' employed to mask the sites' darker past.

An alternative approach is to create an all-encompassing strategy for dealing with the multi-faceted nature of the *Atlantikwall* that would include theoretical and even poetic interpretations of these traces and retell complete historical narratives on site-specific landscapes and urban areas. These places, then would embody a lasting notion of the symbolic significance of the *Atlantikwall* in its entirety. In the midst of social unrest and the rise of nationalism, this former defence line, emblematic of *Totaler Krieg* architecture, would act as a reminder of the temporality of 'Perpetual Peace' (Kant 1795/2005). As such, the remnants of the *Atlantikwall* would, indeed, one day be capable of revealing a Heideggerian truth regarding its past as a silent witness to an ideologically-based crime, to all those who collaborated in its execution and to those countless individuals who suffered as a result of building it.

8.10   *Train Tracks* – Part of the Wall Series taken along the French coastline.

NOTE

1   For an extensive study on civilian evacuations of Cherbourg, Le Havre and Lorient see Torrie 2010.

REFERENCES

Ambachtsheer, H. 1995. *Van verdediging naar Bescherming. De Atlantikwall in Den Haag.* Den Haag: Gemeente Den Haag, Dienst Ruimtelijke en Economische Ontwikkeling, afdeling Monumentenzorg.

Anon. 1942a. Bundesarchiv *Militärarchiv* Freiburg, Germany (RM7/992: 10/3/1941-23/8/1942).

Anon. 1942b. Reports by Urban Development and Housing Commission (Dienst Stadsontwikkeling en Volkshuisvesting (dS&V)) 1942. The Hague. Municipal Archives.

Anon. 1942c. Gemeente's-Gravenhage, cartographic material May.

Anon. 1940–45. German Fortifications. Duitse Verdedigingswerken (collectie 575/ 59-65, 313-316) 1940–1945); Netherlands Institute for Military History (NIMH), The Hague.

Anon. 1943–44. Demolition drawings and tender documents (Sloop percelen), Gemeentewerken cartographic material, 1943–1944. The Hague's Municipal Archives.

Anon. 1945a. Public Announcement poster, *Bekendmaking* 1945, The Hague's Municipal Archives.

Anon. 1945b. HQ First Canadian Army, *Air Recce. 35 Recce Wing RAF*. London: Canadian Military HQ.

BBC Documentary. 2003. *Heroes of the Second World War*.

Benjamin, W. (1936) 2008. *The Work of Art in the Age of Mechanical Reproduction, and other Writings on Media*, translated by J.A. Underwood. Cambridge and London: Harvard University Press.

Bosma, K. 2006. *Schuilstad. Bescherming van de bevolking tegen luchtaanvallen.* Amsterdam: SUN Uitgeverij.

Forty, G. 2002. *Hitler's Atlantic Wall*. Hersham: Ian Allan Publishing.

Gilbert, A. 2006. *POW. Allied Prisoners in Europe, 1939–1945*. Beccles: John Murray Publishers.

Grass, G. 1962. *The Tin Drum*. New York: Pantheon Books.

Heidegger, M. (1953) 1977. *The Question Concerning Technology and Other Essays*, translated by William Lovitt. New York: Harper & Row.

Harff, P. and Harff, D. 2005. *IJmuiden-Den Haag, Atlantikwall 1940–1945*. De Witte.

Harrison, G.A. 1951. *The European Theater of Operations: Cross-Channel Attack*. Washington DC: Office of the Chief of Military History, Department of the Army.

Høgg, I. 1981. *History of Fortifications*. London: Orbis Publishing.

Homze, E.L. 1967. *Foreign Labor in Nazi Germany*. Princeton: Princeton University Press.

Kant, I. (1795) 2005. *Perpetual Peace*. New York: Cosimo Classics.

Kimpel, H. 2006. *Innere Sicherheit: Bunker Ästhetik*. Marburg: Jonas Verlag.

Neufert, E. (Hrsg. von Albert Speer) 1943. *Bauordnungslehre*. Berlin Amsterdam Prag Wien: Volk und Reich Verlage.

Prideaux, B. 2007. Echoes of War: Battlefield Tourism. In Ryan, C. (ed.) *Battlefield Tourism: History Place and Interpretation*. Amsterdam and London: Elsevier, 17–29.

Propaganda Kompagnie. Europa's bolwerk: Atlantik-Wall. In: *Signal*. Nummer 11/1943. Berlin: Deutscher Verlag, 2–5.

Rolf, R. 1982. *Bunkers in Nederland*. Den Helder: Uitgeverij H. Talsma.

Rolf, R. and Saal, P. 1986. *Vestingwerken in west-Europa*. Weesp: Fibula-Van Dishoeck**.**

Sakkers, H. 1993. *Generalfeldmarschaal Rommel – Opperbevelhebber van Heergruppe B bij de voorbereiding van West-Europa, 5 november 1943 tot 6 juni 1944*. Koudekerke: Zeelucht.

Sakkers, H. 2004. *Duitse bunkerbouw vanuit het Rijkscommissariaat – Abteilung Siedlung und Bauten – 1942–1945*. Koudekerke: Stichting Militair Erfgoed.

Schuhmann, H. 1943. *OT. Im Einsatz. Als Kriegsberichter bei den Frontarbeiten*. München: Verlag Knorr & Hirth.

Schut, Bakker P. 1946. Opruiming, herstel en wederopbouw. In: *Den Haag, 1946. Vol. 1*. Den Haag: Bureau voor statistiek en voorlichting stadhuis jaarlijkse uitgave, 28–52.

Seidler, F. 1987. *Die Organisation Todt. Bauen für Staat und Wehrmacht. 1938–1945*. Koblenz: Bernard & Graefe Verlag.

Seymour, W.A. (ed.). 1980. *A History of the Ordnance Survey*. Chatham: W & J Mackay.

The Supreme HQ Allied Expeditionary Force (SHAEF) Counter Intelligence Sub division, *Handbook of the Organisation Todt, MIRS/MR OT/1945, London*. (reprint) Osnabrück: Biblio Verlag, 1992.

Speer, A. 1970. *Inside the Third Reich*. New York and Toronto: Macmillan.

Topham, S. 2002. *Blow-up: Inflatable Art, Architecture and Design*. München, Berlin, London, New York: Prestel Publishing.

Torrie, J.S. 2010. *'For their Own Good'. Civilian Evacuations in Germany and France, 1939–1945*. New York and Oxford: Berghahn Books.

Trevor-Roper, H.R. (ed.). 1964. *Hitler's War Directives 1939–1945*. London: Sidgwick and Jackson.

Virilio, P. (1975) 1994. *Bunker Archaeology*. Princeton: Princeton University Press.

9

Military Intelligence: The Board of Ordnance Maps and Plans of Scotland, 1689–c.1760

Carolyn J. Anderson

Today the complexities of military tactical operations and deployment of troops are such that armed forces are dependent on geographic and geospatial support. Army field manuals include detailed procedures for the production and use of military mapping and for the provision of maps as a source of intelligence. The manuals state that:

> it is necessary to rely on maps to provide information to our combat elements and to resolve
> logistical operations far from our shores. Soldiers and materials must be transported, stored,
> and placed into operation at the proper time and place. Much of this planning must be done
> by using maps. Therefore, any operation requires a supply of maps (US Department of the
> Army 2001).

A study of history reveals that one of the most pressing demands for maps has come about as a result of military needs in the service of the State. The kings of France, in the course of the sixteenth century, are well-known for commissioning maps for the purpose of fortifying their frontiers and planning campaigns, and for more generally recognising the usefulness of maps in war (Buisseret 1992). A similar development took place in England at this time. Henry VIII employed French cartographers such as Jean Rotz to map the coasts and ports of England for defensive purposes. There is also evidence that Henry tried to supervise the conduct of sieges from afar on the basis of information contained in maps (Barber 1992). In Sweden, as in France and England, King Gustavus II Adolphus (r.1611–32) appointed military surveyors including Heinrich Thome, a German *ingeniör* (fortification officer), to produce maps of conquests and fortifications in the Baltic provinces (Mead 2007).

There are many historical examples that illustrate the practice of employing official cartographers for military offensive and defensive purposes. This chapter looks in more detail at one – the British military mapping of Scotland between 1689 and *c.*1760 (Figure 9.1). At this time, engineers, draughtsmen, and associated surveyors were charged with planning, constructing, and recording landscapes of and for military action, and their records – maps, plans and memoirs – were recognised as a particular tool of political surveillance. The period was marked by the Jacobite Risings in Scotland, when clans gathered in an attempt to restore James VII of Scotland and II of England and Ireland, and descendants of the House of Stuart, to the throne (Lenman 1995). The sustained nature of the first rising, from July 1689 to mid-

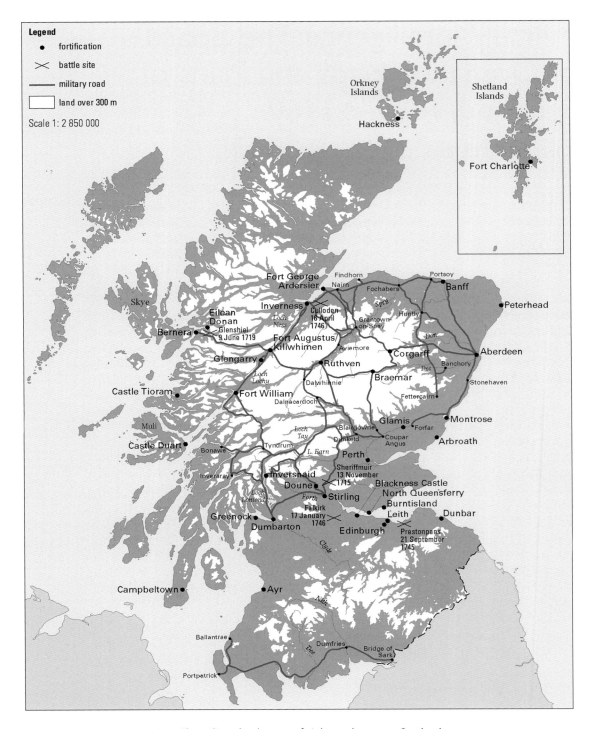

Orkney
Islands

Hackness

Shetland
Islands

Fort Charlotte

Skye

Fort George
Ardersier   Findhorn
                   Nairn   Portsoy
Inverness   Fochabers   Banff
Eilean   Culloden   Spey   Peterhead
Donan   16 April   Huntly
Glenshiel   1746   Grantown-
Bernera   9 June 1719   on-Spey
             Loch   Aberdeen
             Ness   Don
Fort Augustus/   Aviemore   Corgarff
Kiliwhimen   Banchory
Glengarry   Ruthven
                                    Dee   Stonehaven
Castle Tioram   Loch   Dalwhinnie   Braemar
                 Lochy   Fettercairn
         Fort William   Glamis
Mull   Dalnacardoch   Montrose
                        Loch   Blairgowrie Forfar
Castle Duart   Tay   Dunkeld   Coupar   Arbroath
         Bonawe   Tyndrum   Angus
                        L. Earn
                              Perth
Inveraray   Inversnaid   Sheriffmuir
             Doune   13 November   Blackness Castle
                Loch   1715   North Queensferry
                Lomond Stirling   Burntisland
Greenock   Forth   Leith   Dunbar
         Dumbarton   Falkirk
                      17 January   Edinburgh   Prestonpans
                      1746   21 September
                              Clyde   1745

Campbeltown   Ayr
                              Nith

         Ballantrae   Dumfries   Bridge of
                     Dee   Sark
         Portpatrick

9.1   The military landscapes of eighteenth-century Scotland.

1691, turned the government's attention firmly towards Scotland. Warrants were issued for 'Brass Ordnance & … Mortar Pieces with all the ammunition Stores and Equipage thereunto belonging … to be transported to Scotland' (Talbot 1689). It also prompted a concern to map Scotland in an attempt to know the nation to better govern it: 'the Officers of the Ordnance … represented that they had appoynted Engineers to make Draughts and Estimates of what Works would be needfull to be done effectually to secure North Britain' (Anon. 1708: 263). From this time on, military engineers were actively involved in reinforcing the Union of England and Scotland and securing Hanoverian succession. Recurring rebellion – notably in 1715, 1719, and 1745–46 – and abortive invasions by French Jacobite forces in 1708 and 1744 effectively sustained the government's anxiety over Scotland and led to repeated renewals to map the military landscape. These maps informed state and military strategy.

An archive of about 750 manuscript maps is a surviving legacy of the government's activities in Scotland at this time. Using examples from the archive, this chapter examines the institutional nature of British military mapping in the eighteenth century then looks at how different political and military imperatives at different times gave rise to different constructions and representations of Scottish space.

THE RATIONALISATION AND NATURE OF BRITISH MILITARY CARTOGRAPHY

With changes in the art of warfare – the so-called 'military revolution' – military tactics across Europe evolved (Parker 1988). For Buisseret (2003) and Widmalm (1990), the impact of these changes produced changes in the nature of mapping. Advances in firepower transformed the conduct of both offensive and defensive operations, modified the art of fortification and, initially, slowed the pace of warfare. In response, armies acquired new specialists: the artillery emerged as a separate unit to the cavalry and infantry; engineers emerged to design and to construct new types of fortifications and siege works. With the transition in the seventeenth century to more mobile strategies, battles overcame sieges as the decisive element in war and every place became a potential theatre of war. Only then did the *fortificateur* develop into the *ingénieur-géographe* as European States demanded 'knowledge of the whole geography' and began to sponsor large-scale topographical maps of territories and military surveys in preparation for battle (Widmalm 1990: 201, Skelton 1970: 77). By the eighteenth century, military officers in the field were increasingly expected to be cartographically literate, to understand the use of maps for military purposes and eventually to provide the necessary expertise to lead State mapping projects (Edney 1994). Surveyors marched alongside soldiers, mapping for reconnaissance; surveying and constructing fortifications, towns and barracks; building roads and bridges; depicting military action; and systematically surveying national territories (Godlewska 1999, Edney 1997, Duffy 1996, Harley 1978a). The outcome was the growing domination of map making by military personnel, a move Edney (1994: 19) calls the 'cartographisation of the military', the increasing 'map-mindedness' of senior army officials that allowed the use of maps and the practice of mapping for military purposes.

The Board of Ordnance

As the role of maps in government and national defence grew during the sixteenth and seventeenth centuries, the idea of a professional, centralised State institution capable of administrating and coordinating a nation's mapping grew with it. One such institution was the Board of Ordnance, a British department of State and growing cartographic authority. Constituted in 1597 as a ministry of defence, from this time the power of the Board increased greatly and its Office of Ordnance grew substantially. By 1683, the Board had jurisdiction over the construction and maintenance of sovereign fortifications and barracks, control of armament factories, supply of munitions and subsistence stores to the Army and Navy, and responsibility for land surveying. Furthermore, the technical and military establishments of the Artillery, Engineers, and Ordnance Field Trains were commanded by the Master-General of the Ordnance and administrated by the Board (The National Archives 2004, Stewart 1996, Marshall 1980, Tomlinson 1979).

With the growth of the Office in the late seventeenth century, clearer distinction was made between the functions of its military and civil officers. Responsibilities and developments in specialist roles, for example, in military engineering and civilian draughtsmanship, became more acute as cartography emerged as a particular tool of government. In the *Rules Orders and Instructions* issued in 1683, the duties of State engineers and their role in map making is clearly defined for the first time. The Principal Engineer was to take 'Surveys of Land ... to draw and design the Situation of any Place in their due Prospects, Uprights and Perspective'. His knowledge of civil and military architecture was to give rise to 'perfect Draughts of every Fortifications, Forts and Fortresses of Our Kingdoms ... and to know the Importance of every one of them, where their Strength or Weakness lyes'. And, in times of action, he was to conduct sieging operations (Frederick 1683–1760: 52, 54, 55). Although the *Rules* were amended in 1686, the duties of the engineers remained largely unaltered and, thereafter, were approved by every sovereign of Britain from William III to George II. As part of the development of the civil branch of the Ordnance, a Drawing Room was established at the Tower of London, possibly as early as 1683. Crucial in its ensuing evolution was the instruction in the *Rules* to 'cause the Draughts or Designs thereof to be left in the Office of Our Ordnance, there to remain for the Use and Information of Our said Master General and Principal Officers of Our Ordnance as Occasion shall require' (Frederick 1683–1760: 53). In January 1694, the Ordnance engaged its first permanent draughtsman. Lucas Boitout was charged with the sole task of 'Making, Draughting, and preparing such Plans, or Draughts ... as shall bee Required and Directed By the Master General ... or Principal Officers' (quoted in Parnell 1995: 93). From this time onwards, the Drawing Room became a centre of carto-reproduction. Apprentices from the age of 12 were trained as draughtsmen and surveyors to complement the engineers in the field and to help with the compilation, drawing, correction, reduction, enlargement and copying of maps and plans (Harley 1978b).

While cartographic concerns represented only a small sector of the Board's total responsibilities, they nevertheless were important in advancing the conventions and socio-political meanings of British military mapping that were established through the course of the eighteenth century (Anderson 2010, Marshall 1980). Through instruction in the military sciences, including practices associated with cartography, practical experience in the field and drawing room, and the transfer of continental codes of mapping, engineers and draughtsmen under the aegis of the Board of Ordnance adopted drawing styles in their use of colour and symbol that reflected wider European practices. These were most clearly defined in the maps made as part of the 'everyday' engineering work of the Ordnance, namely fortification (Figure 9.2), but the military engineers were also employed in making maps of roads, battles and the wider countryside. Their maps conveyed both a pragmatic function of construction and a

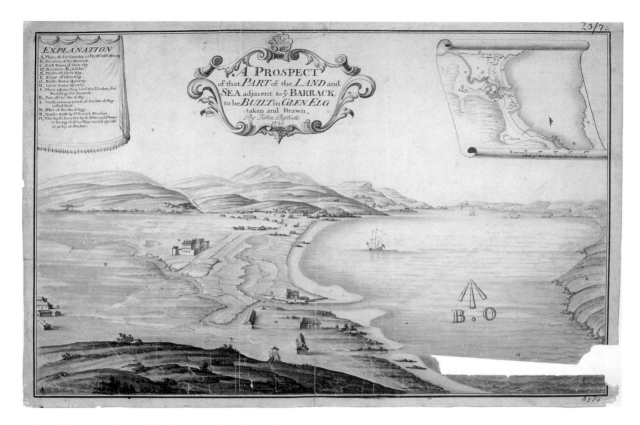

political function for establishing social order. Military maps were intellectual as well as physical tools of access for sending soldiers from the limited disciplinary units of the garrisons and forts in parts of Scotland to the Highlands and, eventually, to the full extent of the nation. As General William Roy (1785: 385) remarked, 'accurate surveys of a country are universally admitted to be … the best means of forming judicious plans of defence … Hence it happens, that if a country has not actually been surveyed, or is but little known, a state of warfare generally produces the first improvements in its geography'. Reliable information about the geography of Scotland was essential for the British state to exercise territorial control.

9.2   John Henry Bastide, *A prospect of that part of the land and sea adjacent to ye barrack to be built in Glen Elg*, 1720.

Cartographic Conventions

'The main skill in all Military Architecture' according to Second Engineer Talbot Edwards (1709/10a: 122), 'is fitting a Design to the Situation'. In fortification, engineers had to consider not only the fort's mathematical and scientific conception but its location and strategies of defence and attack. They used several forms of representation to do this, most popular of which were the horizontal section or plan, the vertical section or profile, and the perspective, axonometric, or bird's-eye view (Figure 9.2). British engineers adopted a practice similar to that used in France since the sixteenth century and extensively rationalised by Vauban (Louis XIV's Commissioner General of Fortifications) in the seventeenth, one based on the hierarchical organisation of cartographic representation through the use of different scales.[1] French maps were generally considered 'logical in treatment, brilliant in design, and clear in presentation'

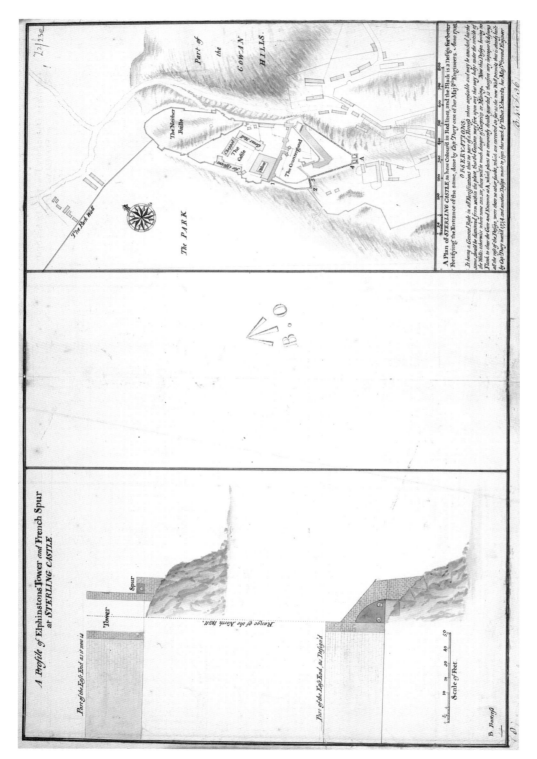

9.3   Theodore Dury, A Plan of Sterling Castle, as here Color'd in Red lines, and the Black is a Design for better Fortifying
       the Entrance of the same; A profile of Elphinstons Tower and French Spur at Sterling Castle, 1708.

(Tooley 1949: 2). Engineers working for the Board did much to emulate French practice. They popularised three main types of fortification map. The first was a medium-scale, topographical plan of a fort's situation (Figure 9.2). The second was a high resolution, large-scale plan of the fort itself, showing the enceinte or main perimeter of the 'attack zone', and parts of the fortification including the bastions, ravelins, and deep defences of the glacis (Figure 9.3) (Duffy 1985). The third type of map represented very high resolution plans of the individual fortress buildings. These plans were frequently accompanied or replaced by cross-sections or vertical profiles (Figure 9.3), and gave particular attention to the inclusion of measurements of elevation. These measurements, when combined with data on distances, could inform an artillery officer of the best position for gun emplacements in order to command the surrounding territory. They were of equal importance to the engineer for estimating martial capacity: designing barracks to accommodate companies of soldiers, and calculating the volume of powder, munitions and stores to be kept in the garrison magazines and storerooms.

Colours used in the maps and plans of Scottish forts similarly suggest standardisation of graphic representation. In practice, the fundamental colour specifications adopted by the British engineers matched those formulated by Vauban:

> The engineer … will produce a plan large enough to allow all its elements to be clearly distinguished … he will be sure to give a red wash to all completed stone-faced structures; Indian Ink or grey if they are simply earth or turf; distinguishing the parapet from the terreplain by a darker layer where it begins (Vauban 1680 quoted in Sanger 1999: 50–51).

Proposed works were to be given a yellow wash. Thereafter, four different colours were used: green for turf-covered parapets and the glacis; brown for roads, dry ditches and earthworks; blue-green for water; and indigo was used to represent iron or roofs of buildings covered with slate. 'This rule must be followed exactly to avoid the confusion that haphazardly colouring plans with all sorts of colours could cause if the meaning of one were mistaken for that of another' (Vauban 1680 quoted in Sanger 1999: 50–51, Muller 1756: 14–15). Topographical maps and some route surveys portrayed features designed to imitate nature. Stylised representations were used for trees, tilled fields, and sands, cultivated fields were yellow and moorland buff. Relief was shown in the emerging style of the time, using hachured lines to indicate the direction of the slope and changing tones to differentiate the gradient; positions were correct even if no elevations were given (Figure 9.9). These graphic codes displayed an artistic convention in depicting military landscapes. But 'beyond scientific instrument and artistic image', the political and military intent behind their production cannot be ignored (Cosgrove 2008: 158). A plan of the town and castle of Stirling, for example, includes a statement that 'the Houses Colour'd Yellow, obstruct the Command of the Castle and ought to be purchas'd by the Government and taken down' (Skinner 1746).

The extent to which all British military maps and plans conformed to standard practices did vary, however, possibly as a consequence of the conditions under which they were commissioned and drawn. The reason for a particular drawing style being favoured at any one time is open to conjecture. A style could reflect the compelling reason for their execution which may have afforded an engineer little time to draft more aesthetically pleasing plans, or his lack of equipment, or greater skill as an engineer than a draughtsman (Fleet 2007). As an English eighteenth-century engineer wrote, 'few surveyors are masters of the art of drawing' (Vallancey 1779 quoted in Marshall 1981: 3). These graphic representations conveyed, however, 'a much truer notion … than what, without such assistance, could possibly be conveyed in many words' (Roy 1793: 155–6).

The stimulus for rationalising military mapping – through institutionalisation and standardisation of representation, scale, and colour – came from the state's desire to establish a common cartographic discourse amongst its engineers and draughtsmen; a form of expression familiar both to producers and receivers and, crucially, one easily interpreted by a distant government for developing strategic policies. Subsequent copying and circulation of maps was a common event in the genealogy of military maps, but both were strictly controlled. William Caulfeild, director of road building in Scotland between 1740 and 1767, instructed the engineers surveying the roads to submit their completed plans '*only* to the General Officer Comanding in North Britain & to the Board of Ordnance' (emphasis added) (Anon. 1749: 358–60). Such explicit practice concerning the circulation of military maps reflected the territorial imperatives of the state. The maps were state secrets for the eyes of governing authorities alone; the majority were not concerned with communicating information of general interest to a civilian audience.

THE BOARD OF ORDNANCE IN SCOTLAND

Jacobite tendencies towards a form of guerrilla warfare prompted changing mapping technologies in Scotland in accordance with altered military and political imperatives. There was not, however, a complete shift from one technology to another. Fortification cartography dominates the representation of military landscapes and reflects the British State's need to secure its medieval castles, establish a military presence, and provide accommodation for its troops in the Highlands engaged in dealing with the threat of Jacobite insurgency.[2] Topographic and route surveys, while considerably less in number, reflect substantial military developments. From 1715, strategies to suppress insurrection and to repel foreign invasion provoked a military expansion into the Highlands that saw not only the design and construction of more fortifications but methods to improve the mobility of the British army. With these came a change in the mapping technologies as engineers were commissioned to reconnoitre the Highlands, choose sites for new military establishments and ensure effective communication between them and with the principal Lowland garrisons.

Between 1689 and 1760, the geographical distribution of fortifications evolved as the State's knowledge of Scotland shifted and expanded (Figure 9.4). The government's principal concern during this period was to command the Highland passes to prevent Jacobite rebels from descending into the Lowlands (Wade 1727). Initial measures were confined to strengthening existing medieval fortifications and establishing a military presence in the most disaffected part of the Highlands, to the south and west of the Great Glen (Figure 9.4a). The second phase, from 1715 to 1745, represented substantial military developments, in the building of barrack forts in the Highlands and fortified garrisons along the Great Glen from Fort William to Inverness, and in securing the medieval castles neglected by George I's Hanoverian government (Figure 9.4b). This phase also saw the first exploration of military surveyors into the mountainous Highland region to the east of the Glen. This area became thoroughly described in the third phase (1746–c.1760) through a period of reconnaissance for suitable new military garrisons for the troops sent to establish social order in the Highlands (Figure 9.4c). Many of the Highland forts damaged by the Jacobite army during the '45 Rebellion were refortified. With the addition of a road-building programme that saw the forts linked by an extensive network of military roads, the Scottish mainland was in effect an occupied country.

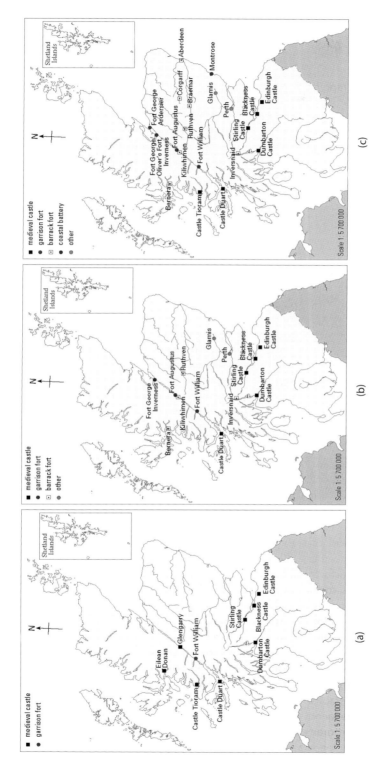

9.4a–c   Distribution of Scotland's fortification cartography in relation to phases of building activity: (a) 1689–1714, (b) 1715–1745, and (c) 1746–c.1760.

'For Preventing an Insult'

In 1690, with troubles to contend with in Ireland and Scotland, Sir Martin Beckman, Chief Engineer to the Office of Ordnance, advised the Board that 'no Monarch, Prince or State has been, nor can be, safe in their government without tenable fortifications for the magazines and security for their respective seaports' (quoted in Barker 1985: 106). With the threat of a second uprising in Scotland, money and men were sent north to rebuild Inverlochy citadel, lying in ruins since the 1660 Restoration (Tabraham and Grove 1995, Tait 1965). In his proposal for rebuilding Inverlochy, John Slezer (1689) provides a reminder of just how effectual the Cromwellian citadels (deliberately destroyed after the Restoration) had been: 'This Fort formerly contributed much to keep the Highlands in Subjection to the Government, and in an intire Peace amongst themselves'.[3] Fort William took only eleven days to build and was, in reality, little more than an earthwork with a palisade on top. Inspecting it in 1710, Edwards (1709/10b: 129–131) reported that 'This Forte for defending it self is indeed but a very ill figure'. Despite its poor state, unfavourable position at the foot of a mountain, and exposure to musket shot, Fort William was the only garrison fort to withstand a Jacobite siege during the '45 Rebellion.

By the beginning of the eighteenth century, military maps of Scotland were scarce.[4] When concerns were raised for the security of North Britain in 1708 following the Act of Union the previous year, the Board confessed to the Privy Council 'that Wee have as yet no Draughts of the Castles of Edenburgh, Sterling and Inverlocky' (Anon. 1708: 266–267). Maps of Scotland's forts in the formative years of the Union were surveyed and compiled by engineers in the Scottish Ordnance Office, by Slezer and Theodore Dury.[5] Since the principal Lowland castles – Edinburgh, Stirling, and Dumbarton – were already strategically situated on volcanic outcrops, the engineers' concerns were to update their defences to contend with 'modern' warfare methods, rather than to build new fortresses. Initial defensive works were proposed by Dury. His plans were ambitious, designed 'for fortifying … to resist an Attack in form with Great Artillery', and proved too expensive for the Board. He resubmitted plans for works that would, instead, fortify 'for preventing an insult' but these still met with criticism. For fortifying the entrance to Edinburgh Castle, Dury proposed a hornwork 'which is a Figure most of the considerable places in Europe are fortify'd with being neither over large for taking up many men, nor so little to contain a sufficient Number to make a good Resistance' (Edwards 1710). His design, however, was found to be too broad for Castle Hill and too short for a counterguard (Edwards 1709/10a: 122). Instead, rocks on the north and south side of Castle Hill were cut away, retrenchments were dug and a 40 foot wide moat was built, the engineers believing 'these advantages will much Lengthen time, and cost an Enemy dear, before they can come to the main Gate of the Castle' (Edwards 1709/10a: 125). Dury's plans for Stirling Castle were equally ambitious (Figure 9.3) and although his proposals were subsequently altered, the castle's strategic location provided good reason to modify its defences:

> there seems to be two great uses in Fortifying it vizt, by Comanding the most Considerable Pass from South to North in that part of the Kingdome over the River Forth, which by its turnings about the Ground near the Castle, makes also a very Convenient Place for a Camp of 10 or 12000 Men Situated in a narrow part of North Brittain between 2 Rivers the Forth and Clyde which by the Map seems not above 16 Myles a sunder (Edwards 1709/1710c: 127).

'Roads and Remarkable Places'

By the time of the Hanoverian succession in 1714, there was pervasive disillusionment with the 1707 Union. Risings in 1715, when over 20,000 Jacobites mustered against the British

Crown, and 1719 had shown just how serious a threat the Jacobites were to the stability of the British state. When attention turned once again to Scotland's defences, the government's intentions were clear – to gain social and political control in the Highlands. This is nowhere better illustrated than in Lewis Petit's 1716 map of a citadel overshadowing the town of Perth (Figure 9.5).[6] Perth was occupied by the Jacobites and heavily fortified by them during the rebellion of 1715. Petit's map relates to unfulfilled intentions to construct a new fort. His plan reveals an imagination for a fortress modelled upon the ideal city – upon 'Euclidian form and central planning, with total social control represented in its architectural composition' (Pollak 1991: xxxv). Two of the citadel's bastions overlook Perth while the remaining three look out over the surrounding countryside. In its depiction, the new citadel was devoted entirely to a military presence, and in its form and situation it served the double function of defending itself from outside attack as well as offering a means from which to subjugate the local populace.

Lingering and often violent demonstrations of Jacobite disaffection following the 1715 rebellion led to a resolution to establish a permanent military presence in the Highlands. Four strategic sites – at Bernera in Glenelg (Figure 9.2), Kiliwhimen in the Great Glen, Ruthven in Badenoch, and Inversnaid near the shores of Loch Lomond – were chosen by Petit as suitable sites to build new 'barrack forts' (Anon. 1717: 361–2). The design of these forts was of particular concern to military engineers, a fact reflected in the numerous large-scale site plans made by

9.5   Lewis Petit, *Plan of Perth & adjacent places, with a projection of a Cittadel*, c.1716.

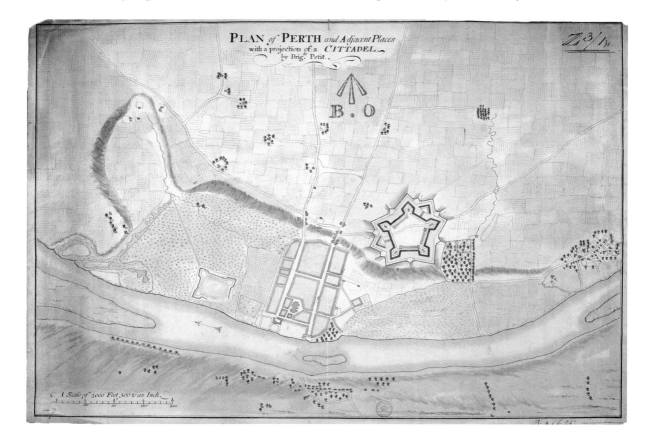

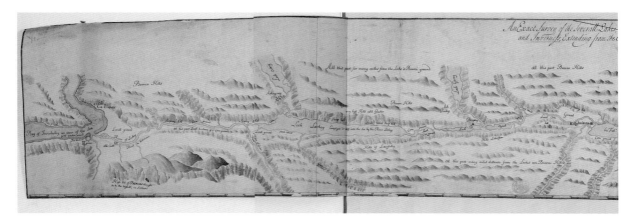

9.6   Joseph Avery, *An Exact Survey of the Several Lakes, Rivers, and Roads, between Fort William and Inverness, Extending from the East to the West Sea, latt. from 57° to 58°*, 1725.

Andrews Jelfe, Director of Barrack Building in Scotland. Each fort had a similar architectural form, standing as a detached, enclosed, self-defensible barrack complex with bastion-like angled towers at alternate corners from which it was possible to cover the whole exterior of the enclosure with flanking musketry fire (Saunders 1998). Two piles of barracks were built facing across a square with the rear walls forming part of the external defences. Although intended to house between 120 and 360 soldiers, the barracks were never fully garrisoned. During his reconnaissance of the Highlands, George Wade (1724: 11–12) reported that there were 'in some but thirty men'.[7] He was particularly scathing about the effectiveness of the barracks: 'It is to be wish'd that … no Insurrection may ever happen to Experience whether the Barracks will Effectualy answer the End Propos'd'.

Wade's arrival in Scotland in 1724 saw a change in cartographic concerns to coincide with changes in the Hanoverian army's handling of Jacobite insurrection. He gathered intelligence on the Highland clans, those for and against government, and described in detail 'the greatest and most unciviliz'd parts' of the Highlands through which he travelled (Wade 1724: 2). Wade (1725: 17) recognised that Loch Ness formed a judicious means of transporting military provisions and troops between Kiliwhimen (then later Fort Augustus) and Fort George at Inverness, and commissioned an exact survey of the Great Glen, 'from the East to the West Sea'. Joseph Avery carried out the survey in 1725; the map at a scale of about one inch to a mile, included the lochs and rivers and 'all Roads & Remarkable places' (Figure 9.6). In 1731, Wade's geographical and political knowledge of Scotland was put to order in a map drawn by Clement Lemprière, senior draughtsman in the London Drawing Room (Figure 9.7). In its outline, the *Description of Scotland* is largely based on the outlines of Scotland published in the Blaeu *Atlas Novus* of 1654 (Fleet, Wilkes and Withers 2011). Yet Lemprière's map makes use of more recent military maps, being one of the first to correctly show the Great Glen as a straight line and record the new military roads being constructed under Wade's command. These ran from Fort William to Inverness (1725–27), Dunkeld to Inverness and Crieff to Dalnacardoch (1728–30), and Dalwhinnie to Fort Augustus by the Corrieyairack Pass (1731) (Moir 1983). Crucially, the map shows the locations of the principal government garrisons in relation to the disposition, loyalties, and strengths of the Highland clans. Combined with the military road network, the map reveals Hanoverian intentions to establish order and 'reduce the Highlands to a more due Submission' (Wade 1724: 15–16).

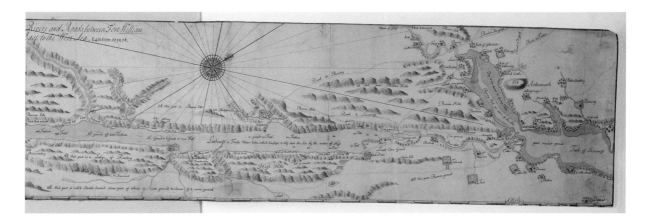

Wade's scheme to control Scotland included building two new fortifications. The first was a new barrack at Inverness to the north of Loch Ness. The second, Fort Augustus, was built at the west end of the loch near Kiliwhimen described as:

> the Centrical part of the Highlands … equally distant from Fort William and Inverness, and where a Body of 1,000 Men may be drawn together from those Garrisons in 24 hours to Suppress any Insurrection of the Highlands (Wade 1724: 17).

Wade was also concerned to improve the mobilisation of troops and material by means of roads and by making use of Scotland's many inland waterways and extensive coastline to connect the forts one with the other. Troop movement generated a need for explicit cartographic materials – for surveys and written descriptions – in order to formalise strategic plans and to achieve, for example, Niccolò Machiavelli's fifteenth-century ambition for a military commander to be able to 'paint out the country through which he must march' (quoted in Buisseret 2003: 120). Regional or relatively small-scale maps were compiled for planning route networks between fortified strongholds (Figure 9.8); large-scale maps were drawn as records of road building (Figure 9.7). Mapping military movement, unlike fortification cartography, was sporadic and exceptional. As Figure 9.8 shows, Wade's work offered a descriptive and utilitarian geography of parts of the Highlands, noting the condition of existing roads and the work necessary to make them suitable for wheeled vehicles, as well as the condition of the ground and nature of the terrain. His maps provided a military commander with a brief physical, social, and military treatise on a planned route. For Wade, it was the content of the maps rather than their appearance that mattered most: military utility functioned as the maps' structuring agent, defining principles of inclusion and exclusion.

In 1740, supervision of road construction devolved to Wade's protégée, Major William Caulfeild, who oversaw a massive expansion of road building, improving, and extending Wade's initial network of roads. Ironically, Wade's roads for a brief time were of greater strategic value to the Jacobites during the '45 Rebellion. In September 1745, it was reported that 'some of [the McDonald] Chiefs stay'd at home [and] were breaking down the Bridges & ruining the Roads' to hinder the Hanoverian army (Hope 1745). As the '45 advanced, the benefit that the roads afforded the Jacobite army caused government troops to destroy their own constructions: intelligence from London disclosed 'an Order from Lord Launsdale for breaking up the Roads [and] doing every Thing [that] can retard the Rebels in their March' (Craigie 1745).

9.7   Clement Lemprière, *A Description of the Highlands of Scotland*, c.1731.

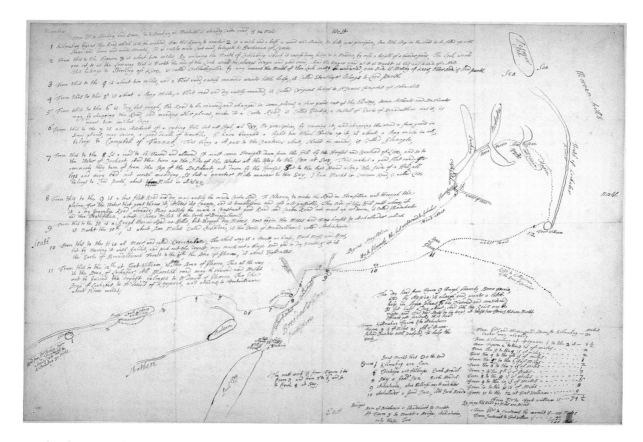

9.8 George Wade, [Sketch and description of the proposed Roads from Callander and Loch Tay to Fort William and Appin including details of mileage and of inns] c.1727–3.

Scotland Surveyed

Events during and just after the 1745 Jacobite Rebellion had made the British government acutely sensible of the 'want of a proper Survey of the Country' (Watson 1770: 10). One map used by officers of both armies during the rebellion was John Elphinstone's (c.1745) printed *Mercator's Map of North Britain*. Copies were variously annotated to show the routes of military roads and locations of camps, barracks and defensive posts. But the map, at a scale of 13 miles to an inch, was too small-scale to provide the topographical detail necessary for tactical and ordnance decisions required of a military map. As Quartermaster-General of the forces in North Britain, it fell to David Watson to supply Cumberland and his Generals with geographical information to plan the systematic suppression of Jacobite loyalists and establish a military strategy for enforcing the rule of law. If Watson was to fulfil his duty to provide adequate military intelligence, he had to know Scotland and to achieve this, he needed a military survey by which the country could be 'thoroughly explored and laid open' (Roy 1785: 386). This is the background to the Military Survey of Scotland, 1747–1755, known to its contemporaries as the 'Great Map'.

In its production, the survey was poorly supported by the Board of Ordnance. For the first two years, William Roy, Watson's assistant, worked alone. Then, in 1749 and in subsequent years, junior engineers, recent graduates of the Royal Military Academy, were engaged to assist Roy in surveying Scotland. The survey was conducted in two parts. The north of Scotland, including the Highlands but excluding the islands, was surveyed between 1747 and 1752, and then the Lowlands in the years to 1755. From the outset, military functionality determined the content of the survey. Roads, rivers and lochs were surveyed along measured traverses, using circumferentors and chains, while the remaining landscape features – towns, villages and hamlets, enclosures, woodland and relief – were sketched in by eye or copied from existing maps during the fair drawing. Each surveyor kept a field book and a sketch book. In the first he inserted the angles and measurements of his stations. In the second, he delineated his stations and the face of the country to form a military sketch (Dundas 1806).

Surveying took place during the summer months. In the autumn, the surveyors returned to the Drawing Room in Edinburgh Castle and through the winter, the separate traverses were collated into a single map, known as the 'original protraction'.[8] The survey artists, chief amongst them Paul Sandby, prepared the original protraction using the engineers' field note- and sketch books. This formed the basis of the fair copy.[9] The difference between the fair-drawn map of the north and the original copy of the south of Scotland is striking. The original protractions were drawn in the most part in black ink with very few features in colour. The Highlands, or fair copy, abounds with colours that reflect the prevailing military colour schemes and conventions (Figure 9.9). Sandby was responsible for the 'Mountains and Ground'. The final 'relief' compilation resulted in a hybrid combination of bird's-eye and perspective views. The overall effect was to produce a highly painterly and decorative interpretation of contemporary military cartographic techniques, one that William Roy (1785: 386–7), its principal surveyor, was to later describe as 'rather … a magnificent military sketch than a very accurate map of a country' but, although an 'imperfect work', it still possessed 'considerable merit, and perfectly answered the purpose for which it was originally intended'.

In 1755, work on the Military Survey of Scotland came to an end when the Survey personnel were called away to the impending outbreak of the Seven Years' War between Britain and France. But for this intervention, the variable accuracy and the nature and quantity of information conveyed by the Survey would have been adjusted over time. This was not lost on Roy (1785: 385–7), who later remarked that 'It would, however, have been completed, and many of its imperfections no doubt remedied' because:

> in the various movements of armies in the field, especially if the theatre of war be extensive, each individual officer has repeated opportunities of contributing, according to his situation, more or less towards its perfection; and these observations being ultimately collected, a map is sent forth into the world, considerably improved indeed.

The Survey was the work of rapid reconnaissance rather than a thoroughly measured topographic survey. In its endeavour, however, it was defined by Captain Hugh Debbeig (1766: 198), one of the Survey's contributing engineers, as 'the greatest work of this sort ever performed by British Subjects and perhaps for the fine Representations of the Country not equal in the World'.

The Survey depicts some medieval castles remodelled as barracks following the '45, including Corgarff and Braemar, as well as several planned constructions, such as Fort George at Ardersier Point which was built between 1748 and 1760. Designed by William Skinner, Chief Engineer in Scotland from 1746, the garrison was the largest in Scotland with a capacity to accommodate over 2000 men (Vyse 1803). In the process of its construction, many plans were drawn of the fort (Figure 9.10) and its location and the pattern of construction provides an indication of the priorities of defence (Ewart and Gallagher 2010). The greatest perceived threat was from the

9.9   [William Roy], *Part of the Reduction from the Great Map, shewing the Kings Road which is express'd by a Red Line & the Country Roads by a Brown Line*, c.1753.

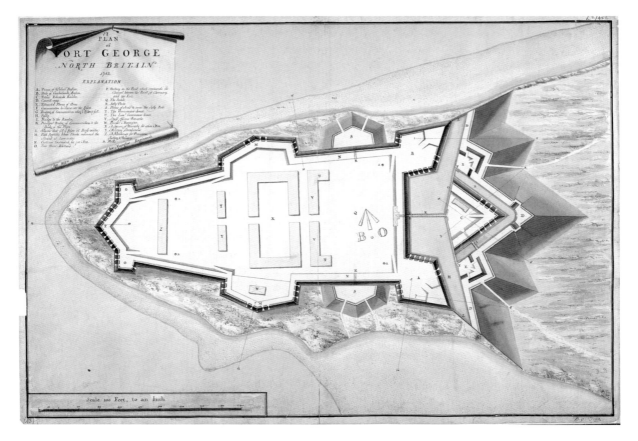

Scale 100 Feet, to an Inch

9.10   William
Skinner, *A plan of
Fort George, North
Britain*, 1752.

land, from rebellion in Scotland. The first line of defence to be erected was the covered way and glacis and the ditch to the rear, protecting the landward approach to the fort. In 1754, attention turned to the Point Battery revealing a shift in defence priorities with the strengthening of the seaward batteries. Skinner, in his design of Fort George, epitomised the art of fortification that had evolved in Britain during the eighteenth century. Fort George was a model of geometric bastion architecture, capable of both mounting and resisting a forceful attack.

CONCLUSION

This review of the Board of Ordnance and its military mapping activities in eighteenth-century Scotland has of necessity been partial. Yet it clearly shows that mapping Scotland became a priority of the Board of Ordnance from 1689 and the start of those Jacobite risings which raised concerns for national security over the following 60 years. Reliable information about the geography of Scotland was essential for the British government to exercise territorial control and to counter insurgency in Scotland. The responsibility for acquiring this information was, according to Roy (1765: 2), 'the Business, and not the least essential part of the profession of Military Men' who, he felt, were able 'to observe and consider Countrys in such a manner as to acquire, at least a General Knowledge of the principal Positions and Posts, which an Army should occupy, when occasionally employed for their Security and Defence'. By the eighteenth century, the British state recognised the skill of military engineers in measuring and reducing the world to paper and the importance of this in territorial control and national defence. As a form of military intelligence, the map was able to stand in for the territory in order that tactical decisions could be made in and over space. Thus cartographic information about Scotland both influenced and adapted to military policy and realities on the ground, allowing new political and social order to be established there during the eighteenth century.

There are many instances in the military mapping of eighteenth-century Scotland where maps conveyed a pragmatic function of construction. Through surveys made using standard instruments – plane table, alidade, theodolite, compass, and chain – and designs executed at standardised scales, an engineer structured space. Coincidentally, he represented the territorial imperatives of the British state. For Mukerji (2003: 657), 'The intelligence of engineering is not just pragmatic, but also deeply invested in social, legal, and moral conceptions of power'. Military maps permitted geographical information to be transmitted through time and across space from a point of origin – a field survey of an event – to interested audiences. When that audience was a political one, cartographic technology acquired an overt power over the society it was representing. As well as forming records of the landscape, the Board of Ordnance maps and plans were an effective means by which to act in and on the land; a tool of government as well as a representation of space.

NOTES

1   Sébastien le Prestre (1633–1707), Marquis de Vauban, was the foremost military engineer of the seventeenth century.

2   Maps and plans of fortifications account for about 72 per cent of the extant archive while maps of military movement make up about 22 per cent.

3   John Slezer shows the fort as originally built by Oliver Cromwell with the part dismantled by Charles II. Slezer, originally from the Low Countries, was commissioned as Chief Engineer of Scotland in 1671. In the revolution of 1688, he fought against the supporters of William, Prince of Orange. After the defeat of the Jacobite forces at Killiecrankie on 27 July 1689, he declared an oath of fidelity to William III, procuring a commission as 'captain of the Artillery Company and Surveyor of Magazines' (Cavers 1993).

4   See TNA WO 55/2281 *Register of Draughts*. The earliest plans recorded in the *Register* date from 1708 (Dumbarton) and 1709 (Dumbarton and Leith). Recorded plans of Edinburgh, Stirling and Fort William (Inverlochy) post-date 1712, although Slezer's and Theodore Dury's earlier plans (1689–1709) were known to the Board of Ordnance.

5   Theodore Dury was designated Chief Engineer in Scotland in *c*.1690, joining Slezer.

6   Lewis Petit was a French Huguenot who escaped religious persecution in France by joining the Board of Ordnance as an engineer. He was sent to Scotland in 1714 to report on the defences at Fort William and the outlying castles of Tioram, Duart, Invergarry and Eilean Donan. In 1715, he was appointed Chief Engineer in Scotland (Fleet 2007).

7   General George Wade was Commander-in-Chief of the British Army in Scotland from 1724 to 1740.

8   BL Maps K.Top.48.25.1a. the original protraction of northern Scotland, north of Edinburgh and Glasgow, mounted as 84 rolls of irregular size and shape.

9   BL Maps K.Top.48.25.1b. the fair copy of northern Scotland; originally 12 rolls but now combined with the 10 rolls of the original protraction of southern Scotland (Maps K.Top.48.25.1c.) and remounted as 38 sheets of unequal size.

REFERENCES

Anderson, C.J. 2010. Constructing the Military Landscape: The Board of Ordnance Maps and Plans of Scotland, 1689–1815. University of Edinburgh: unpublished thesis.

Anon. 1708. Entry Book of Warrants 1705–1709. The National Archives (hereafter TNA WO 55/344.

Anon. 1717. Warrants 1712–1717. TNA WO 55/346.

Anon. 1749. Orders to General Churchil[l] concerning carrying on the Roads in North Britain. Entry Books of Warrants, Regulations and Precedents. TNA WO 26/21.

Barber, P. 1992. England I: Pageantry, Defense, and Government: Maps at Court to 1550 in D. Buisseret (ed.) *Monarchs, Ministers and Maps*. Chicago; London: The University of Chicago Press, 26–56.

Barker, N.P. 1985. The Architecture of the English Board of Ordnance 1660–1750. University of Reading: unpublished thesis.

Buisseret, D. (ed.). 1992. *Monarchs, Ministers and Maps*. Chicago; London: The University of Chicago Press.

Buisseret, D. 1992. Monarchs, Ministers, and Maps in France before the Accession of Louis XIV. D. Buisseret (ed.), *Monarchs, Ministers and Maps*. Chicago; London: The University of Chicago Press, 99–123.

Buisseret, D. 2003. *The Mapmakers' Quest: Depicting New Worlds in Renaissance Europe*. Oxford: Oxford University Press.

Cavers, K. 1993. *A Vision of Scotland: The Nation Observed by John Siezer 1671 to 1717*. Edinburgh; HMSO; National Library of Scotland.

Cosgrove, D. 2008. *Geography & Vision: Seeing, Imagining and Representing the World*. London; New York: I. B. Tauris.

Craigie R. 1745. Letter number 143 to Robert Dundas younger, 14 December 1745. The National Register of Archives for Scotland (hereafter NRAS) 3246, Vol. 34.

Debbieg, H. 1766. Memorial. TNA CO 325/1.

Duffy, C. 1985. *Siege Warfare: The Fortress in the Age of Vauban and Frederick the Great, 1660–1789*. London; Boston: Routledge & Kegan Paul.

Duffy, C. 1996. *Fire & Stone: The Science of Fortress Warfare, 1660–1860*. London: Greenhill Books.

Dundas, D. 1806. Memorial. The National Archives of Scotland (hereafter NAS) RH1/2/523, 2a–f (copy).

Edney, M.H. 1994. British military education, mapmaking, and military 'map-mindedness' in the later Enlightenment. *The Cartographic Journal*, 31: 14–20.

Edney, M.H. 1997. *Mapping an Empire: The Geographical Construction of British India, 1765–1843*. Chicago; London: University of Chicago Press.

Edwards, T. 1709/10a. A Report concerning the Fortifying Edinburgh Castle. Misc Entry Books and Papers 1696–1714. TNA WO 55/319.

Edwards, T. 1709/10b. A Report of Fort William in North Brittain Conserning the Place it Stands in and the usefullness of a small Magazin there. Misc Entry Books and Papers 1696–1714. TNA WO 55/319.

Edwards, T. 1709/10c. A Resport of Sterling Castle in North Brittain. Misc Entry Books and Papers 1696–1714. TNA WO 55/319.

Edwards, T. 1710. A Plan of Edinburgh Castle. NLS MS 1649 Z.03/58a.

Elphinstone, J. c.1745. A New & Correct Mercator's Map of North Britain. British Library (hereafter BL Maps K.Top.48.17–21; TNA MPF 1/247.

Ewart, G. and Gallagher, D. 2010. The Fortifications of Fort George, Ardersier, near Inverness: Archaeological Investigations 1990–2005. *Post Medieval Archaeology*, 44(1).

Fleet, C. 2007. Lewis Petit and his Plans of Scottish Fortifications and Towns, 1714–16. *The Cartographic Journal*, 44(4): 329–41.

Fleet, C., Wilkes, M. and Withers, C.W. J. 2011. *Scotland: Mapping the Nation*. Edinburgh: Birlinn.

Frederick, C. 1683–1760. Rules Orders and Instructions for the future Government of the Office of the Ordnance. BL Additional MS King's 70.

Godlewska, A. 1999. *Geography Unbound: French Geographic Science from Cassini to Humboldt*. Chicago; London: University of Chicago Press.

Harley, J.B. 1978a. The Contemporary Mapping of the American Revolutionary War in J.B. Harley B.B. Petchenik, and L.W. Towner (eds), *Mapping the American Revolutionary War*. Chicago; London: University of Chicago Press, 1–44.

Harley, J.B. 1978b. The Spread of Cartographical Ideas between the Revolutionary Armies in J.B. Harley, B.B. Petchenik, and L.W. Towner (eds), *Mapping the American Revolutionary War*. Chicago; London: University of Chicago Press, 45–78.

Hope, J. 1745. Letter number 41, to Robert Dundas, 2 September. NRAS 3246, Vol. 34.

Lenman, B. 1995. *The Jacobite Risings in Britain, 1689–1746*. Dalkeith: Scottish Cultural Press.

Marshall, D.W. 1980. Military Maps of the Eighteenth-Century and the Tower of London Drawing Room. *Imago Mundi*, 32: 21–44.

Marshall, D.W. 1981. Instructions for a Military Survey in 1779. *Cartographica*, 18(1): 1–12.

Mead, W.R. 2007. Scandinavian Renaissance Cartography. D. Woodward (ed.), *The History of Cartography, Vol. 3, Cartography in the European Renaissance*. Chicago; London: The University of Chicago Press, 1781–805.

Moir, D.G. 1983. *The Early Maps of Scotland to 1850. Volume 2*. Edinburgh: The Royal Scottish Geographical Society.

Mukerji, C. 2003. 'Intelligent Uses of Engineering and the Legitimacy of State Power'. *Technology and Culture*, 44(4): 655–76.

Muller, J. 1756. A treatise containing the elementary part of fortification, regular and irregular. The second edition. London.

Parker, G. 1988. *The Military Revolution: Military Innovation and the Rise of the West, 1500–1800*. Cambridge: Cambridge University Press.

Petit, L. 1716. A Plan of Perth with the Retrenchment made about it by the Pretenders Engineers. NLS MS.1647 Z.03/01d.

Parnell, G. 1995. The Buildings and Works of the Office of Ordnance at the Tower of London, 1660–1722 (Vol. 1). Reading University: unpublished thesis.

Pollak, M.D. 1991. *Military Architecture, Cartography & the Representation of the Early Modern European City*. A Checklist of Treatises on Fortification in The Newberry Library. Chicago: The Newberry Library.

Roy, W. 1765. Military Description of the South-East Part of England July. TNA WO 30/55.

Roy, W. 1785. An Account of the Measurement of a Base on Hounslow-Heath. Philosophical Transactions of the Royal Society of London, 75: 385–480.

Roy, W. 1793. *The Military Antiquities of the Romans in Britain*. London: printed by W. Bulmer and Co. and sold at the apartments of the Society; and by Messrs. White, Robson, Nicol, Leigh and Sotheby, Brown, and Egerton.

Sanger, V. 1999. Vauban et la topographie des places fortes: Brest et Longwy in C. Bousquet-Bressolier (ed.), *Le Paysage des Cartes genèse d'une codification*. Paris: Musée des Plans-Reliefs. 49–63.

Saunders, A. 1998. 1600–1750: Early Evolution in J. Douet (ed.) *English Barracks, 1600–1914: Their Architecture and Role in Society*, London: The Stationery Office for English Heritage. 1–28.

Skelton, R.A. 1970. The Military Surveyor's Contribution to British Cartography in the 16th Century. *Imago Mundi*, 24. 77–83.

Slezer, J. 1689. Innerlochie or Obrian Fort, in Lochabor. BL Maps K.Top.50.37.2.

Skinner, W. 1746. Plan of the Town and Castle of Stirling with the Bridge over the Forth and part of the Country Adjact. TNA MPHH 1/204.

Stewart, R.W. 1996. *The English Ordnance Office, 1585–1625: A Case Study in Bureaucracy*. London: The Royal Historical Society; The Boydell Press.

Tabraham, C. and Grove, D. 1995. *Fortress Scotland and the Jacobites*. London: B. T. Batsford; Historic Scotland.

Tait, A.A. 1965. The Protectorate Citadels of Scotland. *Architectural History*, 8: 9–24.

Talbot, C. 1689. Warrant No. 16 [a] issued on 12 April. Warrants 1642–1744. TNA WO 55/424.

The National Archives. 2004. *Ordnance, Board Records*. Military Records Information, 66.

Tomlinson, H.C. 1979. *Guns and Government: The Ordnance Office under the later Stuarts*. London: The Royal Historical Society.

Tooley, R.V. 1949. *Maps and Map-Makers*. London: B. T. Batsford.

US Department of the Army. 2001. Map Reading and Land Navigation, Field Manual, No. 3–25. 26.

Vyse, R. 1803. Defences of Great Britain: report on various points of defence of North Britain. TNA WO 30/66.

Wade, G. 1724. Report on Wade's journey taken in pursuance of royal instructions dated 3 July, 1724. BL Additional MS King's 100.

Wade, G. 1725. Report of Wade's journey of the following year (under instructions dated June, 1725). BL Additional MS King's 101.

Wade, G. 1727. Report of Wade's journey in 1727 under instructions from George II. BL Additional MS King's 103.

Watson, J. 1770. Memorial. NAS RH1/2/511.

Widmalm, S. 1990. Accuracy, Rhetoric, and Technology: The Paris-Greenwich Triangulation, 1784–88 in T. Frangsmyr, J.L. Heilbron, and R.E. Rider (eds), *The Quantifying Spirit in the Eighteenth Century*. Berkeley: University of California Press, 179–206.

10

Commanding the Rivers: Guarding the German Railway Network in Peace and War

Volker Mende

A STRATEGIC ADVANTAGE

In the middle of the nineteenth century, many theories on the integration of the railways into the existing system of German fortification were discussed by military authorities. While the methods involved in this discussion were often complex and difficult to realize, by the beginning of the First World War their principle objective had been achieved: the creation of a sophisticated network of fortified railway stations, railway city gates, mountain tunnels and bridges. The development of specialised fortified railway bridges is an especially complex story, often involving disputes between private railway companies and military strategists. In 1856, the Prussian Chief of Staff, Karl von Reyher, objected to a proposed railway bridge on a new line from Prussia to Hannover. He insisted that a new fortress should protect the bridge planned for the Elbe river crossing, just north of the fortress at Magdeburg. The costs involved, meant the company could not progress with the project. But the War Ministry thinking was clear: if rail companies wished to cross a great river, the bridge must to be protected either inside an existing fortress, or with a completely new fortified bridgehead.

In 1870 von Reyher's successor, Helmuth von Moltke, advised the Prussian King: 'Every newly built railway line is a strategic advantage' (Grabau 1935: 137). The application of modern analytical techniques to technological developments – particularly the introduction of powerful artillery – led to a new approach in military thinking. The next war, von Moltke argued, would be decided at the German borders. Following the German victory against France in 1871, in the period before the First World War, military authorities designed many fortified railway bridges in Prussia and along the borders to France and Russia. Bridges were prepared for war.

RAILWAY NETWORK AND THE MILITARY IN GERMANY

By the beginning of the First World War there were more than 58,000 kilometres of railway lines in the German Reich with the extent of the network doubling between 1871 and 1914. These developments were a direct consequence of the political unification of the German states to form the German Empire in 1871. Historians describe communication as a primary factor in

10.1 Bridge over the river Elbe (built in 1847–51), Wittenberge – Remains of a casemate with embrasures for rifles and guns.

this phase of German nation building. While conservative elements among the military first thought that an increase in railway lines could jeopardize the security of the state, other military commanders – such as von Moltke – recognised the benefits and new opportunities of the expanding railway network (Grabau 1935: 80). The inclusion of German railways in planning the preparations for war had been envisioned in the constitution of 1871. The incremental nature of the developments meant, however, that when the King of Württemberg wrote to the Emperor Wilhelm II in 1903 he surmised that, 'The great national idea to administer the German railways as a unified network still awaits its realisation' (Mitchell 2000: 218). In fact, there was no unified railway in the German empire until 1918.

In the beginning of the railway age, German military authorities planned according to the following basic strategic principles. First, continuous east-west lines, where large rivers were crossed using bridges protected by fortresses. Second, north-south routes, connected to the North Sea and Baltic Sea ports. Third, several secure bridge crossings over the rivers Rhine and Vistula. Fourth, the provision of essential facilities for military stations such as loading points, water tanks and reserve depots for locomotive coal. One of first military strategists of the railway age, a Prussian General Staff Major, named Fischer, served as the military representative on the official Expert Commission that planned the route of the Prussian Royal-Eastern Railway Line, from Berlin to Königsberg. For a crossing of the wildly meandering river Vistula, this

commission decided upon a bridge at the small town of Dirschau. The next bridge in the line, over the river Nogat was situated inside the old fortification works of the town of Marienburg. While neglected by military historians, both bridges retain an outstanding position in European architectural and military history. Located near the Russian border, they are characterised by a sophisticated array of defensive elements, such as artillery positions, blockhouses and pivot-bedded guns.

From the late 1840s onwards, the potential threat to bridges at the borders grew in significance. The expansion of the German railway network was concentrated at the borders of the most likely enemies; in the west, France and in the east, Russia. During the last years of the nineteenth century, German General Staff were well informed – via a French civilian railway officer – of the French railway mobilisation plan (Zuber 2002: 115–17). The risk to highly strategic larger bridges, for which reconstruction would require months or years was particularly high. It became absolute that wherever a major railway bridge was built, a strong fortification had to be created. However, no one organisation was able to carry these enormous construction costs. Surveillance and maintenance during peacetime would also have cost millions and the liberal Prussian parliament – and later the German Reichstag – would never have approved such expenditure. The solution that emerged in the 1850s, saw the Prussian Military authorities experiment with securing the railroad bridges with small, but strong forts, which were to be deployed with military personnel only in the case of war. According to Adolf Wermuth (the secretary of state for the treasury) from 1887 onwards, the German Empire began to spend on average twelve million marks per year on strategic railway buildings (Wermuth 1909).

10.2   Bridge over the river Nogat (built in 1857), Malbork/Marienburg on the Polish border – The *Blockhaus* at the right bank secures the forefront of the abutment.

EARLY FORTIFIED RAILWAY BRIDGES

The potential use of railroads by the military varied. With the notable exception of work by Bremm (2004), who has discussed the connection between network formation and fortresses, current studies concerning the railway and war focus largely on the influences on the transport of matériel and its relationship to strategy (Köster 1999). Accordingly, there remains a gap in our knowledge of the impact of tensions between the railway companies and the military on the structure and design of the network. On the 1 March 1847, for example, a Prussian Military Delegate Officer, Colonel From, wrote to the Federal Military Commission in Frankfurt on Main:

> *If the railroads exercise this influence on the conduct of war, they have to follow the nature of war ... it will be advantageous to the network nodes or intersections of the military railway lines or their transitions across main land sections, as rivers, reception lines and ditto to fix where possible in order to stay under all circumstances, in possession of the Hinterland (From 1847).*

In the following years, the great river railway bridges over the Rhine, Elbe, Oder and Vistula, increasingly came into the focus of the Prussian War Department. The crucial question arising was how railway bridges could be protected with defensive mines which, in the event of an enemy attack, could be detonated.

In 1852, the Military Commission of the German Confederation stipulated that railway lines at the border should be controlled by secured river bridges, borderline fortifications and defensive positions.[1] For the first time in Prussia, this principle was applied to the river Elbe. Within the fortress of Magdeburg, four new fortress-works, built 1845–1848 and privately owned by the Berlin-Magdeburg Railway Company, secured the bridge. A little later in 1847, the bridge at Wittenberge, also over the Elbe, was constructed. This bridge was the first in Germany to be defended by reinforced blockhouses. Even as construction was being completed in 1849, military instructions were being sent to the civil government to regulate the area around the bridge as a Zone of Servitude but its status as fortress was not settled, possibly due to the revolutionary events of 1848.[2] Completed in 1851, Wittenberge had six fortification towers arranged in pairs, the highest number of any German fortified bridge (Mende 2010). This form of defensive strategy became widespread. In 1857, the Austrian War Department wrote to railway companies stating that they had to provide strategically important railway bridges with permanent mine chambers for demolition (Köster 1999: 276). Similarly, in 1858, the Federal Assembly of the German Confederation in Frankfurt am Main forced the government of the German State of Baden, to insert mine chambers into the railway bridge at Waldshut over the Rhine (Anon. 1858).

Throughout the German Confederation, a number of bridges built over the Rhine such as the Fortress of Mainz, and in Prussia in particular, such as Fortresses Cologne and Koblenz had been planned at the end of the 1850s. It was here that the perfection of structures for the defence of railway bridges primarily emerged, principally equipping the bridge pillars and abutments with mine chambers. But in the southwest of the German Confederation there was a problem. The Grand Duchy of Baden had concluded a treaty with France in 1857, to build a railway bridge across the Rhine at Kehl, but had failed to acquire permission from the Military Commission of the German Confederation. Opposite the Rhine was the French border fortress of Strasbourg (Mitchell 2000: 49). In a protracted diplomatic struggle the German Confederation ensured that defensive works were installed by 1861.[3] The Grand Duchy of Baden finally funded

its own fortification, during both peacetime and wartime, secured with troops from Baden and equipped with eight guns and tons of explosive powder to load the mines in case of a French occupation.[4] However, the final form of the fortifications at the bridge at Kehl Baden was regarded as ineffective by Prussian military command. And, in order to deny the French a bridgehead, the German Confederation concluded that, as a last resort, the iron-lattice construction of the bridge would have to blown to pieces with defensive artillery.

On large rivers and near the borders, military strategy necessitated that a bridge had be defended until the demolition squad had loaded all the mine chambers and destroyed the crossing. It could, however, also be possible that the bridge would be needed for one's own troop movements later. In this case, a blockhouse or a tall tower was installed to defend the bridge. In the 1850s, the towers were expensively decorated, had simple wooden beam roofs and embrasures designed principally for rifles, with some designed for heavier guns. Some of the most vulnerable bridges, such as the Rhine bridge in southern Cologne and the Vistula bridge in Thorn, had embrasures in their river pillars. In 1838, the Prussian government passed a new law ruling that the defensive measures had to be paid for by the railway companies. For instance, the Rheinische Railway Company had to pay the enormous sum of 296,000 taler to lay tracks through the fortress of Koblenz and to secure the Railway bridge over the river Moselle, a condition they described as an 'exceptional sacrifice' (Anon. 1860).

10.3   Bridge over the river Rhine (built in 1862), Mainz – View of left abutment, the pair of towers is set on multi-storied gun casemates.

10.4   Bridge over the river Rhine (built in 1861), in Kehl – View from the left bank to the right bank in Baden. *Note*: On the right a *caponier* secures the turning bridge at the abutment.

10.5   Bridge over the river Oder (built in 1908), Stany/Aufhalt on the Polish border, guarded by two pairs of very old-fashioned brick blockhouses. Note the left bank abutment blockhouses are preserved. The roofs are made by reinforced concrete. Both are connected by a basement infantry corridor, equipped with loopholes.

In about 1865, Prussia introduced a simple standardised building type for blockhouse with vaulted ceilings with soil on top to dampen bomb blasts (Mende 2007). Subsequently, these ceilings were replaced with more sophisticated bearing systems constructed from iron. There were variances in the building style of the various Prussian Fortification Offices. Because of this and also the different tactical positions of the bridges and other local site conditions, a variety of shapes of fortification emerged. Up to four Blockhouses could be constructed at any bridge. The novel and efficient use of these structures eventually ensured the usage of the German word *Blockhaus* passed into international fortification terminology.

With the introduction of concrete the form taken by these fortifications became more standardised with basic structures, smooth walls and embrasures for machine guns defining the architecture. In the beginning of the twentieth century, blockhouse roofs were strengthened with reinforced concrete and after 1910, they were also equipped with pillars for anti-aircraft-guns. Gates of wood or iron, installed between the blockhouses could be locked to block off the rails.

These gates were later reinforced and had infantry loopholes installed. Some blockhouses also utilised other defensive elements, such as pitfalls, infantry barricades and barbed wire. These structures were often enhanced with fortified multi-storied infantry blocks. On the eve of the First World War, barracks, ammunition magazines and field artillery positions were installed near the bridges. Each abutment had a telephone, connected to the adjacent railway station command centre. Thus, bridges were incorporated into the fortress defence system.

HIGHLY DEVELOPED BRIDGE FORTIFICATION

State intervention in the railway sector was particularly conspicuous in the expansion of the network in 1871. It is noteworthy that all the bridges paid for by the Empire had, for the most part, a unique architectural style of their own. The German Reich railway bridges were well built and strongly martial in their architectural style. The bridges over the river Rhine at Hüningen and Roppenheim clearly illustrated this. However, by 1900, German authorities realised that the fortified bridge had to be modernised, because military technology was developing numerous new and more powerful armaments. Instead of ordinary blockhouses, larger scale forts began to be built as part of bridges. These new forts were equipped with concrete dug-outs and barbed wire, modern 53mm guns and infantry minefields. In 1899, the Prussian Minister of War, Heinrich von Goßler suggested that to provide cover for the river Vistula, the Marienburg bridge in the east had to operate as a regular fortification (von Goßler 1899). The bridge at Neuenburg in the west was similarly constructed to matched the defensive power of a conventional fortress. In the contested region of Alsace-Lorraine, the German Reich enlarged border-fortresses at Metz and Diedenhofen. At the latter the two railway bridges over the Moselle – both protected by sandstone blockhouses built in 1878 – were by 1904, supported by strong, concrete multi-storied blockhouses. These were amongst the first generation of fortification structures made of concrete fronted with dressed stone. The inner city of Diedenhofen lost its status as a fortified area in 1904 but the same year saw the construction of three new crossings over the river Moselle – a road bridge and the two railway bridges – all with accompanying blockhouses. These developments can be interpreted as a show of power by the German Empire in this conquered area of its territories.

After the constitution of the German Reich in 1871 and following demands made by von Molkte, Chief of Staff, the pillars of significant railway bridges on the internal lines of the

10.6   Bridge over the Moselle (left bank blockhouse built in 1904), Thionville/ Diedenhofen on the French border. Note the construction used reinforced concrete with dressed stone facade, covered by a roof armoured with concrete.

German railway network were also mined. This was also paid for by private railway investors (Grabau 1935: 139). For instance, all major viaducts of the Upper Lusatia District, Saxony, were retrofitted with mine chambers. For the masons involved in the installation, this was extremely difficult and dangerous work. The explosive powder was stored in external powder houses next to the bridges. The viaduct near the village of Niethen, for example, received additional mine chambers with a segregated powder magazine.[5]

In East Prussia, at the Russian border, the German Reich had a specific problem. Intelligence reports suggested that, in the event of war, Russian troops aimed to quickly cross the border and destroy strategic elements of the German infrastructure. In 1894, during a military exercise, the General Staff simulated a Russian cavalry raid destroying the East Prussian rail system (Zuber 2002: 147). These threats encouraged the construction of a dense network of defensive works, such as concrete blockhouses, artillery positions and barracks (Bujas 1997). Small, fortified railway bridges were also part of this system. As a consequence, between 1900 and 1913, a deep, tiered cordon of fortifications was erected – using a mixture of concrete, soil and barbed wire. Railway bridges in this region were strategically integrated into this militarised network, making a significant contribution to national defence.

PREPARING FOR WAR – GUARDING THE BRIDGES

After 1913 the last three major bridges across the Rhine, at Rüdesheim, Engers and the famous 'Brücke von Remagen', were built and the first instalment for their construction totalling millions of marks was paid by the German Reich.[6] These three bridges were distinguished by a new and

unique architectural structure – artillery and the gun defences were reduced and loopholes positioned behind steel panels because now, an entirely new offensive weapon had to be accounted for: aircraft.[7] In addition, as of 1912, the German military began taking the increased range of gunnery into account. At Phillipsburg, a military training area, they practised 'shooting at flying targets'.[8] Blockhouses on railway bridges were soon re-planned and rebuilt for the installation of permanent air-defences. The Blockhouse on the bridge in Breslau-Carlowitz over the river Oder, for example, had pivots for machine guns on its roof.[9]

   The Rhine river bridges at Rüdesheim, Engers and Remagen were the last newly built major bridges in the German Empire. Their filigreed concrete supporting structure was clad with imposing black volcanic stone a design reminiscent of the medieval castles and town gates which were being carefully preserved across Germany. But this is an architectural illusion. The bridge towers were roofed with hidden armoured plates which doubled as anti-aircraft platforms to contend with airships and aircraft. This is why they needed such high towers.[10] By the beginning of the First World War, all major bridges over the Rhine and on the eastern border of the Reich could quickly be secured with machine guns or temporarily converted field guns. Bridges would no longer be defended in the traditional manner. Instead with conventional fortresses they became part of a system, pillars in the tactical territorial defence against invading aircraft. Moreover, offensive action against enemy railway infrastructure was also planned. In 1915, the German Army was well prepared to conduct rail demolitions to delay the Russian advance (Zuber 2002: 300). These preparations were coordinated by the General Staff, who published a list, for internal use only, of all the main bridges and tunnels of the 36 railway lines in western Russia (Anon. 1915).

10.7   Bridge over the river Oder (blockhouse built in 1868, rebuilt in 1913), Wroclaw/Breslau on the Polish border. Note the remnants of the right-bank concrete blockhouse with anti-aircraft-platform.

10.8   Bridge over the river Rhine (completed in 1919), Remagen. Note, the right-bank abutment was constructed using reinforced concrete with dressed stone facade, topped with anti-air-raid platforms.

Plans were also put in place to ensure the defensive capacity of the rail network in the interior of the country would be properly secured, not by troops, but railway employees. On 27 August, 1914, the Chancellor of the German Empire, Theobald von Bethmann-Hollweg, ordered secret 'enhanced rail security' throughout the Reich. From that moment, railway officials and workers had to guard bridges, tunnels and stations. Every civilian guard was supplied with a rifle and cartridges and had to wear white armbands. In addition to the main bridges, the rivers themselves were patrolled by boats.[11] Men who were too old to be sent to the front, guarded the whole railway system. They had become combatants and the interior of Germany was secure.

RAIL AND SWORD

In the mid-nineteenth century, there was no all-encompassing country called Germany, but rather a collection of largely independent states, within which there was little political unity. These states were members of a loose confederation, the German Confederation. In the aftermath of the Napoleonic Wars, Prussia realised that the connection between eastern and western provinces had to be supported by railways. Accordingly, it developed a mixed railway system including commercial railway companies and State-owned railway lines while other

States created State-owned systems. Over time, this railway network was prepared for war, the so-called policy of 'Rail and Sword' as first expressed by a German nobleman and military officer under the nom-de-plume, Miles Farrarius (1893: 42).

To secure the railways in Prussia, a mixture of solutions was settled upon. The first element of plan was to run the railway lines through the existing river fortresses. The Prussian Chief of Staff, von Moltke, wrote in 1861 that the principle task of a river fortress is to protect the bridges. In his opinion these bridges would constitute a 'connected system' (Frobenius 1906: 30). Secondly, the plan sought to expand the use of permanent mine chambers. On the eve of the First World War, this relatively inexpensive option was being used in about 900 road and railway bridges across Germany. Plans to deploy personnel to load the chambers and deliver ammunition were put in place, with Prussia the most organised in this regard. For example, at the end of July 1870 – the beginning of Franco-German War – the civil Transportation Authority of the Grand Duchy of Baden had concerns about loading the mine chambers of the bridge over the Rhine at Mannheim. The construction engineer for this bridge loaded the powder into the chambers himself (Anon. undated). After the war, civil railway officers were obliged to check the mine chambers regularly and to coordinate their inspection with the Fortification Inspection Offices which were distributed throughout the German Empire (von Kameke 1880).

10.9   The *Landsturmbataillon* No. 2 Rastatt Guard at the bridge over the river Rhine (built in 1895) Roppenheim in 1914, after outbreak of the First World War.

The third part of the plan involved the use of what can be described as the 'forgotten fortress'. For the first time in 1847, fortified Railway bridges, designed in Prussia, were installed on the main rivers. In this way, a network of defence works was established over the country. It was, however, a network which was hidden in plain sight. Anybody who went by train or tended sheep on the riverside saw these structures. Yet a fortified railway bridge could not be found in national budgets because they never fully qualified as a fortress and, most of time, this network was funded by the private shareholders of the railway lines. With few exceptions, they had to pay the enormous costs for the networks and, thereby, for the defence of the State.

Predictably, many German railway shareholders and engineers protested against the high costs of military works on the railway line. In 1854, the chief engineer of the Magdeburg-Wittenberge Railway Company, Hans Victor von Unruh, wrote about the exorbitant costs of many fortifications the company had to install near bridges (Mende 2010: 47). In Koblenz, the Rheinische Railway Company was forced to place part of the station outside the town resulting in the building of two terminals: one for passengers inside town and the other for freight outside (Mende 2011). On the other hand, to bring the railway to their city, many mayors and railway shareholder companies wrote pamphlets in a heroic military style. Most of them argued that the homeland would be more secure if the railway line passed through *their* town, rather than an neighbouring one.[12] In times of war, civil and military administrations cooperated. It is well known that in Prussia a lot of public railway officers served as military consultants during mobilisation and war in 1859 and 1866. The Prussian military was not alone in this. In 1866, in the Kingdom of Württemberg, the civil Chief Engineer of the Royal Railway Administration took

10.10   Bridge over the river Spree (built in 1866), Cottbus. Note, the standardised blockhouses on each side of the river were erected in 1868, right-bank *Blockhaus*.

the initiative and schooled the War Minister on how to destroy the railway network in case of a Prussian invasion.[13]

Visualising these plans on a map something interesting emerges, namely that each element complements the others. If one river falls due to enemy action, the next one will stop their advance. The entire country is a fortress. If one part of this fortress is captured, the aggressors become mired in a tangle of mines, blockhouses and homeland troops. The whole country was defended by a ring of 'sharp swords', installed in peacetime and fully available by August 1914. The crossings over the major 'German' rivers – Rhine, Elbe, Oder and Vistula – changed their function over time. Some of them started out as civilian railway bridges and ended as fortified structures. This makes one of the essential objectives in German military planning clear – the creation of a network of small fortresses, guarded in peacetime by civilian rail workers and in wartime by the same men – now in uniform. These measures had a strategic importance that lasted until contemporary times. Only in 2004 did NATO's control over the mines and fortifications on the railway system in Germany officially end.

NOTES

1   It is noteworthy that the next memo dated 1853, which dealt with the planned changes to the German railway system, was laid out by the Fortification Department of the same Military

Commission (See the introduction in: Report, 26 January 1853. Hauptstaatsarchiv Stuttgart (HSTA), E 271c, Bü 2236, document No. 132).

2   Geheimes Staatsarchiv Preußischer Kulurbesitz GSTA PK, I. HA, Rep. 77, Tit. 1308, Nr. 1.

3   Generallandesarchiv Karlsruhe (GLA), Abt. 238, Nr. 501.

4   Bundesarchiv Berlin (BA), DB 5/II, Nr. 240.

5   The powder magazine is still preserved (Sächsisches Hauptstaatsarchiv Dresden,(SäHSTA), 11230, No. 5820).

6   The planning for the first of these three bridges, at Rüdesheim, started in 1909 (GSTA PK, I. HA, Rep. 151, HB, Nr. 1319, 79).

7   The anti-aircraft-armament at the bridge over the Rhine at Rüdesheim was planned in advance, in 1912 (GSTA PK, I. HA, Rep. 151, HB, Nr. 1319, 195–197).

8   Bundesarchiv, Militärarchiv Freiburg (BAMA), PH 3/755, 253 *et seq.*

9   BAMA, PH 3/758, 107 and BAMA, PH 3/758, 228.

10   BAMA, PH 3/744, PH 3/745, PH 3/746 and PH 3/747.

11   Landeshauptarchiv Koblenz (LHA), Abt. 418, Nr. 1127, 107; LHA, Abt. 418, Nr. 1127, 141. For the Rhine, see record: LHA, Abt. 418, Nr. 1127, and LHA, Abt. 418, Nr. 1127, 111. It lead to embarrassing situations – in peacetime, authorities had forgotten to produce enough armbands for every civilian guard and water patrol.

12   Examples of this can be found in a various German railway records from the 1830s until the eve of the First World War. In 1856, the city of Crossen emphasised their proximity to the fortress of Posen (Städtische Sammlungen Cottbus, Stadtarchiv, D 34, Rundschreiben des Magistrats Crossen vom 2. April 1856). In 1866, the rural district assembly of Altmark argued that near, Stendal (their county council centre) would preserve a railway bridge over the Elbe better than the neighbouring county because the Stendal garrison would be ready for action faster (GSTA PK, I. HA, Rep. 90 A, Nr. 4284, p. 214). In 1907, the villages of the Saarburg district applied for a licence to install a railway line because of the strategic advantages associated with the line (Gemeindeantrag vom 15. 12. 1907, BAMA, PH 3/755).

13   See the record: HSTA, E 211c, Bü 2244.

REFERENCES

Anon. 1852. Military Commission of the German Confederation. Hauptstaatsarchiv Stuttgart (HSTA). E 271c, Bü 2236.

Anon. 1858. Protokoll der Deutschen Bundesversammlung vom 25. Februar 1858. Bundesarchiv Berlin (BA), DB 5/II, Nr. 240.

Anon. 1860. Railway Company to Royal Commissioner, 16 October. Geheimes Staatsarchiv Preußischer Kulurbesitz (GSTA PK), Berlin. I. HA, Rep. 90 A, Nr. 4277.

Anon. 1915. Kunstbauten im westlichen Rußland. Anlage zur Eisenbahn- und Telegraphenkarte des preußisch-russischen Grenzlandes, aufgestellt in der Eisenbahnabteilung des großen Generalstabes. Berlin.

Anon. undated. Mannheim Garrison to War Department, Generallandesarchiv Karlsruhe (GLA) Abt. 238, Nr. 2032.

Bremm, K.-J. 2004. Von der Chaussee zur Schiene: Militär und Eisenbahnen in Preußen, Frankreich und der Habsburgermonarchie bis 1848/50, *Militärgeschichtliche Zeitschrift*, 63 (1), 1–52.

Bujas, P. 1997. Blockhauzy wiezowe wezla oporu Ruciane-Guzianka, *FORTECA*, No. 1, 24–31.

Ferrarius, M. 1893. *Studien* über *die heutigen Eisenbahnen im Kriegsfalle*. Wien-Pest-Leipzig: Hartleben.

Fischer, Major. 1841. Die Eisenbahnen zwischen Oder und Rhein, nördlich der österreichischen Grenze und des Mains. 18 April. GSTA PK, I. HA, Rep. 75 A, Nr. 1251, 1–41.

Frobenius, H. 1906. *Napoleon, Moltke und die Festung*, Berlin: A. Bath.

From, Colonel. 1847. (HSTA) Stuttgart, E 271c, Bü 2232.

Grabau, A. 1935. *Das Festungsproblem in Deutschland und seine Auswirkung auf die strategische Lage von 1870–1914*, Neue Deutsche Forschungen. Abteilung Kriegswissenschaft, Band 1, Berlin.

Köster, B. 1999. *Militär und Eisenbahn in der Habsburgermonarchie 1825–1859*, Militärgeschichtliche Studien, Band 37, München.

Mende, V. 2007. Blockhäuser an der Speebrücke bei Cottbus – eine Untersuchung zu Planungsgeschichte, Bauablauf und Bedeutung einer außergewöhnlichen Eisenbahnbrücke, *Niederlausitzer Studien*. Cottbus. 33, 105–21.

Mende, V. 2010. Einhundert Jahre im Verborgenen – eine Kasematte der fortifizierten Eisenbahnbrücke Wittenberge/Elbe (1847–51), *Festungsjournal*. Marburg. 37, 43–51.

Mende, V. 2011. Die fortifikatorischen Anlagen der Mosel-Eisenbahnbrücke Koblenz-Lützel, *Neue Forschungen zur Festung Koblenz und Ehrenbreitstein*, Band 3, Regensburg: Schnell & Steiner, 43–62.

Mitchell, A. 2000. *The Great Train Race: Railway and the Franco-German Rivalry, 1815–1914*. New York: Berghahn.

Passarge, L. 1990 (1857). *Aus dem Weichseldelta. Reiseskizzen*, new edition. Berlin (Danzig): Hartmut.

von Reyher, H. 1856. Gutachten des Generalstabes über die projektierte Anlage einer Eisenbahn von Genthin nach Uelzen. 14 January (GSTA PK) I. HA, Rep. 90 A, Nr. 4286.

von Goßler, H. 1899. Sächsisches Hauptstaatsarchiv Dresden (SäHSTA), 11250, No. 127, 10.

von Kameke, G. 1880. Prussian Minister of War to Chancellors' Office, 2 February, BA, R 4201, Nr. 351.

Wermuth, A. 1909. Correspondence to Chancellor Bethmann-Hollweg, 30 November 1909; GSTA PK, I. HA, Rep. 151, HB, Nr. 1319, 79–83.

Zuber, T. 2002. *Inventing the Schlieffen Plan: German War Planning 1871–1914*. New York: Oxford University Press.

11

Forteresse Invisible: The Casemates of the Maginot Line in Alsace-Lorraine

Lisa Haber-Thomson

Most young Frenchmen ask if it still exists … I can't confirm: for some, it never existed (Anthérieu 1962: 7).

INTRODUCTION

The Maginot Line

Between 1936 and 1939, the French *Service Technique du Génie* poured over one and a half million cubic metres of concrete to realise the Maginot Line. Located in eastern France – primarily in Alsace, Lorraine, and the Alps regions – the line was conceived as a permanent barrier between France and her neighbours. This barrier to be the first line of defence at the outbreak of the Second World War. But few of the structures saw battle: the infamous topological miscalculation of its planners left the fortifications almost entirely outside the theatre of war. As a result, most of them remained undamaged in 1945. In the following decades, the French military made several attempts to reassign the fortifications as Cold War silos and spy stations. But when the escalating costs of the Algerian war in the 1960s forced the French government to give up on re-using the structures, the casemates of the Maginot Line were largely abandoned.

Invisibility

Today, eastern France is littered with these structures. Given the defining characteristics of the fortification – its monumental scope, its overt typology (mirrored in the bunkers of the *Atlantikwall*), and its placement tracing the political boundary of France – one would expect the structures to have a specific and overt relationship to the history both of the region and of the Second World War. This is not the case.

Throughout France, many former military sites have been repurposed to commemorate the past: the fortified city of Neuf-Brisach, the monument raised for the fallen at the Battle of Verdun, and the beaches of Normandy, are among the most conspicuous examples. These places have become part of the *patrimoine* of monuments, museums, and sites of collective memory. Other obsolete defensive walls – used as promenades and gathering spaces – have become vibrant urban spaces and locate collective memory by marking the sites of historical significance. Defensive walls, in particular, lend themselves to becoming what Pierre Nora (1984) has called *lieux de mémoire*: they are the places where the nation's territorial integrity was won or lost.

With the exception of a few *ouvrages* that have been transformed into museums, the Maginot Line has been treated differently, its bunkers remain unmarked, invisible in this lineage of national landmarks. Once meant to be a literal realization of the territorial boundary of France, the Maginot casemates are located along the current political border. Yet they are not even seen as a symbolic gesture demarcating territory. They are forgotten memorabilia: a graveyard of architecture. And so, if they are not, as Paul Virilio (1994: 47) once suggested, 'proof to the citizen that his territorial limits will remain impermeable', then what are they proof of?

Despite their ubiquitous presence in the region, no one seems to notice they are there. Why is this? After all, the Line traces the territorial extent of the country; what better marker for the 'site' of nationality? One could claim that the story is simply an embarrassing episode that France would just as soon forget. But given the sheer volume of leftover concrete that is hidden in plain sight, and the fact that the Maginot Line was highly publicized as a 'secret' innovation before the war, it can be argued instead that a certain *mythology of invisibility* has, in fact, been inherited from the pre-war historicization of the fortifications.

This mythology can be seen in the context of two specific shifts in the relationship between the French military apparatus and the home. First, the traumatic loss of life in the trenches of the First World War led to mounting pressure for the military to develop innovative ways to protect the French soldier. This, combined with a necessity to react to early twentieth-century's modernization of warfare, resulted in a desire to develop a system of fortified structures that would not only protect but even replace the body of the soldier. Second, this system of fortifications was meant to be contiguous with the political boundary of France, yet hidden within the domestic landscape. Rather than enforcing a separation between civil space and military space, the fortified political boundary was embedded within the towns and farmlands of eastern France. These two shifts in strategy – the blurring between bodies and concrete, between civilian and military – was propagated throughout France during the inter-war years via a popular press which represented the new modes of defence as pervasive but invisible, hidden, and secret.

IN PLAIN SIGHT

Name Replaces Objects

The Maginot Line is perhaps the most infamous failure of military strategy of the last century. Built on the cusp of a radical transformation in the conduct of warfare, these structures demonstrated the limitations of a fixed (no matter how powerful) defensive line against a mobile and strategically unknown enemy. The infamy of the strategic failure of the line has eclipsed discussion of the structures themselves, whose solid inflexibility precipitated the failure in the first place. And while the phrase 'Maginot Line' has been appropriated countless times as a synonym for failure, discourse regarding the actual Maginot Line is fairly sparse.

Most of the academic literature regarding the Maginot Line covers French politics of the interwar period. Apart from these texts, technical pamphlets (requisite of any large

11.1 A rural casemate, of the type frequently found in technical pamphlets. This is an unambiguously military landscape: no sign of civilian life encroaches. *Sector Haguenau*, Casemate 24 (*Aschenbach Ouest*).

11.2 The new football field of Hatten, next to a Maginot casemate. Its gun cupola has been disguised as a football. *Sector Haguenau*, Casemate 31 (*Hatten Sud*).

military installation) are mostly written by amateur military hobbyists. These pamphlets are filled with measurements of artillery ranges and rifle calibres, and of photographs that show solitary bunkers in an otherwise empty landscape, without people, in black and white (Figure 11.1).

These photographs are widespread but misleading. While some casemates are located in rural areas,[1] the slow creep of suburban growth has left many of them on municipal land. These suburban casemates have a very tangible and direct physical relationship to the towns they were once meant to protect. The Maginot Line has become an exemplar of hiding in plain sight (Figure 11.2)

Suburban Bunkers

At the intersection of what are now the *Rue de la Chasse* and the *Impasse du Renard*, in the small Alsatian town of Plobsheim, a school boasts a bright-orange fence. Beyond, a bunker-shaped grassy mound is equipped with table-tennis and a pair of benches (Figure 11.3). Casemate 23 is completely ignored by the neighbourhood in which it finds itself, and the integration of the structure yields nothing too different from what would have been there, had the bunker not been: a bright-orange school yard fence and tables-tennis, *sans* bunker-shaped mound. Throughout Alsace and Lorraine, a landscape of suburban bunkers like Casemate 23, either buried or fenced off, creates an eerie network of house-sized mounds and ruins.[2]

11.3   This school yard accommodates the casemate by simply covering it with earth. The gun cupola can be seen to the right of the image, at the highest point of the mound. *Sector Bas-Rhin*, Casemate 23 (*Plobsheim 20/3*).

Stumbling upon one of these buried bunkers, it is difficult not to think up a variation of Adolf Loos's proclamation (Figure 11.4).

> *If we find a mound in the forest, six feet long and three feet wide, formed into a pyramid, shaped by a shovel, we become serious and something within us says, someone lies buried here. This is architecture (1975: 45).*

11.4   A grave of architecture. *Sector Haguenau*, Casemate 92 (*Kilstelt 16/3*).

These funereal-like mounds are so obviously present, and yet so wilfully ignored. Unlike their rural counterparts, their proximity to inhabited space, makes it impossible to render these urban bunkers as autonomous monoliths. Furthermore, the bunkers do not disrupt the familiar pattern of the suburban plot. Their scalar similarity to a small single-family house allows the casemates to be seamlessly incorporated within the suburban fabric. But this integration is complicated by incongruities, both in external appearance and in programmatic inflexibility. The nearly solid block of concrete contains no space for a home. Each casemate, while relegated to its own suburban-sized plot, is specifically devoid of domestic space within. The network of bunkers forms a landscape that is simultaneously overtly militarized and innocuously suburban. This was precisely the intent of its builders (Figures 11.5 and 11.6).

The Substitution of Concrete for Men

On August 19, 1935, a statue of André Maginot was unveiled at Verdun. Though he would not live to see it completed, Maginot (a decorated veteran of the First World War who served as Minister of War up to his death in 1932) had been a major advocate of building a permanent

Germany →

11.5   Site plan, showing the casemate in its new suburban
context. *Sector Haguenau*, Casemate 27 (*Oberroedern Sud*).

11.6   A suburban casemate. The scalar similarity to its neighbours, and the ease with which the town is planned
around it, is countered by its typological specificity. *Sector Haguenau*, Casemate 27 (*Oberroedern Sud*).

system of fortification along France's eastern border. Albert Lebrun, the last President of the Third Republic, spoke of Maginot's motivations for championing the fortifications that were to bear his name: '[He wanted] to substitute the logical rampart of concrete and steel for the rampart of bodies, for he did not want the French to know those horrors again, nor be subjected anew to that painful Calvary' (quoted in Panouillé 1985: 8).

While the soldier couldn't be replaced entirely – as a minimum squad was necessary for the operation of each bunker – the Maginot Line was billed as a modern innovation that would minimize the need for manpower by relying on communications systems and artillery range to complete a network of fortified bunkers, and protect the required soldiers through the solidity of concrete. Conceived as a system of interconnected points, the 'line' was composed of several types of independent forts, which were distributed along 25 sectors. Each major *ouvrage* which housed the large artillery, could also support infantry of between 600 to 800 men and included all of the infrastructure necessary to remain fully autonomous from the civilian grid. An *ouvrage* was likened to a submarine on land, or a new kind of military creature: 'This organism … like a battleship, should be capable of living alone and of its own means' (Cadilhac 1939: 10). Buried between 20 and 25 metres underground, the *ouvrage* itself was a linear element that surfaced only for entrances (separate for men and ammunition) and gun cupolas. They also held the command centre for each sector and buried telephone lines connected each *ouvrage* to the rest of the system. *Casemates*, *cloches*, and *tourelles* housed smaller machine guns or observation posts and were independent monoliths. The forts were positioned such that each one was within visual and artillery range of its neighbours. In the most vulnerable areas, overlapping fields of fire extended one fort over in each direction, so that an incapacitated bunker would never leave a vulnerable gap.

Thus a line was formed, though continuous only when manned and armed. It is important to note that the continuity of the line depended on the soldiers who operated the guns and the communication centres – though this was not at all clear to most civilians at the time. Throughout its construction and up until the Battle of France in May of 1940, most French people believed that the line was, in fact, physically continuous and contiguous with the political boundary between France and Germany. This illusion was propelled by the nicknames given by the press, for example, '*forteresse France*' or, '*la Muraille de France*', which served to convince the population that France would be protected by an infallible technical barrier.

Of course, the military leadership knew that manpower was critical. Those who were sceptical of investing the majority of available resources on fortifications made that clear – at least behind the closed doors of the *Superior Council of War*. As General Foch put it, at a session in May 1920: 'fortifications are inert matter which has value only to the troops that put it there' (quoted in Doughty 1985: 47). But after the traumatic losses of the Great War, the French public needed to believe that a new system of fortifications would substitute for the need to risk the lives of yet another generation of young men. This was articulated by an unnamed officer in an article in *l'Illustration* in the early 1930s which responded to the outcry over escalating costs: 'I'd rather they put concrete than the bodies of our children in front of the enemy's cannons, for this would cost even more dearly!' (Anon. 1933: 36). Reinforced concrete, rather than the lives of men, was to be used to defend the territory.

Political Manoeuvres: The Decision to Build

The fixation on manpower was understandable. Although France had emerged victorious from the Great War, she had suffered a severe loss of about ten per cent of her population. Most of those dead were men between the ages of 20 and 45 (Huber 1935). And although their army was officially disbanded, the German threat had never really faded from the minds of the military leadership. This was a threat that could be measured: 'In face of 70 million Germans, we are here with our open border and our 28 million people' (Anon. 1919 quoted in Panouillé 1985: 10). Articles in periodicals like *L'écho de Paris* urged the public to take the threat of depopulation seriously. Without seeing corresponding results, the tone of these articles became increasingly urgent, and new incentives were introduced: a ban on birth control and abortions was reinstated in 1920 (see Hughes 1971). Also instated in 1920, the *Médaille d'honneur de la famille française* gave civil honour to mothers (French or not) who raised four or more children with 'French nationality'.[3]

Even as child rearing was becoming a publicly nationalistic act, increasing pressure was put on the government to reduce the mandatory military service from two years to one: men could be born for France, but not die for her. Whatever other measures were taken, the government needed to reassure the traumatized public that new defensive techniques were being developed to reduce the likelihood that their sons would be the next generation of cannon fodder. The 'open border' was addressed by the formation of the *Commission de défense des frontières (CDF)* which was to decide how best to modernize its protection. The CDF concluded in its 1926 report that the frontiers must be solidified with 'ultra-modern, permanent fortifications' (quoted in Hohnadel and Truttmann 1988: 2).

Many in the military and government were opposed to this plan, arguing that permanently fortifying the borders was tantamount to transforming the country into a fortress, and would not allow military commanders enough flexibility. *Forteresse France* would also give a sense of false security to reserve forces and citizen troops. These objections show that it is not just with the advantage of hindsight that the weaknesses of the Maginot Line were apparent. While the advanced telecommunications networks and the machine-like operations of the system were cutting-edge, the solidity and inflexibility of the system were incongruent with the rapid transformations in technology and new forms of mobility that were the hallmarks of early twentieth-century modernity and its expression in warfare.

But those in favour of 'permanently solidifying the borders' argued that this would give France a chance to hold out at the opening phases of a new war. If a conflict arose, they would be able to use the time gained to transform additional assets into military power (Brawley 2010). In addition, it seemed sensible to spend money where it would allow the faltering economy to grow, rather than on equipping and training a large standing army. This was the beginning of the 'defensive doctrine': a military structure whose purpose was keeping the peace. The words of the antimilitarist Jean Jaurès were remembered: 'the organization of National Defence and the organization of Peace are the same (Colonel X 1939: 12). The doctrine rapidly gained support, and soon the safeguarding of territory and citizens through defensive action would be the primary objective of the military. In July 1927, Paul Painlevé, Minister of War and a major advocate of the Maginot Line, summarized: 'safeguarding the integrity of national territory is the essential purpose of the country's military organization' (quoted in Panouillé 1985: 9).

Construction was permitted for a permanent system of forts that could, in case of emergency, quickly become operational with a minimum of soldiers. It was decided to concentrate military preparedness on the protection of the valuable natural resources and industry in Alsace-Lorraine. In terms of physical geography, this border was also the most open. Unlike the western and southern borders, the east did not have the natural barriers of ocean or mountains. There was an additional reason for the attention they gave to this region: France had just regained these territories from Germany and was not about to let this part of her *territoire* go undefended. Regional human geography studies, like Paul Vidal de la Blache's *La France de l'Est* (1917), called attention to a different kind of national threat. Alsatian, a Germanic dialect, was (after French and Occitan) the third most spoken language in France. Just as the Maginot Line was intended to keep the Germans out, it was also for keeping the French in. Although perhaps not as explicit as the advertisements calling for public support of the Maginot Line, pamphlets with titles like *L'Alsace et la Lorraine Veulent Rester Françaises!* (Alsace and Lorraine Desire to Remain French!) – which showed images of destruction left behind 'after the retreat of the Germans', along with young Alsatian schoolgirls learning French – were printed and distributed. The concentration of military resources in the region coincided with an explicit push towards the 'French-ification' of the locals.

Embedded Landscapes

If the publicity surrounding the Maginot Line served as a patriotic call for the local population to identify with France, the physical construction of the system served to encircle that population along with its land. The actual delineation on the map, and the precise marking of the individual objects, can be seen as a contemporary example of what James Scott (1998) describes as 'seeing like a State', centralized authority imposing an abstract system of measurements on local particulars: the construction of the casemates required giving Cartesian coordinates to terrain – a universalizing system of abstraction. This abstraction was reflected in the way the terrain itself was seen from within, as soldiers who lived inside the forts needed to rely on coordinates and drawings in order to 'see' the landscape. These soldiers were *internalized*, protected by metres of concrete. So too was the terrain. As described by Rudolph Cheminski (1997), 'inside each cannon turret, a diorama of the surrounding countryside was drawn (and often prettified and coloured by bored gunners) along the circular wall, allowing artillery crews to visualize the targets corresponding to the numbered coordinates sent up to them by fire control'. Within the *ouvrage*, the French countryside was abstracted, reduced to a set of coordinates.

The abstraction of the terrain within the *ouvrage* was reciprocated by the erasure of the *ouvrage* within the landscape. Typical camouflage techniques, consisting of vegetal or painted fabric screens, hid the structures from the casual observer. But even as the structures were buried and hidden, the press made it clear that the Maginot Line could be anywhere. Here is an example of a fairly typical description, published in 1938: 'The fortresses, today, are underground. They lurk in the depths of the soil, under the false appearance of inoffensive fields. They inter themselves invisibly in the flanks of the hills, carved out like molehills' (Anon. 1938: 128). Or: 'You must be just a few metres from its gaping entrance to see it. Its exterior silhouette takes on the folds of the soil in which it is buried, and its turrets are cleverly concealed in the uneven terrain' (Leroux and Lucien. 1940: 281). Sometimes, these articles are accompanied by photographs of nondescript tunnels, but without any indication of context or location. Or the author has included a foggy sketch of a hill, where one can just discern the twin turrets of a casemate. These texts and images give the impression that, since you cannot see them anyway, the fortifications could be anywhere. While the physical terrain was subsumed within the *ouvrage* – and given its military form, by way of measurements, charts and figures – the *ouvrage* was itself absorbed into the folds and flanks of this very terrain.

As the threat of conflict grew nearer and as resources dwindled, the idea of the line encroached more closely on the nearby towns. The knowledge that fortified houses – camouflaged to look

11.7   A local museum reconstructs a 'typical' household preparing for the arrival of the Germans. *Sector Haguenau*, Casemate 33 (*Abri de Hatten*).

like normal homes – were being constructed in ordinary towns was widespread. It would be impossible to tell the difference: an ordinary-looking house could be, under its illusion of domesticity, an integral part of the defensive ring surrounding the region (Figure 11.7). Because the Maginot line was 'secret' and unseen, ordinary towns suddenly had military significance, regardless of whether or not they contained fortifications. The line of defence was placed back in the home, even if not through the lives of the soldiers. Through the media campaign to inform the public of the innovative ways in which they were being protected, the *in*visible structures of the Maginot Line were highly visible in the public imagination.

INVISIBLE BY IRRELEVANCY: THE BATTLE OF FRANCE

From the Romans to Vauban

Between 1930 and 1940, popular newspapers continuously and proudly published images of France's 'battleship built on land', and informed the public of the German, Czech and Romanian copy-cat fortifications. *Forteresse France* was unbreachable. But we all know how this story ends: Germany invades the Low Countries in May, 1940. Circumscribing the Line to the north, the German army crosses the 'uncrossable' Meuse (it was an exceptionally hot summer and the river was low). The Battle of France was over in a few days.

In order to understand how this strategic blind spot could have been overlooked by the *Commission de défense des frontières*, it is perhaps instructive to look briefly at how a French historical tradition of national defence was mobilized to justify the fortification. From its inception, the Maginot Line was propagandized as the direct descendant of both the Roman defences along the Rhine, and Vauban's geometric forts. Indeed, the idea of a territory as fortified earth had, in the minds of the military establishment, a specifically French heritage. Establishing France's Roman legacy (and the territory that went with it) as distinct from the Germanic tribes to the east with the use of fortifications was a tradition that went back to the Roman *Limes Germanicus*. This defensive system, consisting of a series of temporary camps in the Roman military tradition, sketched out the rough extents of the Maginot Line (Anon. 1940: 219). Though these camps frequently became permanent, they were constructed with the explicit purpose of supporting a mobile infantry and could therefore be built and demolished with relative ease.

By the time Sébastien Le Prestre de Vauban became Marshall of France in the late seventeenth century, the extent of France's territory was generally established (albeit with some contested border lands). The temporary military camp in the Roman tradition was no longer the logical method of defence of territory. With the establishment of a national *territoire* came more permanent constructions. The focus of fortification moved away from supporting the mobile attacking armies of an expanding empire towards permanent structures that would outlive its soldiers (Viollet-le-Duc 1978). Vauban was an expert at attacking strongholds and had used his expertise in the offensive to transform the way forts were built. Revolutionary in how he applied the rigours of mathematics to terrain to assure victory, using his doctrine, a military strategist would analyse the land to plan the angles of a stronghold such that all possible enemy approaches were visible and under fire. The debt owed to Vauban's mathematical construction of landscape can be clearly seen within the Maginot Line's system of *ouvrage* and casemates.

Both the temporary Roman camps of the *Limes Germanicus* – which drew the first territorial division between France and Germany – and Vauban's contribution to the development of military architecture, which used strategic analysis of terrain to construct permanent fortifications, were consistently cited to explain the historical lineage of the Maginot Line. The press was quick to adopt these precedents: "'City besieged by Vauban, city taken – city fortified by Vauban, impenetrable city". Today, we are permitted to say: *Ouvrage* fortified by Maginot, impenetrable *ouvrage*;' we could even add: 'invisible *ouvrage*.'" (Anon. 1940: 219). In a series of maps accompanying this same article, entitled 'Vingt Siècles D'histoire Autour du Rhin', we see a pre-France GAULE, protected by the *Limes Germanicus* against the invading arrows of the 'Germanic Tribes'. Over the sequence of eight maps, GAULE is gradually transformed into modern FRANCE. The final map zooms in on the eastern border: the Maginot Line has replaced the ancient Roman one.

But despite these historical references made by those who wished it built, the Maginot line was a categorically different idea. Neither a temporary camp nor a single fortified point in the form of a city, its construction implied the solidification of the entire border of a sovereign territory. Unlike both historical examples, this meant that the political border was to be *permanent* and *inflexible*. In addition, as discussed above, its sole purpose was as a defensive barrier. This lack of flexibility and the focus on the defensive position at the expense of the offensive were both critical factors in its failure.

Modernity and the Maginot Line

French post-war interpretations of the failure of the Maginot Line are all quick to note how the individual bunkers functioned perfectly. The forts are described as being *so* strong that the German army had to find a way around it and that the strength of the line was never in question by either side. That the line failed had nothing to do with the construction of the fortifications themselves. This sentiment is expressed in many of the post-mortem analysis published in France after 1945: 'Everywhere else, this line played its role' (quoted in Anthérieu 1962: 147). In other words, everywhere that the line was confronted *as it was intended* by its planners, it performed as planned. But as described above, it was for the very reason that it was not confronted as planned that led to its massive failure.

The defeat of France was the result of a clash between two totally opposite doctrines of warfare: one slow, heavy, and methodical; the other, fast, mobile, and unpredictable. These opposing methods operated on different temporal scales entirely. As noted by Virilio (1994), 'The *war of real time* has clearly supplanted the war in real space of geographical territories that long ago conditioned the history of nations and people'. When the *Commission de défense des frontières* was called to modernize border protection, the solution they came up with operated within the tradition of French territorial control. But was it 'modern'? Their idea of modernization had led them to examine the specifications of war technology – the range of artillery, the blast impact of aerial bombs. They responded by calculating the thickness of concrete and depth of burial that would be required to resist these attacks. It was a logically calculated protection of brute force, but one that only anticipated an enemy approach of equally logical and calculated moves. Their idea of modernization was to appropriate technological solutions to the implementation of a historically grounded theory of defence.

France's defeat was not due to German technological superiority, but to France's misuse of history and geography to believe that she could, in fact, physically seal her borders. So its very attempt at continuity – which was one of the innovative differences of the Maginot Line – was also the thing that failed. This was a topological error – a misunderstanding not of the *scale* of modern warfare but of the very type of warfare. The encircling of sovereign territory by means of a fortified structure was simply not a relevant move. The Maginot Line was not considered as a barrier by the invading force – and was therefore invisible to them – because its planners did not anticipate this irrelevancy. The Line was conceived as a variation on a historical idea of a line of defence, grounded in the static Cartesian geometries of Vauban. It was advertised explicitly as such, even as it was being advertised as being 'modern'.

BURIED HISTORIES

Bunker Tourists

Today, it is possible to visit a few of the *ouvrages* which, apart from the addition of a few stage-sets of cheap mannequins eating plastic food and examining laminated maps, are untouched from their original conditions (Figure 11.8). At the *Ouvrage Schoenenbourg*, I take a tour given by a local retiree whose father fought in the war. Also on the tour are about 20 Germans, and a young Italian couple. We learn about the clever ways the *ouvrage* could survive any number of attacks by an advancing German army. Despite the almost total lack of typical sprucing-up gloss for the tourists, the tour is strangely disconnected from the larger history of the place. On this tour, an elderly Alsatian guide patiently describes inter-war French military innovations to a group of Germans, depicting the victory of a battle that never took place. This place is the setting of a story that never happened.

11.8   A mannequin in the *Ouvrage Schoenenbourg* slowly accumulates mould.

11.9   The entrance to this *ouvrage* is closed, but a French flag is flown.
Sector Lauter, Petit Ouvrage de Rohrbach, Bloc 2 entrance.

The story of the Maginot Line that is told on such a tour is one in which a people could easily place their national pride. The constructions are truly impressive: in their (literal) scope and depth, and in their technical ability to withstand any number of the dangers of trench warfare that had decimated the armies of the First World War. But while these facts are true, the story of their construction and innovation have little bearing on the one that played out immediately after. Part of what complicates the history of the Maginot Line is that both of these stories are true. From the outside, it is a disgraceful episode in French military history, which perhaps explains the lack of French tourists. But here, 20 metres below ground at Schoenenbourg, it is a story of truly innovative technologies that happened to be built at the wrong time. In the narrative of this place, it is the Germans who were outfoxed by the clever French. But more than that – the Germans in this story are not called *Nazis* and France has not suffered that profound embarrassment of miscalculating her *territoire*. This story picks up before all that: when two armies, great enemies from long ago, stand face to face. The *ouvrage* where we stand should be the orderly conclusion (in the French tradition) of that story. That other history, the one that is shameful for French and Germans alike, is not here (Figure 11.9).

Burial

There are several factors that distinguish the remains of this particular built-border. In itself, France/Germany does not currently have a problematic boundary. In addition, there is not a real discrepancy between France's state-border and the nation it circles. Unlike, for example, the borders of post-colonial States which were literally drawn in the twentieth century as empires ceded power, the placement of this border is congruent with the construction of territory and national identity as described by social theories of nationhood, like those of Benedict Anderson or James Scott. In other words, the border was circumscribing a territory that was simultaneously 'becoming' inscribed with national identity.

Nor are these structures the brain-child of a hated tyrant. While similar in typology to the bunkers of the *Atlantikwall*, or to Hoxha's bunkers that litter the Albanian coastline, the Maginot Line was built explicitly in the French rationalist tradition. Unlike these other examples, these structures can't really be seen as symbols of failed ideology.

The factors that usually give ruins their unambiguous cultural significance are complicated in the case of the Maginot Line. It is explicitly French, both in its inscription of territory and in its rationalizing tendencies inherited from Vauban. But it is also an explicit failure, in that it is a militarized space that is not defensively functional. In the remains of the Maginot Line, we can see, unresolved, the tension between the French historical lineage of mathematizing territory, and the contemporaneous global developments in the modernization of warfare. Today, these structures are not explicitly integrated within their new suburban context with reference to their relationship to the *territoire* of France. But the historical use of domesticity as camouflage, and the deliberate image of invisibility propagated by the press before the war, roots them in a legacy of obfuscation of the boundaries between military and civilian. This effacement is reflected today by the uneasy placement of the remains of the Maginot Line in the popular imagination. Without easily falling into either category, they are seen neither by those looking for military nor domestic space.

An important aspect of the professed modernity of the line was the fact that it was buried, 'into the very thickness of the planet and no longer along its surface' (Virilio 1994: 39). In fact, many of the structures were not originally buried – the 352 casemates, the cloches of the 142 ouvrages, and the thousands of blockhouses were all built above ground. But Virilio is right, in a

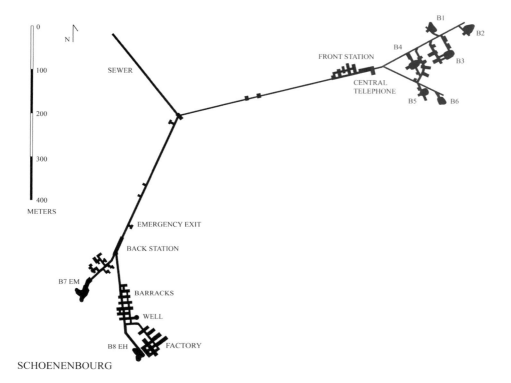

way. The burial has been happening gradually, and not just in a literal sense. Highly circulated, images published before the war of nondescript corridors and pastoral landscapes devoid of any discernible structures gave a false impression that the line was solid but unseen. During the war, the Line's topological irrelevance made the structures invisible to the Blitzkrieg. Over time, inconvenience has left the structures in the middle of towns, but without anyone noticing them. The casemates of the Maginot Line are not functionally useful, nor can they bear the symbolic weight of the territorial boundary they demarcate.

The retreat continues – both by the literal burial of the offending structures, and by the casting of the Maginot line within the narrative of France's military history without being able to account for its failure as such. By publicly attempting to replace the soldier with the bunker, and by permanently encircling territory in an age of highly mobile war technologies, the Maginot Line was both immediately obsolete and permanently entrenched within the domestic landscape.

NOTES

1   In these cases, ownership has reverted back to the farmer on whose field the structure stands; too big to be removed and useless for farm storage, they lie as they were left.

2   At times, the willing blindness to these structures is so overt as to take an even comic tone: in the outskirts of Strasbourg, Bas-Rhine Casemate 7 is located at the center of a new urban park and outdoor sports center. A developer's map at the entrance to the park indicates an *espace liberté* to be located at the site of the bunker – maybe an indication that the casemate had been transformed

into a commemorative space. Wrong: Casemate 7 had been buried, like all the others, and the *espace liberté* was a pleasant bunker-shaped doggy park, where the canines of Strasbourg could feel free to take care of business.

3   Bronze medal for 4 or 5 children; silver medal for 6 or 7 children; gold medal for 8 or more children. *Fédération Nationale de la Médaille de la Famille Française.* Available at: http://www.medaillefamillefrancaise.com

REFERENCES

Anderson, B. 1983. *Imagined Communities.* New York: Verso.

Anon. 1918. *L'Alsace et la Lorraine Veulent Rester Françaises!* Paris: Les Images de France.

Anon. 1919. L'ennemi interieur: le fléau de la depopulation, in *L'écho de Paris*, 2 January, Frontpage.

Anon. 1933. L'armature defensive de la France. *L'illustration*, 9 September, 35–7.

Anon. 1938. Une colline fortifiée d'après le principe de la 'Ligne Maginot. *L'illustration*, 1 October, 128–9.

Anon. 1940. Vingt Siècles D'histoire Autour du Rhin. *L'Illustration*, 2 March, 219.

Anthérieu, E. 1962. *Grandeur Et Sacrifice De La Ligne Maginot*. Paris: G. Durassié.

Brawley, M.R. 2010. *Political Economy and Grand Strategy: A Neoclassical Realist View*. Routledge Global Security Studies; 13. London; New York: Routledge.

Bruneau, P. 1940. Vingt Siècles D'histoire Autour du Rhin: de la Gaule a Hitler. *L'Ilustration*, 2 March, 219–21.

Cadilhac, P. 1939. Sur le front et dans les entrailles de la ligne Maginot. *L'Ilustration*, 7 January, 6–11.

Cheminski, R. 1997. The Maginot Line. *Smithsonian*, 28: 3 June, 94–7.

Colonel X. 1939. *La Ligne Maginot: Bouclier De La France*. Paris: Nouvelles Éditions Excelsior.

Doughty, R.A. 1985. *The Seeds of Disaster: The Development of French Army Doctrine, 1919–1939*. Hamden, CT: Archon Books.

Hohnadel, A. and Truttmann, M. 1988. *Guide De La Ligne Maginot: Des Ardennes Au Rhin, Dans Les Alpes*. Bayeux: Editions Heimdal.

Huber, M. 1937. *La Population De La France; Son Éolution Et Ses Perspectives*. Paris: Hachette.

Hughes, J.M. 1971. *To the Maginot Line: The Politics of French Military Preparation in the 1920's.* Harvard Historical Monographs, V. 64. Cambridge, MA: Harvard University Press.

Leroux, G. and Lucien, J. 1940. Quelque part sure la Ligne Maginot. *L'illustration*, 23 March, 280–81.

Loos, A. 1975. Architecture, in *Form and Function: A Source Book for the History of Architecture and Design 1890–1939*. Edited by T. Benton, C. Benton, and D. Sharp. London: Crosby Lockwood Staples.

Nora, P. 1984. *Les Lieux De Mémoire*. Bibliothèque Illustrée Des Histoires. Paris: Gallimard.

Panouillé, J-P. 1985. Autopsie de la Ligne Maginot. *L'histoire*, #77 April, 8–17.

Scott, J.C. 1998. *Seeing Like a State: How Certain Schemes to Improve the Human Condition Have Failed.* New Haven, CT: Yale University Press.

Vidal de la Blache, P. 1917. *La France de L'Est*. Paris: Colin.

Viollet-le-Duc, E. 1978. *Histories d'une forteresse*. Brussels: Mardaga.

Virilio, P. 1994. *Bunker Archeology: Texts and Photos.* Translated by George Collins. New York: Princeton Architectural Press.

Part IV
Trauma: Spaces of Memory

12

Defending the Irish Border: The Map of Watchful Architecture

Garrett Carr

INTRODUCING THE MAP

My cartographical work charts the Irish border. I am attempting to remap it in ways that question nationalism rather than reinforcing it with a simple borderline, which applies us/them, here/there and other binaries. My maps seek to encourage a new reading of the Irish border, a process that may give rise to fresh thinking about this border and political borders in general. Anssi Paasi (1999) has drawn attention to the recent academic focus on borders and border regions, not just to the material consequences of borders but also their cultural weights and meanings. Paasi writes that the main instigation of this interest has been the fall of the Iron Curtain and the resulting reconfiguration of many national and regional identities. He also highlights the roles of globalisation and migration flows. This is all pertinent, but within Ireland we are also reacting to a local and more specific history. Decades of intransigent politics and violence, much of it fuelled by issues of identity, are giving way to a slow process of relationship building. This has included much bridge and road building across the border, literally and metaphorically. The meaning of the Irish border is in flux. It is proving to be a much more complex and interesting place than the standard line on the map might imply.

The Map of Watchful Architecture charts military and defensive structures, ancient and recent, found in the Irish borderland. In its development I discovered my own working methods required a certain amount of fresh thinking. The graphic elements on most maps, including mine, tend to be built up through a process of addition. First the base landscape is laid down, then the rivers are added, then the roads, etc. But *The Map of Watchful Architecture* was created with processes more akin to subtraction, conflation and uncovering. In the latter's case, the uncovering of the points that can underpin lines. These processes may be worth discussion in this essay because they were not just behind-the-scenes methodologies. Rather, these reductions and distillations form the map's very mode of expression. They are how the map works. I will focus on the processes shortly, explaining to what ends I used them. But first, what are the subjects of the map? What is actually charted?

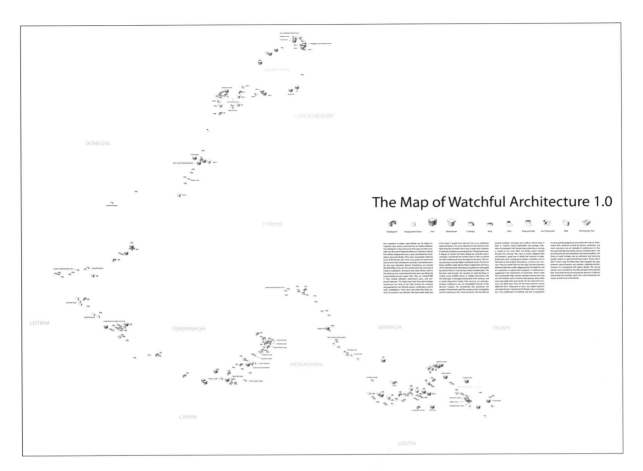

SUBJECTS OF THE MAP

At first glance *The Map of Watchful Architecture* may appear to portray a borderland busy with defence but in fact the illegal immigration checkpoint, deployed by the Garda Síochána (the Irish police force) in north Co. Louth, is the only element on the map currently engaged exclusively with the management of the border. Everything else is, to one degree or another, historic. Operation Banner began in 1969 and has ended recently in Northern Ireland. It was a deployment of the British military in Northern Ireland to support the local police force. It involved patrolling the border and the building of watchtowers and other installations along its length. After the 1998 Good Friday Agreement the operation began a gradual scaling down. Most of the installations, including all of the watchtowers, are now gone. On *The Map of Watchful Architecture* Operation Banner installations are marked OB. This military deployment was reflected south of the border too. Installations such the Irish Army's barracks in Co. Monaghan, also decommissioned recently, are also mapped. The Second World War saw the construction and manning of many military installations. Structures were built inland, close to the relatively new international frontier, but were distinctly concentrated around Lough Foyle. Figure 12.2 focuses on the Foyle basin: the defensive forms marked WWII include pillboxes, observation posts, and anti-aircraft batteries. There are almost no structures of that vintage anywhere else along the border.

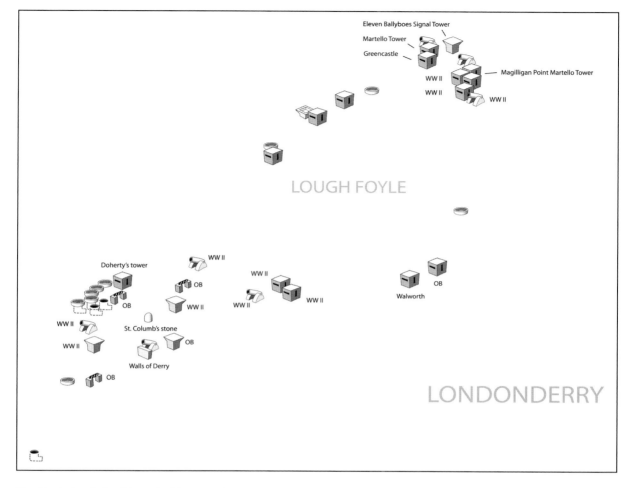

Eleven Ballyboes Signal Tower
Martello Tower
Greencastle
Magilligan Point Martello Tower
WW II
WW II
WW II
LOUGH FOYLE
Doherty's tower
WW II
WW II
OB
WW II
WW II
WW II
WW II
Walworth
OB
WW II
St. Columb's stone
WW II
OB
Walls of Derry
OB

LONDONDERRY

12.2 Detail, Foyle basin.

The Foyle basin had long held strategic importance. For most of the nineteenth century its entrance was guarded by two Martello towers, still to be seen on the land and charted on *The Map of Watchful Architecture*. Londonderry and its walls, completed in 1618, were sited where the Foyle narrows. This town was a large-scale cohesion of colonial architecture emerging from a feudal landscape. A degree of control had been forged by Lord Mountjoy's campaign. To take an example from the map, he built the fort at Moiry Pass in 1601 to control the main north/south route through the hills. It was joining an already highly castellated terrain. The forts at Newry, Taaffe's Castle, Narrow Water, Ardgonnell, and many others had been built, destroyed, occupied and reoccupied by various forces in the previous 300 years. These and many others are on the map. It was the Normans who had brought the concept of castle-building to Ireland, using fortified points to solidify themselves into the landscape. In Donegal, Greencastle, built in the fourteenth century, and in Louth, King John's Castle, built in the twelfth century, are just two examples. Giraldus Cambrensis was the embedded historian of the Norman invasion. He commented that previously the people of Ireland had used the woods as their strongholds and the marshes as their entrenchments (Cambrensis 2000: 82) but that did not exclude building. One structure he was probably thinking of were crannogs.

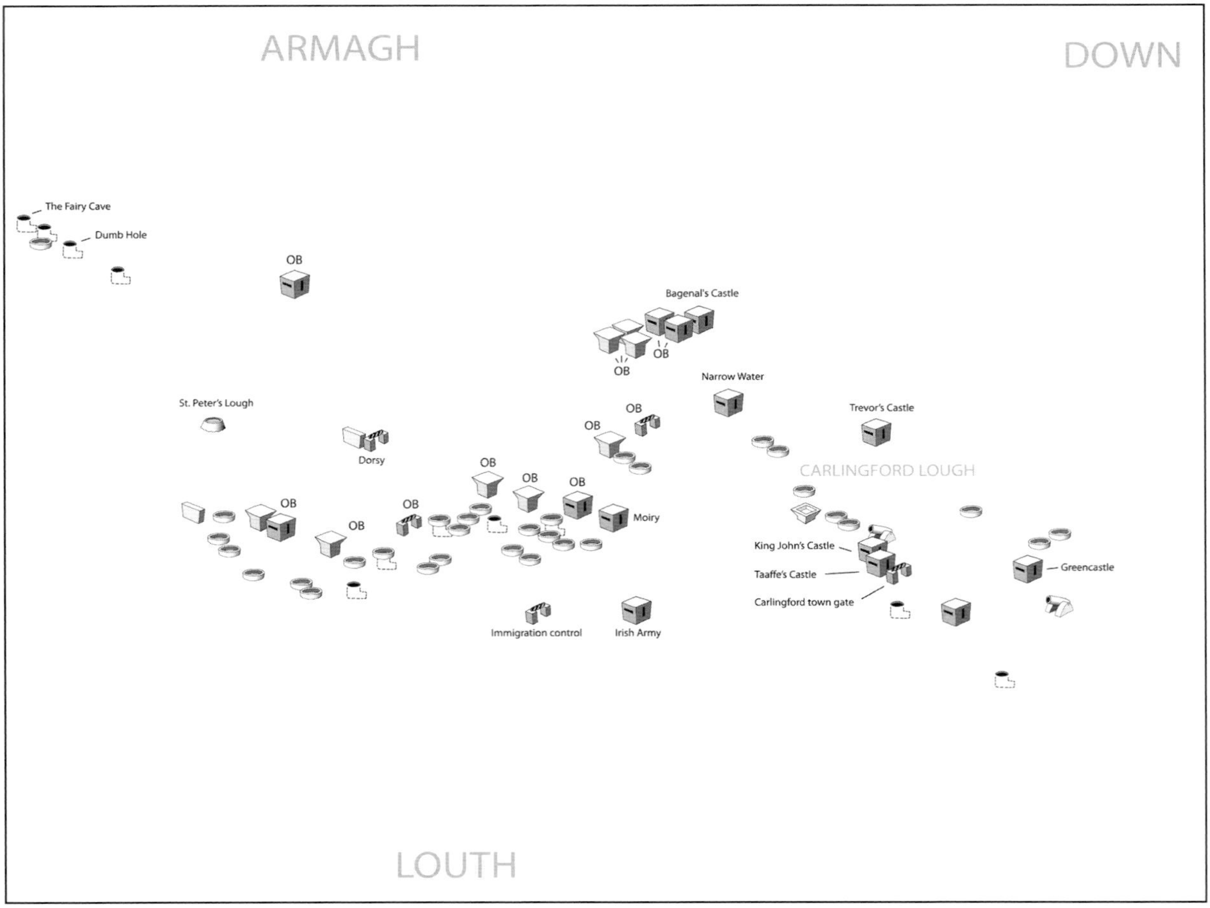

ARMAGH   DOWN

The Fairy Cave

Dumb Hole

OB

Bagenal's Castle

OB

OB

Narrow Water

St. Peter's Lough

OB

Trevor's Castle

OB

CARLINGFORD LOUGH

Dorsy

OB   OB   OB

OB   OB

OB

OB   Moiry

King John's Castle

Taaffe's Castle

Greencastle

Carlingford town gate

Immigration control   Irish Army

LOUTH

12.3   Detail, South Armagh.

These were artificial islands built in lakes or marshes, highly defendable and perhaps high-status homesteads. Each border lake containing a crannog is named on *The Map of Watchful Architecture*. Often the border passes straight through the crannog. They were an easily mapped point and perhaps a good way to divide the resource of water. Souterrains are also charted. These were underground shelters, probably used to hide food or the homesteaders themselves in times of danger. Areas of volatility are suggested in the their distribution. North Louth has a particularly high number, perhaps because this area was the interface zone of several tribal groups (Buckley 1989: 37).

As can be seen in Figure 12.3, this area of the borderlands has received highly consistent attention over the centuries. North Louth and South Armagh have some of the oldest and newest defensive structures and much of them are densely packed. The very name South Armagh still carries the bloody tinge of recent conflict. Many of the Operation Banner structures marked on the map in that area are hilltop watchtowers, a much more assertive deployment than the low-lying installations and checkpoints which tends to be the norm elsewhere along the border. This area's role as interface is even charted in ancient literature, being the backdrop to the epic story *Táin Bó Cúailnge*. It was here that the warrior Cúchulainn took his stand against

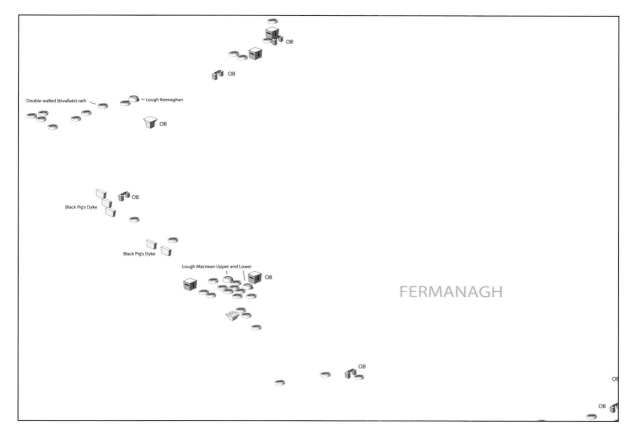

12.4 Detail, western tip of border.

the invasion of Ulster by a southern horde. This tale of violence, land, cattle and kinship was passing from the oral tradition to the written around the Early Medieval period, the time many of those souterrains and raths were being dug.

The most common basic architectural form on *The Map of Watchful Architecture* is the ring. Rings made of earth, stone or both. Thousands of raths, also called ring-forts, were built all over Ireland and the border area is no exception. When I first began collating the coordinates of all the elements on this map there seemed no doubt that raths belonged on a map of defensive building. Many are large, proudly crowning a hilltop and have double or even triple earthwork rings. However, many other raths are of small diameter and in uncommanding locations. Victor Buckley writes that raths are actually better thought of as domestic structures of the Early Medieval period. Excavations 'have shown that these sites contained the houses and farm-buildings of an extended family. It would be better, therefore, to view the enclosing ramparts not as defensive but as delimiting the extent of the home farm and as an effective means of keeping out wild animals, thieves and wandering farm animals' (Buckley 1989: 35). So, while raths are defensive they are perhaps no more defensive than the average bungalow. Nonetheless, raths are on version 1.0 of *The Map of Watchful Architecture*.

Dorsey and the Black Pig's Dyke are probably the oldest elements on the map. South Armagh's Dorsey can be seen in Figure 12.3. It is an earthwork that once funnelled people toward an approved entrance point. Dorsey means *door* or *gate*. Further west the Black Pig's

Dyke plugged the gaps between natural barriers and created a border. Sections of it can be seen in Figure 12.4. It is a series of ramparts and ditches and parts of it correspond roughly with today's international frontier. The natural barriers were, and still are, the hills and lakes of the drumlin belt and the two loughs at each end of the border.

MISSIONS OF THE MAP

The Map of Watchful Architecture seeks to do two things. One task is to uncover the way the Irish border, although generally represented on maps as a line, is in fact managed via points. On *The Map of Watchful Architecture* the cartographical sign of the borderline is dug up, leaving points that form outposts, nets, and rows. The second task is to de-familiarise. The map takes certain structures, perhaps constructed a thousand years apart, and puts them in the same category. The map seeks out what they have in common and uses it to make links across time, making comparisons that may sometimes surprise. *The Map of Watchful Architecture* conflates specificity and instead represents broad themes from the border's long narrative.

First, the uncovering of points underneath the borderline. Most of the raw data for *The Map of Watchful Architecture* was gathered from various databases. Coordinates of heritage sites in the Republic of Ireland are available from the National Monuments Service. In Northern Ireland I got them from Built Heritage. I got the coordinates of the Operation Banner installations directly from the Ministry of Defence, via the Freedom of Information Act. I am still trying, and still failing, to get checkpoint information from the Garda Síochána. Should this ever be forthcoming or if I glean the information some other way then those elements will go on future versions of the map.

When I used map-making software to project raw data onto digital maps the whole island was rendered thick with dots. Some of the defensive sites came packed with burial sites, monasteries and a host of other unsuitable elements. Also, I was only interested in the border corridor, but none of my sources demarked information that way. The databases gave me far more elements than I needed. I had to prune them back. *The Map of Watchful Architecture* is carved from this mass of information, a subtractive process. Sets of points were revealed.

Even during the most violent periods of its history the Irish border was never fenced. Although the aspiration of a closed border was occasionally voiced it seems that only once was anything like it ever attempted. That was with the creation of the Black Pig's Dyke around 2,000 years ago. However, the strength of these earthworks vary greatly and they are not strung together continuously. Archaeology tells us that they never were. The earthworks were more likely intended as local statements or to control an important crossing (Mitchell and Ryan 1997: 243). I have mapped these constructions as points.

There is no doubt that during Operation Banner the military deployment along the northern side of the border was focused on points, watchtowers and checkpoints, backed up by barracks. Donovan Wylie's *British Watchtowers* (2007) and Jonathan Olley's *Castles of Ulster* (2007) record of some of these strong points. They are collections of photographs of military installations built and staffed during Operation Banner. They show architecture that is watchful and wary. They are concreted strong points in the battle against enemies that are shifting and mobile. With the watchtowers' high visibility, tall on hilltops, and barricaded checkpoints on lower ground, on border roads, Operation Banner was a tough assertion of a border as a defended line. But even then it was not a solid line. They were strong points but just points nonetheless,

merely implying a line. This porosity gave room to the possibility of Bandit Country, smuggling, terrorists' cross border insertions and occasional southern straying of the British Army.

Graham Burnett's study of the colonial mapping of Guyana, *Masters of All They Surveyed* (2000) helps frame the point/line dichotomy theoretically. He follows the geographer Robert Schomburgk and reveals a border drawn by joining the dots between landmarks. His survey left a breadcrumb trail of nodal-points behind him, mapped and named, such as the stone column *Puré-Piapa* (Figure 12.5).

These were not built points, at first they do not seem to have much in common with the structures that concern *The Map of Watchful Architecture*. These were naturally occurring geological formations. Schomburgk merely charted them, illustrated them and, in that sense, used them. But they may shed light on another form of power present in, for example, a watchtower. A power that is rooted deeper than the cameras and the guns. When *Puré-Piapa* and other distinctive sites were charted and illustrated they became nodal-points in the organisation of space. Most of the border Schomburgk was attempting to draw was impenetrable jungle. So a borderline was instead implied by linking points of distinction. These included waterfalls, hillocks, oddly shaped rocks, but most especially elevated sites. The 'landmark objects' were often:

> … *promontories or elevations, points that offer a view of the place itself … So constructed, the landmark can become a nodal point in the construction of the colony, a position of relative stability in multiple fields – geographical, social and political. By differentiating space and*

12.5   Paul Gauci after Charles Bentley, (1806–1854), 'Pure-Piapa: A remarkable basaltic stone in Guiana', from Twelve views in the interior of Guiana by Robert H. Schomburgk, (1804–1865), London, Ackermann, 1841, hand-coloured lithograph.

organizing it hierarchically, such nodes foster the regime of colonial control, install regions and boundaries, and give permanence to individual experience. They allow individuals to situate themselves with respect to privileged positions and constitute a powerful technique for capturing space (Burnett 2000: 129).

These nodal-points are often how a border is enacted – how space is captured – and such points are what is charted on *The Map of Watchful Architecture*. It may be protested that a stone column and a watchtower, although sharing a certain loftiness, are hardly the same. The watchtowers of Operation Banner were manned, armed and equipped for surveillance, capable of dealing out real force to control the borderland. A perceptive leap may be required to see that both *Puré-Piapa* and a military watchtower can be used to claim space but making that leap is rewarding. Deep power is not just set on battlefields but, to use Burnett's phrase, 'in multiple fields'. This is not a new notion, nor is it new to Ireland. Irish Inauguration stones were always on high ground, the new king or lord invited to behold their territories during the inauguration ritual. They were often naturally occurring but distinctive boulders. The inauguration stone now know as Saint Columb's Stone, in Derry, juts only a few inches out of the soil (Figure 12.6). It is not defensive, not architectural, but a nonetheless it was a meaningful stone that was charged with political power.

The O'Neill inauguration stone, near present day Cookstown, was considered so important that it featured prominently on a map by Richard Bartlett, the cartographer who travelled with Lord Mountjoy's campaign to subdue mid-Ulster. In 1602, Lord Mountjoy had the stone

12.6   Saint Columb's Stone.

smashed. Its destruction was an attempt to clear the land of the network of nodal-points representing the old order in case it should ever reawaken and reconnect. Certain landmark objects could have such power. Smashing the stone was a first step in the deployment of new strong points, such as Mountjoy's fort at Moiry, casting a Tudor net over the area. There is a story, reflected in Scotland too, that a piece of the stone was sent to England and inserted in Queen Elizabeth's throne. Such was the enchantment of stones. Even these defenceless rocks can reinforce proposed territories. As such, I have included 'Inauguration Stone' as a category on *The Map of Watchful Architecture*. The only one on the map can be seen in Figure 12.2.

As part of a network of control 'Inauguration Stone' is at home among the other categories; 'Checkpoint', 'Fort', 'Watchtower', 'Crannog', 'Ring', 'Hide', 'Gun Placement', 'Wall' and 'Promontory Fort'. Most of the individual elements of each category were not built in one historical phase. Most of them span centuries but I have conflated them to contribute to the map's mission of de-familiarisation. *The Map of Watchful Architecture* looks at the basic forms of defensive architecture underlying centuries of building. Newly categorised, a castle or tower can be allotted new meanings. The artist John Byrne did something similar with his project *The Border Itself* (Byrne 2001). He did not use maps. Instead, he worked with photomontage and wit. The creations he exhibited include fictional postcards attempting to promote the border area, some featuring border castles. On the postcards the images were fore-grounded with flowers and accompanied by phrases in the style of clichéd touristic sentiment. But the images are not the Norman or Elizabethan Castles normally found on postcards, they are Operation Banner installations. In his playful way Byrne is looking at questions of nostalgia but the postcards may also invite us to ponder the difference between a Norman tower and an Operation Banner installation. We may conclude that the differences are slim.

Likewise, to take one example from *The Map of Watchful Architecture*, compare the earthwork at Dorsey and the Immigration Control in Co. Louth. They are close to each other and can be seen

12.7   John Byrne. Border Postcard from *The Border Itself* exhibition, 2001. Photographic print with text.

THE OLD FORTIFICATIONS AT CROSSMAGLEN REALLY SET OFF THE MAIN SQUARE in Figure 12.3. The Dorsey site was built in the first century and may have operated as an official entrance into Ulster (Buckley 1989: 26). Currently the Garda Síochána check the passengers of buses crossing the border into the south. This is not a permanent structure but it is a highly consistent deployment. They are looking for illegal migrants and may not know they are part of a 2,000 year tradition. Instead of two categories, First-century Gate and twenty-first century Immigration Control, we have just one; 'Checkpoint'. To distinguish them chronologically textual labelling is used but the symbol is the same. In this way immigration control is revealed as inheritor of a long tradition while at the same time an ancient site is instilled with contemporary resonance.

For *The Map of Watchful Architecture* I hammered together many different forms into one category. I use the brutish term 'hammer' deliberately, the conflation was often a crude process. Strong arguments can be formulated against almost every grouping decision made in on the map. Could not a promontory fort be as well described as a wall? It could. It could also belong in the category 'Rings'. I sought a single common trait of multiple forms, isolated it and called it the defining trait. But structures will have more than one trait and the process of definition still goes on. Future visits to sites and further research may mean that forthcoming versions of *The Map of Watchful Architecture* will feature different configurations.

EXHIBITING THE MAP

In conclusion, I should mention that *The Map of Watchful Architecture* has received some divergent reactions from viewers. I have been told it is Republican, an argument for the unification of Ireland, in that it seems to suggest the border is artificial and brutally maintained. I have also been told it is Unionist, pro-partition, for pushing the division of Ireland back an unshakable two millennium. Both these reactions seem and predictable. They may have gotten space because the symbols on *The Map of Watchful Architecture* are sometimes conventional and susceptible to brisk readings. But they are arranged in an unconventional grammar, arrangements that can and do stimulate with even brief study. The conflation of pillboxes and Norman strong houses, anti-aircraft batteries and cannon placements make connections not found on many maps. Perhaps on no other map. The breaking up of the borderline into points shows it is not an evenly spread phenomena but actually subject to long-lived trends. The map is clotted and busy in some key places and stretched thin in others.

I believe the notion of a border being not a line but a series of points is an idea worthy of exposure through cartography. I chose defensive architecture as subject but other ideas could have been explored. For example, a map of petrol stations could also have formed a description of the border. They too tend to be found close to it, taking advantage of price variations in both states. It was because I wanted a longer historical view and because of the Irish border's association with trouble that I alighted on defensive architecture. This subject seems to have loaded the map with *appeal*, that hard-to-measure dimension. I have observed people poring over it, studying it in great detail, when it has been exhibited.

Defensive architecture can readily be seen to have contributed to the creation of the border rather than to have been simply placed in reaction to it. However, elements on *The Map of Watchful Architecture* always seems to have had some precursor. For example, a Norman structure will have often been built on the site of a cashel. Underlying this is the near constant value of high ground in claiming space. This theme was most recently expressed in the placement of

Operation Banner watchtowers. It is a theme that may have begun in the earliest formations of human society on this island. Ultimately the partition of Ireland seems rooted in a landscape well designed to support the formation of mental borders, the drumlin belt, the loughs of Foyle and Carlingford and the rivers that make up about two thirds of the border's length. *The Map of Watchful Architecture* seeks to cast a cold and close eye on how we reinforce such lines.

REFERENCES

Buckley, V.M. 1989. From the darkness to the dawn: The later prehistoric and early Christian borderlands, in Gillespie, R. and O'Sullivan, H. (eds) *The Borderlands. Essays on the History of the Ulster-Leinster Border*, 23–39.

Burnett, G. 2000. *Masters of all they Surveyed: Exploration, Geography and a British El Dorado*. Chicago, IL: University of Chicago.

Byrne, J. 2001. *The Border Itself*. Exhibition. Dublin: Temple Bar Gallery.

Cambrensis, G. 2000. *The History and Topography of Ireland*. Translated by Thomas Forester. Cambridge, Ontario: In Parentheses Publications.

Gillespie, R. and O'Sullivan, H. 1989. *The Borderlands. Essays on the History of the Ulster-Leinster Border*. Belfast: The Institute of Irish Studies.

Mitchell, F. and Ryan, M. 1997. *Reading the Irish Landscape*. Dublin: Townhouse.

Olley, J. 2007. *Castles of Ulster*. Belfast: Factotum.

Paasi, A. 1999. Boundaries as social practice and discourse: The Finnish-Russian border. *Regional Studies*, 33(7), 669–80.

Schomburgk, R.H. 1841. *Twelve Views in the Interior of Guiana*. London: Ackermann.

Wylie, D. 2007. *British Watchtowers*. Göttingen: Steidl.

13

British Soldiers' Graves in the Crimea and the Origins of Modern War Commemoration

Andrew Keating

INTRODUCTION

The transformation of battlefields into spaces of remembrance containing the individually marked graves of dead soldiers forms one of the uniquely modern facets of war. Scholars have demonstrated how systematic and bureaucratically organized burial of military fatalities originated with the American Civil War in the mid-nineteenth century and the First World War in the early twentieth (see, for example, Laqueur 1994 and Winter 1998). Gettysburg, according to the historian Drew Gilpin Faust, 'signalled the beginning of a new significance for the dead in American public life'. Battlefield cemeteries organized by the government meant the soldier dead could no longer be considered 'the responsibility of their families' since 'they, and their loss, now belonged to the nation' (2008: 100–101). Similarly, in Europe after the First World War, commemoration became 'a universal preoccupation' and the need 'to put the dead to rest, symbolically or physically, was pervasive' (Winter 1998: 28). Although different factors resonated during each of these conflicts, high fatality rates and mass death proved necessary preconditions to the transformation of battlefields from spaces of war into places of remembrance. The emphasis on these wars and their relationship to modern commemoration leads to the assumption, at least somewhat erroneous, that the British did nothing for their soldier dead of the nineteenth century. Or that the transformation of battlefields into cemeteries necessarily began with organized State projects.

Britain's first battlefield burial grounds actually originated during the Crimean War of 1853–6. The processes by which sites of war became transformed into those of remembrance that manifested a new type of patriotism illuminate alternative mechanisms through which modern war commemoration developed. The marked soldiers' graves originated from the actions of individuals who cared about their comrades. Narratives and visual representations of the burial grounds prompted Britons in the metropolis to care for dead soldiers far from home and to articulate the idea that they deserved proper burial in perpetually maintained cemeteries. Although the British government began to understand its obligation to maintain these spaces of the dead, it developed plans for cemeteries in response to pressure from the public. The idea of war cemeteries as patriotic spaces imbued with national meanings thus originated from the care of the dead itself and an interplay between public and governmental efforts to provide for those killed at war.

The Crimean War shared some of the military, technological, diplomatic, and cultural characteristics of the Napoleonic conflicts 50 years earlier and the First World War, 60 years later. Religious tensions and the controversy of the guardianship of the Holy Places as well as geopolitical rivalry between the Great Powers provoked the conflict (Figes 2011). Militarily, the British experienced the war through the siege of the Russian city of Sevastopol they undertook with their allies for roughly a year beginning in September 1854. A relatively static front line led to the extended presence of military camps. The British public's conceptions of the common soldier transformed during the siege: pre-war debates about flogging and military discipline provided the basis for compassion and depictions of the suffering of sick and wounded men manifested unprecedented concern for soldiers' welfare. Accounts of Florence Nightingale's efforts to improve conditions at the Scutari Hospital reinforced the notion that soldiers deserved decent care. War reporting in newspapers as well as books provided the reading public familiarity with the people and places of the conflict as well as the ability to empathize with soldiers' experiences. Telegraph dispatches gave newspapers timely updates on battles and fatalities. Sketches, lithographs and, for the first time, battlefield photographs illustrated these accounts to give the public the impression they could see the war.

Burials in the Crimea featured prominently in visual and literary depictions as a way of demonstrating the sacrifices soldiers made for 'queen and country'. George Brackenbury's well-known anthology narrated the battles and eulogized 'the illustrious dead, whose unforgotten graves lie thick in the fatal plains of Balaklava' (1856: 41). William Simpson's lithographs accompanying the text depicted numerous funerals, graves, and burial grounds. In particular the image 'Hospital and Cemetery at Scutari' provided the public with a visual representation of the site where Nightingale laboured. The Christian funeral procession, the orderly and well-marked graves, military men viewing headstones, the gravediggers engaging in Muslim prayer present a scene dominated as much by the burial ground as the imposing hospital on the hill. The cemetery ground appears to be a rambling and unenclosed space containing a variety of gravestones (Figure 13.1).

In addition to the soldiers interred near the Scutari Hospital thousands more were buried near where they fell on the battlefield or adjacent to military camps. Death and burial of comrades formed a significant part of soldiers' experience of the war. An officer lamented, 'our camps are one gigantic graveyard', and he meant it literally as well as figuratively. One soldier's grave, he noticed, had 'a simple cross of limestone … solid enough to stand for ages' (Hawley in Ward ed. 1970: 35). Crosses began to represent dead British soldiers generally rather than a particular Christian confession. Roger Fenton's photographs depicted some of these burial sites, such as the graves on Cathcart's Hill that he captured on several occasions in 1855 (Figure 13.2). Many more graves, marked with stone or wood, dotted the landscape.

13.1   William Simpson's lithograph, 'Hospital and Cemetery at Scutari'.

RELIGION, NARRATIVE, AND THE BRITISH SOLDIER DEAD

The numerous marked soldiers' graves which sprang up around Sevastopol did so because of several characteristics of the Crimean war. Besides the military reality of the static front line, social and cultural factors prompted new ways of caring for the dead. Aspects of the Victorians' attitudes toward death that had been developing at home influenced the way soldiers and civilians believed the dead should be treated. Additionally, the reconciliation of religious faith with military service and the rise of new forms of Christianity among soldiers and the public at home inaugurated a new religiously defined experience of death. The linking of military service, 'queen and country,' and Christianity brought about idealized understandings of the war's purposes (Anderson 1971: 46). One officer's career and the subsequent literary representation of it epitomized the changes within the British military as well as in the public's understanding of soldiering.[1] The book, *The Memorials of Captain Hedley Vicars, Ninety-seventh Regiment*, originally published near the end of the war, sold hundreds of thousands of copies in multiple editions in Britain. Circulated around the British Empire, it became widely known in the English-speaking world and was translated into several European languages. This literary account reveals the emergence of a new ethical norm for proper treatment of the soldier dead, especially those who died on battlefields far from home.

Like most Evangelical narratives it begins with an account of Vicars' experience of Christian salvation. According to the author Catherine Marsh, he proved 'the reality of his religion beyond

13.2   Roger Fenton's photograph, 'The cemetery Cathcart's Hill – the Picquet House, Victoria Redoubt and the Redoubt des Anglais in the distance'.

question' by presiding over the funerals of his fellow soldiers, by seeing that they received proper burials, and by tending to their graves (1856: 158). At one burial he 'intended speaking a few words to [his] men over the open graves of their dead messmates; but it was as much as [he] could do to get through the service'. Vicars began 'crying like a child' while 'the men cried and sobbed' around him because of their grief. He could not continue the funeral and he 'ordered them to 'fall in,' and [they] went mournfully back to the barracks' (1856: 172–3). While the level of emotion expressed typified religious writing, distraught soldiers mourning dead comrades in this way formed an entirely new type of war reporting. Paradoxically, it did not engender pacifism or a reluctance to fight but instead validated sacrifice and death in battle.

Narrator Marsh presented Vicars' concern with the dead as an aberration within the military, which served to accentuate her hero's Christian virtue. Because 'no spiritual instruction was provided for either Protestant or Roman Catholic soldiers, the field was his own. He began his work by undertaking the command of funeral parties for other officers, who gladly relinquished to him a task so little congenial to their feelings'. Although in fact there were some military chaplains, Vicars' interest in the care of the dead made him noteworthy. Consequently 'he obtained frequent opportunities of addressing the living around the graves of the dead' (1856: 167–8). Soldiers proved a captive audience for the Christian officer preaching heavenly salvation, and the death ritual provided an opportunity to reach them with his spiritual message. Ensuring proper burial for soldiers also meant replicating the mournful graveside scenes that formed such integral parts of Victorian death rituals in Britain. By contrast, the 'horrid sight' of an Orthodox funeral in which priests carried the corpse in an open coffin 'without even a mock air of grief, but looking rather jolly than otherwise' exemplified an improper way to care for the dead (1856: 152).

The moral claim about proper treatment for dead soldiers gains even more exigency when Vicars himself perishes. His burial scene receives more elaborate description than the captain's non-heroic death. One of Vicars' comrades observed 'soldiers digging a grave' and realized 'it was his'. Overcome with grief the officer 'stood beside them, and spoke to them as well as [he] could for sorrow … Oh! how [his] heart bled for [Vicars'] dear mother and sisters at home!' Numerous mourners arrived, including: 'All the officers of the 97th … with some friends from other regiments, and a large number of the men of his own regiment'. The mood seemed mournful, and 'A deep, very deep solemnity prevailed, as the Chaplain read the Funeral Service' (Marsh 1856: 303). The burial scene appeared similar to a respectable Victorian funeral at home. Even if this description represented an attempt by a military man to make battlefield death comprehensible to civilians or even if it resulted from the mediation of a civilian narrator, it became the way that the reading public understood a proper burial scene for a dead soldier. It would be inconceivable for Vicars' body, or indeed any British soldier's body, to be thrown into a ditch and forgotten after reading this kind of personal and emotional account. Instead, a Christian soldier-hero like Vicars deserved a proper burial service, mourning, and a marked grave. This manifested a new moral landscape for the British public and the government as well: an articulation of the obligation to care for soldiers' graves, especially those on battlefields far from home.

The published account of Vicars' life and death reinforced the idea of proper care for soldier dead in yet another way, through the image and hymn depicted on its frontispiece. The verses, by the prolific Scottish hymn-writer James Montgomery, originally were intended to memorialize a minister 'cut off in his usefulness' (Montgomery 1825: 422). Although many dirt mounds of burial places appear, only Vicars' has a gleaming white tombstone with a cross and an inscription. The other graves are arranged in tidy rows and the hills in the background of the scene are clear and clean as well. The image simultaneously presents Vicars as the exceptional individual – his grave stands apart – and as a part of a larger whole; the battlefield burial ground is neat, tidy, orderly. Yet the entire space does not seem enclosed or bounded. The battlefield has taken on some of the characteristics of a cemetery but does not appear to be a space of patriotic commemoration (Figure 13.3).

THE TRANSFORMATION OF BATTLEFIELD BURIAL GROUNDS INTO COMMEMORATIVE SPACES

Following the conclusion of peace in 1856 the British Army had no plan for maintaining the roughly 140 burial grounds scattered around Sevastopol containing the graves of officers such as Hedley Vicars or those of common soldiers and some civilians. Two officers, John Colborne and Frederic Brine, recognized that the graves lacked permanency and attempted to catalogue the epitaphs before embarking on their voyage home. This effort still centred on the dead individually, recording information about them so that their families and the public at home would know that they had received dignified interment. Colborne and Brine identified approximately 5,000 graves in the various burial grounds, but they only recorded information about those that they found with legible grave markers. In addition to reminding the British public about the existence of war graves and cemeteries, the book presented stylized visual representations of them that set

13.3   Frontispiece to *The Memorials of Captain Hedley Vicars, Ninety-seventh Regiment.*

the public's expectations about the proper appearance of battlefield burial grounds.

Despite the catalogue of inscriptions on the graves and monuments, Colborne and Brine produced a vision of collective commemoration. The authors declared their attempt 'to excite an interest relative to the last earthly tenements of those gallant ones who, while they lived, were their country's noblest pride, and, now that they can fight her victories no more assert a just claim to her undying remembrance' (Colborne and Brine 1856: v). Relatives of the deceased presumably already had such an interest, so Colborne and Brine seemingly wanted to reach a broader public. They understood their printed work as a means of ensuring a permanent record of the soldier dead because the physical monuments to them would inevitably decay.

Although only a short time had elapsed since the end of the war, the authors declared 'few traces of our presence in the Crimea remain … save those very cemeteries and monuments of which the present work humbly proposes itself to be a register'. Cataloguing information about the dead would provide a way to remember the individual soldiers as well as the collective accomplishments of the British Army during the war.

The account of individual graves also served to present the spaces of the dead in the Crimea to the British public in a way that educated them on the proper care of battlefield burial grounds. Colborne and Brine emphasized the neatness, orderliness and enclosure of the cemeteries as a way to ensure dignified respect for the dead contained therein. They explained, 'all cemeteries were … enclosed and made neat, in many cases being surrounded by a dry boundary stone wall, with a small ditch outside, the earth from which was thrown against the wall within'. While this type of treatment might have been the Army's intent, in actuality there was no systematic method for ordering the cemeteries, much less an effective or comprehensive implementation of any uniform treatment. The illustrations that Colborne and Brine included with their burial register nonetheless depicted these types of neat, orderly, and enclosed cemeteries that resembled what respectable Victorians would have been familiar with in Britain (Figures 13.4 and 13.5).

13.4   The Cathcart's Hill burial ground.

The responsibility for maintaining the actual burial sites fell upon the British government, yet despite the presence of consular officials in the region the sites languished unprotected.

E. Walker, lith.   London. Published by Ackermann & Co. 96, Strand .W.C.   Day & Son, Lith⁵ to The Queen

CATHCARTS HILL

E. Walker, lith.   London, Published by Ackermann & Co. 106 Strand.   Day & Son, Litĥⁿ․ to the Queen.
1   23   14   16
SECOND BRIGADE, LIGHT DIVISION,
(LOOKING TOWARDS SEBASTOPOL.)

Although diplomats received assurances from the Russian government that the burial grounds would be respected and consuls in the area frequently relayed reports of their condition to London, neither effort amounted to an effective on-going maintenance policy. Visitors frequently complained about problems like 'the ruinous condition of the Burial Ground of the 1st Brigade of the Light Division of the British Army, also of the Burial Ground of the Royal Engineers'. These cemeteries appeared in horrible condition because 'some isolated graves [were] wholly unenclosed and unprotected' (Letter from Reverend Darling to Consul Murray 1859). Additionally, visitors would inevitably compare the cemeteries to the lithographic representations in *The Last of the Brave* and see the actual sites as dilapidated compared to their stylized representations. A dispatch from the Consul-General concurred with visitors and reported, 'the truth of the forcible representations constantly made' about the condition of the graves (Anon. 1859a). He sent several photographs to the Foreign Office in 1860, depicting enclosed cemeteries with crumbling or breached walls (Figure 13.6). The British government attempted to pay a local monastery to care for the burial grounds, but the Order declined to assume the responsibility. Chiding the Foreign Office, they declared it 'the duty of every Christian to respect the Burial place of the dead, but … the office of keeping the graves in repair belonged to laymen' (Anon. 1859a). Presented with this setback, the Foreign Office attempted to hire a guardian for the cemeteries.

13.5   The Second Brigade, Light Division Cemetery.

13.6   Photograph of the Engineer's Cemetery from 1860 showing breaches in the stone boundary wall. The Consul-General sent several photographs to the Foreign Office with his written report on the cemeteries.

Officials continued to receive information from travellers in the region about desecration and neglect of the burial grounds. The Consul at Kerch learned 'that the grave yards of our brave countrymen in the neighbourhood of Sevastopol are falling into a state of Dilapidation from neglect' and directed a vice-consul to investigate their condition. He took action without consulting London because he understood 'the intention of Her Majesty's Government and the wish of the British Nation that due respect should be paid to the last resting places of those who fell honourably fighting for their country at the siege of Sevastopol' (Anon. 1859b). British officials, travellers, and the government increasingly articulated the idea that caring for the burial grounds amounted to a collective, national responsibility when they lamented their condition. The Vice-Consul's report provided a detailed account of the cemeteries in the period immediately following the war. He observed significant damage even though the British Army departed their camps less than four years earlier. In many cemeteries 'the inclosing walls … [have] broken down … by cattle going over them to graze' and 'the monuments were considerably dilapidated, inscriptions wantonly effaced and the whole of the cemeteries in want of extensive repairs without which the traces of many of them will soon be utterly lost' (Anon. 1859c). In addition, he provided information about individual burial grounds and graves, summarizing extensive damage to them and recommending the government spend thousands of pounds on repairs.

Some cemeteries remained in good condition because of an American resident who unofficially maintained and landscaped them. John E. Gowen of Boston arrived at Sevastopol in 1857 to raise Russia's sunken Black Sea fleet (Anon. 1857). He 'took an interest in the British graves', and as a result, 'if many of [them] … are still in a comparatively good state of preservation it is entirely owing to [his] zealous care and philanthropic and Christian feeling' (Anon. 1859c). A visitor who toured the region explained, 'it was his Sunday recreation to visit the surrounding cemeteries, and to note down whatever repairs they needed. These were done entirely at his own expense' (Anon. 1862: 307). British newspapers also noted Gowen's work and his willingness to give travellers tours of the burial grounds. One visit resulted in discovering 'the slabs that covered [a] grave … had been turned over and the remains … entirely exhumed, the bones as well as some remaining portion of the uniform being scattered around the grave'. Despite the 'heart-sickening spectacle to behold the last mortal remains of this brave officer [lying] bleaching in the sun', the visitor took comfort in assurances from Gowen 'that on the following Sunday he would have the remains carefully restored to their former peaceful state'. For this work, the traveller declared, 'the sincerest thanks of every true Englishmen are due'. The British government, by contrast, seemed to be doing nothing, and the visitor insisted that officials should 'take such speedy and necessary measures for putting our graveyards in the proper state of repair as to preserve from oblivion the last resting-places of so many brave men' (Anon. 1860a: 12). Gowen's activities seemed like what should be done by officials. Reporting on them served to critique government inaction and to articulate the collective patriotic responsibility for battlefield burial grounds.

Gowen provided care for the graves and comfort for families in Britain in a way that all respectable Christians should behave. He reassured interested relatives and the public in Britain with information about the cemeteries and specific graves, comforting one correspondent, for instance, with the information that his relative 'reposes peacefully in Cathcart's Cemetery'. Gowen planted rose bushes there 'as well as round other graves of your lamented countrymen' (Anon. 1861b: 12). Other cemeteries, by contrast, remained in a 'barren state … entirely destitute of trees' (Anon. 1860b: 12). Published in *Macmillan's Magazine*, one visitor explained, 'Mrs Gowen … also had taken her share in care for the graves'. In particular she seemed 'deeply interested in the life of Captain Hedley Vicars' and consequently 'she had done her utmost to decorate his grave in the Woronzoff Road with flowers'. The visitor explained, 'she had even carried sacks of rich earth up in her own carriage, in the hope of making plants grow. Every variety of flower and shrub she had tried, and had even gone to the expense of paying a Russian labourer daily to water the plants through the summer heat' (Anon. 1862: 307). The Gowens' efforts reflected a continuation of the attitude espoused by Vicars during the war and expressed by Catherine Marsh in her religious biography of the 'Christian soldier'.

The public and private recognition of Gowen's efforts underscored the idea that his activities served the British national interest. He 'had the honour of receiving a beautiful gold snuffbox' from local consular officials in acknowledgement of his work to preserve the cemeteries (Anon. 1861a: 5). In addition, he received 'a piece of plate' paid for 'and sent to him by the officers of the British Army and the friends of those who fell in the Crimean war'. Those who witnessed the gift approved wholeheartedly, declaring Gowen's actions 'worthy of the public and liberal acknowledgement of a nation's gratitude'. His care of the graves resulted in the Cathcart's Hill cemetery being 'so neatly and prettily … kept' that it 'would do credit to an English town' (Anon. 1861c: 10). Recognition of Gowen's work reveals the developing consensus that caring for soldiers' graves amounted to a collective responsibility and a patriotic duty, albeit one not effectively undertaken by government officials.

Even the British government's successive failures to care adequately for the dead reinforced the developing notion that they were the responsibility of the nation. Following initial attempts to engage the local monastery to care for the graves, the Consul-General hired a retired Russian officer for the job in 1860. Although he introduced the caretaker as 'an artillery officer of English descent, who had high testimonials', others in the government displayed much less enthusiasm for the selection (Anon. 1867b: 8). Gowen did not approve either, disparaging him as 'an old … booby, over sixty years old … who cannot speak one word of any language but Russian'. Furthermore, he thought it was 'a great mistake to appoint a Russian, for Englishmen … would take an active interest in looking after the graves of their lamented but gallant countrymen'. A senior Foreign Office secretary agreed, Gowen, he wrote, 'is quite right, and it is a national duty to see that the graves of our fallen heroes are kept decently in order' (Cavendish 1913: 353). Although no Englishman took over his responsibilities, the Russian's 'appointment was cancelled', and the cemeteries again lacked an official custodian (Anon. 1867c: 8). The attempt to hire a guardian ultimately failed because of this nationality requirement. Gowen, their unofficial overseer, left Sevastopol in the mid-1860s.

The British public became increasingly strident that these sites deserved care and attention from their government. *The Times* published an editorial in 1867 which presented the case in favour of official maintenance, declaring, 'There are few spots so sacred to Englishmen as the burial-grounds around Sebastopol'. The newspaper explained by appealing to personal sentiment and asserting 'To many a mother and widow the burial-grounds of the Crimea are as dear as the family hearth, and those lonely graves are more sacred than the family tomb in an English churchyard'. Thus, the country had a duty to them that should not be abjured to the Russians because 'such an arrangement would … seem like abandoning our own responsibility for this sacred trust'. The British government alone could 'bestow the care and labour necessary to maintain the graves as English affection would wish' (Anon. 1867a: 6). Pressure on the government to repair and maintain the cemeteries involved conflating personal sentiment with collective duty.

THE ADYE-GORDON INSPECTION TOUR

Parliament and government bureaucrats responded to this outcry and dispatched Brigadier-General John Adye and Colonel Charles George Gordon to inspect the burial grounds and recommend a maintenance policy. Elite opinion wholeheartedly supported the tour. *The Times* declared, 'The public cannot now be satisfied unless this inquiry is made … It concerns the honour of the Government to take the matter in hand without delay' (Anon. 1867a: 6). Adye and Gordon arrived in Sevastopol on 29 August, 1872 and spent ten days 'making a careful inspection of every Cemetery and Memorial of the British Army in the vicinity'. They observed how much the burial grounds varied 'in their position and size' as well as 'in the number of graves and monuments' contained within them. In addition to the graves they found 'three commemorative obelisks' as well as 'a few general memorials to brigades and special regiments' (Adye and Gordon 1873: 1). Most of the marked graves they encountered belonged to officers, but they also discovered some for common soldiers. Despite the tremendous concern about the desecration and neglect of these sites, their report emphasized the relative preservation of the graves and made recommendations for renovating them to create permanent commemorative space.

They attempted to locate and catalogue all of cemeteries of which the government had a record. Finding all but eleven, which they dismissed as 'small ones … contain[ing] no tablets', they recorded detailed information about each cemetery: its position, the names found within it, the state of the individual graves, the condition of the boundary walls and miscellaneous remarks. More than half they found 'in good order', and they recorded vague descriptions of damage, such as 'tablet broken' or 'name illegible', for those that were not. Explicitly addressing concerns about 'the alleged desecration of the tombs', they 'made careful inquiries' and 'close inspection' (Adye and Gordon 1873: 2). Discovering only haphazard problems, they concluded that deliberate desecration had not been widespread.

Adye and Gordon confirmed the commemorative nature of the cemeteries as well as their national significance. In constructing a rationale for the damage they encountered, they explained that the 'wild uneducated people' of the Crimea who 'allowed their flocks and herds to stray amongst the graves' or engaged in 'idle mischief' caused most of the damage to the burial grounds and graves. 'Wilful malice' had not occurred. In some 'exceptional cases in which monuments have been violently overthrown,' they concluded, 'the desecration has been the act of persons who have hoped to find money or valuables on the bodies of the dead'. Ordinary acts of grave robbing or uncivilized behaviour by local inhabitants seemed preferable to systematic destruction of British burial grounds. They recommended reorganizing the battlefield cemeteries as well. Because the 'officers and men were buried by their comrades on the ground where they fell', they concluded, 'the whole scene is sacred and historical, and the remains of the dead should not be disturbed'.

Battlefield burial grounds thus became defined in an official document as sacred space for the British nation. For the 'numerous small isolated burial-grounds … the monuments [should be] removed to the nearest large Cemetery'. Rather than attempting to collect isolated human remains and re-interring them in one location, they declared it important to leave the dead buried on the battlefields. Headstones and monuments would form the locus of commemoration. In addition, 'the larger Cemeteries should be preserved', though the erection of 'a substantial wall … round them' and the repair of 'all monuments, tablets, and crosses', along with the 'renewal' of all inscriptions. Cathcart's Hill, they decided, 'deserves special attention'. Not only did Adye and Gordon recommend restoring that cemetery, but they also proposed its expansion as the single site to commemorate all the British war dead. The location, on a hill overlooking Sevastopol, made it an ideal spot for 'a large obelisk or general memorial' which would be 'made in England of granite or other durable material, and sent out to the Crimea' (Adye and Gordon 1873: 5–28). Rather than simply preserving what had been erected during the war, Adye and Gordon proposed a new monument that would represent the post-war memories of the dead and substitute for years of official neglect of the actual graves.

Ultimately it was not the government alone but instead a combination of official and civic efforts that implemented most of these recommendations. Lord Hertford, a Tory courtier and related by marriage to Queen Victoria, began a voluntary committee to raise funds for the Cathcart's Hill memorial. After Hertford's death in 1884, the Duke of Cambridge, a grandson of George III and Commander-in-Chief of the British Army, took over the cause. Himself a Crimean War veteran, he solicited other military figures to join the effort. The voluntary group, technically a private subscription, but clearly well connected to government, military, and the Crown, oversaw 'a collection from the many scattered cemeteries of outlying memorials'. These monuments 'had been replaced in the Cathcart's-hill property, where, too, an addition had been made to the custodian's house. The ground had been levelled and smoothed over, and other work carried out' (Anon. 1884: 14). This private initiative with the leadership of prominent individuals succeeded in implementing the provisions of the report from Adye and Gordon,

13.7 A representation of the Cathcart's Hill burial ground as neat and well-ordered commemorative space following publication of the Adye-Gordon Report.

which itself manifested a consolidation of the area of focus. Maintaining and expanding the single site of Cathcart's Hill became the only possibility after years of neglecting the numerous smaller, scattered burial grounds in the region (Figure 13. 7).

CONCLUSION

During the Crimean War soldiers and officers within the British Army manifested a new commitment to burying the dead in marked, individual graves that mimicked those of respectable Victorian cemeteries at home. Following the conflict, with the publication and popularity of *The Memorials of Captain Hedley Vicars*, the reading public in Britain and throughout the English-speaking world became introduced to the soldier's grave as a site that compelled a new affective relationship. The retelling of Vicars' life, death, and burial on the battlefield functioned like other nineteenth-century humanitarian narratives: it prompted readers to care about suffering at a distance, in this case about the graves of those who died in battle. Scenes of military leaders dying in battle – like Wolfe at Quebec, Nelson at Trafalgar, Abercromby at Abukir, Moore at Corunna – had always mattered to the British public and fostered pride in country. *Hedley Vicars* demonstrated how the graves of all who died in their country's service should be considered sacred.

The graves and burial grounds of British soldiers received continuous attention following the Crimean War. The government's efforts to maintain them proceeded haphazardly and without much success. Work by concerned private citizens provided most of the care for the graves initially, while consuls catalogued damage and pressed their superiors in London for the money and the authority to maintain them permanently. Through reporting on the neglect of the burial grounds, newspapers began to identify them as commemorative sites that demanded care and attention from the government. Once understood as such, editorials and elite opinion in Britain began to demand action by the government and to articulate the view that the nation had a moral obligation to care for its dead soldiers.

The public agitation culminated in the expedition by Adye and Gordon to assess the condition of the burial grounds and to recommend how to preserve them. Their report codified the beginnings of what would become in the twentieth century the norm for British war commemoration. Bodies should be buried on the battlefield and left there, even if headstones and monuments could be located elsewhere. The report additionally confirmed that effective commemoration required continual state involvement as well as orderly and bounded physical space. Bodies on the battlefield made the space sacred but effective commemoration could take place without bodies. Combined action from prominent veterans, the Royal Family, and the government in the 1880s led to the implementation of most of the report's principles and the universal acceptance of the view that caring for soldiers' graves amounted to a collective moral responsibility.

The effort to maintain not only the Crimean graves but also those of soldiers who died in wars of the late nineteenth century reinforced the sense of collective obligation to care for the soldier dead. The Army promulgated regulations directing officers to mark out battlefield burial grounds and supervise the decent interment of corpses.[2] The combination of public and private care for British soldiers' graves reached its apex with the South African War of 1899–1902. Civic organization paid for and erected crosses on all the graves and the military produced detailed registers of burial locations. The South African and British governments assumed financial responsibility for these graves after the war. British efforts to commemorate the war dead changed dramatically during the First World War and produced the bureaucratically organized commemoration style associated with the world wars of the twentieth century. Nevertheless, the policies and practices toward the soldier dead of 1914–1918 initially drew upon the traditions and beliefs that emerged during the Crimean War and its aftermath.

ACKNOWLEDGEMENTS

I wish to thank Professors Thomas Laqueur and James Vernon for their unceasing support of the project from which this chapter is drawn. British Studies colleagues at Berkeley, especially Desmond Fitz-Gibbon and Caroline Shaw, read drafts and provided useful feedback.

NOTES

1   Anderson argues that *Hedley Vicars* represented 'a new departure in religious biography' which was not only 'an instrument of evangelism among young men and soldiers' but also an offering to 'professional soldiers [of] biographical proof that a man of their own day could be a zealous Christian without being any the less good a soldier' (1971: 46–7).

2   For instance, Garnet Wolseley's *The Soldier's Pocket-Book for Field Service*. Page 114 explains 'There must be [a graveyard] in the vicinity of each large hospital station' (1882: 114). Under 'Staff Duties after an Action' Wolseley directs officers to 'see to the burial of the dead' (1882: 138).

REFERENCES

Adye, J. and Gordon, C.G. 1873. *Report on the Crimean Cemeteries*. Cd. 719. London: HMO.

Anderson, O. 1971. The growth of Christian militarism in mid-Victorian Britain in *The English Historical Review*.

Anon. 1857. Raising of the Russian War Vessels at Sebastopol. *New York Herald,* 3 March.

Anon. 1859a. Odessa Consular Despatch No. 4. 9 March, TNA: PRO FO 65/1508.

Anon. 1859b. Kerch Consular Despatch No. 64. 8 December, TNA: PRO FO 65/1508.

Anon. 1859c. Theodosia Consular Despatch No 19. 17 December, TNA: PRO FO 65/1508.

Anon. 1860a. The Graves at Sebastopol. *The Times*, 28 April.

Anon. 1860b. Sebastopol. *The Times*, 27 July.

Anon. 1861a. Sebastopol. *The Times*, 25 March

Anon. 1861b. The Crimean Graves. *The Times*, 2 June.

Anon. 1862. Ten Days in the Crimea. *Macmillan's Magazine*, February.

Anon. 1861c. The Tombs Before Sebastopol. *The Times*, 23 November.

Anon. 1867a. Editorial. *The Times*, 26 September.

Anon. 1867b. The British Burial-Grounds at Sebastopol. *The Times*, 3 October.

Anon. 1884. British Graves in the Crimea. *The Times*, 7 June.

Brackenbury, G. 1856. *The Campaign in the Crimea*. London: P. and D. Colnaghi.

Cavendish, F.W.H. 1913. *Society, Politics and Diplomacy 1820–1864: Passages from the Journal of Francis W. H. Cavendish*. London: T. Fisher Unwin.

Colborne, J. and Brine, F. 1856. *The Last of the Brave; or Resting Places of Our Fallen Heroes in the Crimea and at Scutari*. London.

Drew Gilpin Faust, C. 2008. *This Republic of Suffering*. New York: Knopf.

Figes, O. 2011. *The Crimean War: A History*. New York: Metropolitan Books.

Gillis, J. (ed.) 1994. *Commemorations: The Politics of National Identity*. Princeton: Princeton University Press.

Laqueur, T. 1994. Memory and Naming in the Great War, in Gillis, J. (ed.) 1994. *Commemorations: The Politics of National Identity*. Princeton: Princeton University Press.

Letter from Reverend Darling to Consul Murray. 2 February 1859, The National Archives (TNA): Public Record Office (PRO) FO 65/1508.

Marsh, C. 1856. *Memorials of Captain Hedley Vicars, Ninety-seventh Regiment*. London: Nisbet.

Montgomery, J. 1825. *The Christian Psalmist*. Glasgow: Chalmers and Collins.

Wills, G. 2006. *Lincoln at Gettysburg*. New York: Simon & Schuster.

Winter, J. 1998. *Sites of Memory, Sites of Mourning*. Cambridge: Cambridge University Press.

Ward, S.G.P. (ed.) 1970. *The Hawley Letters: The Letters of Captain R.B. Hawley, 89th from the Crimea, December 1854 to August 1856*. London: Gale and Ward for the Society for Army Historical Research.

Wolseley, G. 1882. *The Soldier's Pocket-Book for Field Service*. London: Macmillan and Co.

14

Contested Spaces: Invisible Architectures

Reenie (Karin) Elliott

INTRODUCTION

Accepting Bernard Tschumi's (1996: 100) statement that 'architecture is defined by the actions it witnesses as much as by the enclosure of its walls', the invisible architecture studio – a collaboration between students and architects at the University of Greenwich – sited design projects in the contested military and ex-military zones of three cities: Dunkirk, Berlin and Nicosia. Analytical drawings, imaginary spatial projections, irony and other forms of narrative, were deployed to investigate and respond to the ephemeral and invisible in the sequential occupation of these contested spaces, exploring their emerging social conditions and measuring the potential of such territories to define the developing city.

Dunkirk's Second World War beach bunkers and eighteenth-century batteries remain unoccupied, appearing as tilting ruins, decaying amongst the sand dunes. The territory has been declared a 'wildlife sanctuary' and a national museum. The future of the divided city of Nicosia, Cyprus, is currently being negotiated politically, with the opening up of border crossings, the dismantling of bridges and the return of an airport. Since the fall of the Berlin Wall in 1989, Berlin's 'No Man's Land' has been largely assimilated invisibly back into the city fabric via a series of urban design projects, despite some radical forms of urban life which flourished temporarily in the political and spatial void.

In these scenarios, the rhetoric of conflict resolution seeks either to fully conceal any physical and spatial reminders of the contested space, or to memorialise them. This has resulted in the colonisation of contested space by bland commercial programmes and structures: offices, malls and shopping, sprinkled with the occasional ill-defined 'democratic' public space and a handful of 'museums of tragedy' (see, for example, Phillips, 1997: 98, 212, 242). The official reclamation of 'No Man's Land' in Berlin, for instance, can be seen as a process of papering over the cracks, where the redeployment of military architecture is restricted to a series of museums, or else total erasure. Are these the only alternatives?

THE DESERT[ED] HOTEL, DUNKIRK

Just outside Dunkirk in northern France, in the early twenty-first century, we ask students to design a hotel on the site of a series of concrete bunkers built during the Second World War.

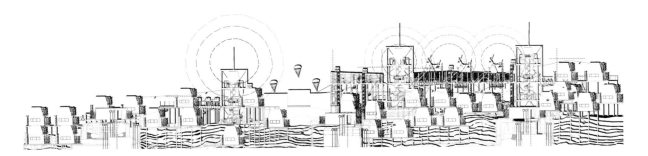

14.1   The Desert[ed] Hotel, Dunkirk.

Flanked by a ruined eighteenth-century military barracks, it's a contested territory that's been occupied by Belgian, French, German and British armies over time. Dunkirk, the last pocket of unoccupied territory as the Nazis advanced, saw the evacuation of 340,000 British troops in three weeks in 1941. We try to imagine the previous occupants of these spaces, French officers amidst chestnut horses burning fires at night, British foot soldiers waiting for boats to bring them home, Germans parachuting in from the sky or arriving in a panzer tank. Hours spent looking out to sea from a bunker: a vast expanse of landscape regulated by a crosshair target on the horizon, revealing the next chapter of your life. The site evokes a multiplicity of occupants, signs written in a cacophony of languages and architectures, violent but beautiful, impersonal yet intimate.

The manner of its historical occupation was not unlike the programme for a hotel. Absence follows bustling presence, follows absence again. The paths of movement inscribed in the project are derived from the military manoeuvres which took place on the site. When the visitor arrives at the hotel, they take the same path as the German tanks took when they commandeered the fortress. The rooms are positioned where the parachutists landed, randomly blown across the dunes by winds. The pathways to the rooms retrace the movement of the anti-aircraft guns. On the gun emplacements, guests dine and gaze at the horizon between sea and sky, mimicking the viewpoints of the gunners targeting this same vista. Barbeques replace exploding shells. War is replaced by play, but not forgotten. This is not a museum, a memorial or an evolving species of contested space. The Desert[ed] Hotel is a place to erase the past and create alternative futures, the replication of a game but with different rules. New sounds intrude upon the silence, it is a progressive shift from one reality to the other. The hotel is a dream, and a nightmare. In *Architecture and Disjunction*, Tschumi expands the modernist understanding of function and functionalism to encompass a broader sense of cultural purpose and temporal flux in terms of programming, de-programming and re-programming. These tactics are set against the modernist paradigm, in an attempt to redress the reductive aspects of technological determinism and notions of progress.

In one project, aircraft, salvaged from 'airplane graveyards', are recycled to construct The Desert[ed] Hotel. The hotel is a stage onto which contested space is projected, extending boundaries of event, communication, operation and visibility. Necessity gives way to luxury. The hotel speaks the language of machines, visible yet invisible. The hotel is a baroque tapestry of fictions in search of an author. As time passes, the occupants move on and are replaced by new occupants. Year upon year, the list of guests who stay at the hotel will get longer, one day the register will be lost, and with it the memory of the original occupants. The Desert[ed]

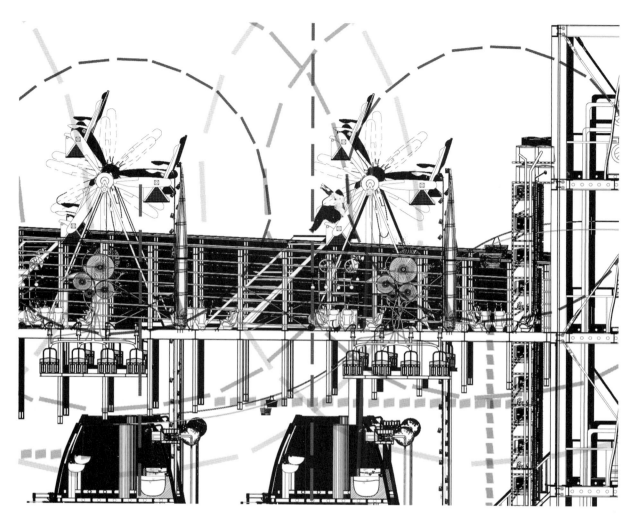

Hotel is composed of strange programmatic sequences: guests can dive into the fuselage of an airplane, attend a mechanised tea party, walk home along the sand dunes, or sleep on an airplane wing. This is neither a linear or a progressive sequence, determined by rational development. All space is contested by its occupants and future unpredictable generations of occupants.

14.2   War is replaced by play at the Desert[ed] Hotel, Dunkirk.

BERLIN: EXCURSIONS IN BLANK SPACE

The invisible architecture studio emerges during a journey through the former 'No Man's Land' in Berlin, an excursion in blank space. By making our observations and recording the current uses of previously inaccessible places, we developed an urban anthropology technique for invisible architectures, often using photographic evidence as a flawed record of social histories. For example, on inspecting the brick arches of a railway viaduct which crossed from East to

14.3 'Redirecting Light' across the border in No Man's Land, Berlin.

West Berlin, we observed bullet holes in the brickwork. These were evidence of the hundreds of people who we discovered had been shot at as they tried to escape into West Berlin from a hospital in the East. A series of mirrors was constructed to redirect light into the dark recesses of the railway viaduct, so that the bullet holes in the shadows would be made visible. New crossings were proposed at these junctures. A floating archive was launched. We set up a picnic (a space for repose) in this, one of the most contested spaces in Berlin. We deduce that 'contested space' could be projected and reflected, moulded and manipulated, contained and released, concealed and revealed, and transported across boundaries.

Such small acts of rebellion, as well as public moments of negotiation, were observed and recorded throughout 'No Man's Land'. Selected micro-spaces were documented. On our return, with 20 students engaged in the process, a full-scale city in a box was constructed: The Berlin Cube. This is the space for a three dimensional urban game of snakes and ladders, where restrictions, and means of escaping them, are inter-played. The means of escape were the elements of a typical Medieval German town: a bridge, a well, an inn, a dungeon, a stair, a maze and a ladder: we had managed to shrink the contested space that we had observed. An appearance of modernist simplicity and clarity of construction belied the true experience of the space and its structure. The lower storey was designed to be lower than the player would expect, and therefore claustrophobic. The circulation route through the structure was deliberately confusing, and difficult to negotiate. What you saw was not what you got. This ambiguity was intended to embrace the inclination towards propaganda in the architecture of contested space. The Berlin Cube, constructed as a mobile archive of such space, floated around Oxford during the summer of 2001. A yellow line (parking restriction) was redirected into the

14.4   The Berlin Cube (construction by Oxford Brookes University).

cube, re-programming it to become the route through the installation. Ironically, it became part of the Oxford City Tour upon its arrival at the Ashmolean Museum allowing contested space to expand further into a new, 'uncontested' host. The installation, by bringing its own restrictions and means of escape to Oxford, and interacting with new ones, suggested to its occupants that contested space is everywhere.

CYPRUS: THE HOUSE DIVIDED

The Buffer Zone is a residual military space between two ceasefire lines in the ancient walled city of Nicosia, delineating Greek Cyprus from the Occupied or Turkish Zone. The boundary infiltrates streets, walls, gardens and even domestic spaces. The emergence of invisible political boundaries has resulted in residual spaces and constructions, showing evidence of conflict and strange architectural collisions. We invited students to join an invisible architecture studio, to explore and draw the spatial conditions of the buffer zone, its observation posts, medieval fortifications and its contemporary United Nations monitored spaces. We invited them to imagine the ancient Greek rooftop festivals where boundaries dissolved and people merged in the moonlight. We asked them to distinguish between shared moments and situations, and the political. We asked them to act constructively rather than cynically.

   We set the students a project to design a theatre. The theatre was also a political allegory. It was a spectacle to be viewed from one side. However, a wholly different interpretation would emerge when it was viewed from the other side. The theatre programme allowed us to explore the uses of techniques such as realism, 'method acting', artifice and posturing, street theatre, 'theatre of the absurd', and 'les mystères'. These theoretical, theatrical positions were placed

14.5   Abandoned objects in the buffer zone of Nicosia.

among other urban design tools which came from understanding the site and its role as an everyday space for habitation, how it's used, and speculations as to what it might become.

Remembering the televised spectacle of the city's division, the theatre would operate as a microcosm of the city, consist of a stage set and an audience and become a form of exchange, a border crossing, a cultural exchange, but most importantly a spectacle. We discerned that the contested space here was subject to observation by multiple audiences and that the process of observation altered the operations and configuration of the contested space. But once the global audience lost interest in this war, the contested space froze. As the media spectacle vanished, the contested space stopped mutating. In this frozen contested space, redundant modernist master-plans were ditched in favour of observing micro-spaces of politeness, and the city retroactively re-structured around them. The observation of gestures, critical moments of negotiation and rebellion, became a strategy for development. But for all its politeness and amiable collisions, the contested space in Nicosia remained frozen. War and politeness made uncomfortable companions.

MEAT AND TWO VEG THEATRE

This 'theatrical landscape' is situated in the Buffer Zone a site is currently divided between Greek Cyprus to the south and the Turkish Occupied Territory to the north. The theatre of war has delineated that which is Turkish from that which is Greek along the Green Line, a ceasefire line within the city limits. But the line is actually a space with observation posts on either side of it, in a state of ceasefire for 35 years. The project imagines how exiled Cypriots will be re-housed in the Buffer Zone. Gun slots around the contested space frame a series of miniature theatres. Contested space is hereby fractured and fragmented. The appearance of any occupant could result in deadly gunfire. It is proposed to replace the guns with the accoutrements of a feast, a shared dining space, a public kitchen, and a vanishing banquet, stored in the observation posts atop the batteries of the Venetian fortifications.

Once the United Nations post has been vacated, vegetables are sent in from the gun slots on the Greek side to tables suspended over the space, where the banquet takes place. The trajectories of gunfire are replaced with slow moving tomatoes, courgettes and sumptuous olives. Market stalls with abundant produce set up below, while grapevines and lemon groves infiltrate the buffer zone. Ali the Greengrocer re-programmes US Big Dog quadruped robots to farm inaccessible spaces. Once the mines are cleared, he sends in robotic farmers to grow vegetables for the feast. Crops are watered using rotating irrigation arms emerging periodically from the observation posts. Remote harvesting techniques are employed. Remote controlled triggers signal the need for more provisions, the use of fertilizers, the dusting and spraying of crops, and harvesting. Sheep grazing on the ancient battlements are farmed by Mohammed the butcher, and sent across the ceasefire line for the annual feast. The Butchers' cleaver comes down on the sheep on the exact line of the border. Over time, the wall of blood in the housing/butchery will be drained. In its place will grow the richest of red flowers.

14.6   Pop up illuminated market and other landscapes subvert militaristic functions.

14.7   The butcher's shop: The knife comes down on the exact line of the border.

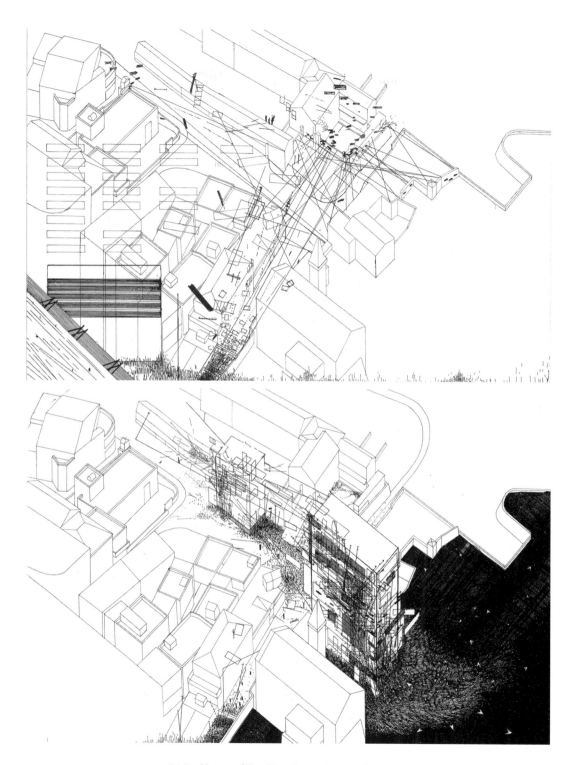

14.8   Meat and Two Veg: Gun trajectory drawings.

This theatrical landscape tampers with nature to create a spectacle and a shared space for people, plants, and animals. It is a place where people from both sides of the Buffer Zone can meet. The theatre re-programme the spaces and accoutrements of warfare with a more benign purpose, 'putting flowers in the barrel of guns' if you will. These 'Pop up landscapes' subvert militaristic functions to achieve an aesthetic purpose, sometimes comical but always eerily prescient. In their world, they explore modernist technologies over which our control has clearly lapsed. The consequences are exposed with wit and imagination. A lightning field, a faraday cage, or a storm can be created by tampering with nature, and yet so was the minefield. Through cloud seeding we may accelerate precipitation. By growing agricultural produce in a minefield, we risk flying figs and grain showers: occasionally a watermelon might explode. A hint of the invisible processes shaping our contested space is revealed: a temporary dining space exposes age-long tectonic plate shifts, a geographically advantageous site for observation. The structural core of a housing project is a wall of blood. Meat and vegetable market stalls are positioned in the strategic trajectories of gunfire. Dining tables are spectacles viewed from gun slots. In the aftermath of military operations, why not reconfigure a permanent housing project on the temporary barricades of the buffer zone? In the theatre of war, the vistas are considered with more care than those of many post-war housing developments.

In combining access to the remote and the everyday, the Meat and Two Veg theatre project unfolds with a rigour and internal logic that eventually challenges our sense of propriety. We are aware of the uncomfortable spatial proximity of meat and 'home' – why is meat transported through the housing project? This is coupled with our distaste at the 'wall of blood'. Nor is the replacement of idyllic rural farmers with US military robots and similar paraphernalia our idea of utopia. Yet the festival, the vegetation, the landscapes of light, and the market suggest real possibilities for shared space and communication in the contested zone. These are the messier strategies of war and reconciliation, not so distant from the rituals of everyday life – meat and two vegetables, the friendly greengrocers stall at the market, a shared dinner table. The 'last supper' space is never drawn, but only hinted at. Its absence refers to one of the most potent symbols of Christianity, anticipating a resurrection of the city. It is never drawn because it represents the acquisition of control by only one side in this sectarian battle. This would result in the loss of contested space, and its reversion to being *uncontested*, just an ordinary place.

THE APPARATUS OF DISAPPEARANCE

Among the ruins of the Venetian walls of Nicosia, you will find abandoned objects and spaces, 'the buffer zone cabinet', a disappearing kit, and many streets where every house is divided in two. You enter these houses from the Greek side, but when you enter their back gardens, you are in Turkey. Each house is a mirror of itself. In the Buffer Zone, doors have been blocked up to become walls and walls have been torn asunder to become doors. Washing machines, televisions, sofas and staircases migrate across the wild landscape of weeds and dust. A kitchen countertop jostles for space with doors and chairs in a spectacle of abandonment. This is another theatrical landscape in the contested space of Nicosia. It is a disintegrating cloth, worn through with holes: the fabric of the Buffer Zone. It is wrapped around the abandoned spaces and the mud buildings on the Turkish side of Paphos Gate. It is equipped with traps, decoys and escape routes, tunnels and mirrors, and is sewn with a silver thread. One strand of thread will

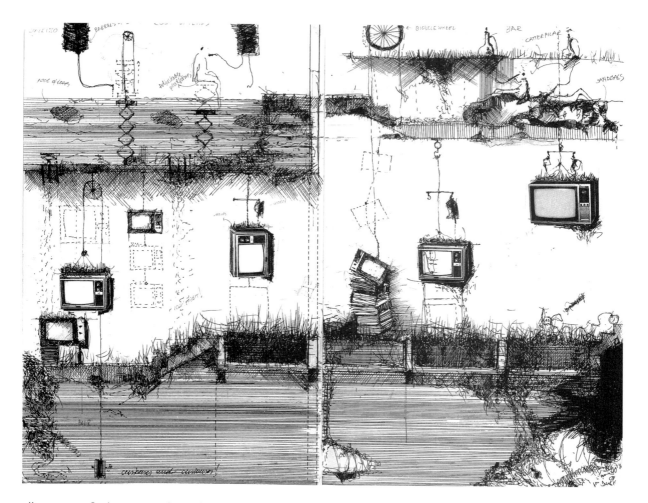

allow you to find your way through the labyrinth, to where you can disappear forever. Here are your instructions:

1. The rules of transformation (which tend to rely on devices) in rotation, reflection, projection and sliding.
2. How to use the television garden.
3. How to leave the pool of tears.
4. Tools for shrinking and stretching.
5. How to view the curiosities of the labyrinthine city.
6. The mobile UN tower and other magic tricks.
7. Sleight of hand, subversion and infiltration.
8. Conceptual tools in the theatre of war.
9. Border controls and buffer zones.
10. On the use of a depository for the divided house.
11. How to access the department of nostalgia.
12. Spaces to 'slip through' from one country to another.

14.9   In the Television Garden.

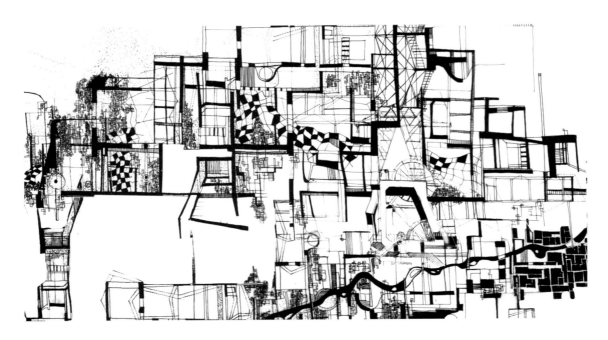

14.10   Magic Tricks Decoys and Traps.

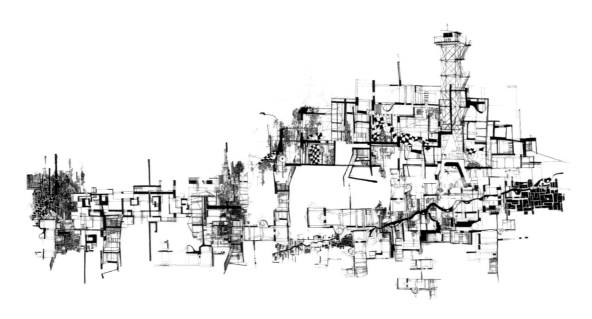

14.11   The Apparatus of Disappearance, Nicosia.

13. Tools for escape: stairs, chairs, ladders, tunnels, dugouts, gun slots and cups of tea.
14. Escaping to wonderland.
15. The public kitchen: a tale of subterfuge and marmalade.
16. Re-claiming wonderland: 70 cars in a bonded warehouse.
17. Re-using dismantled sandbags, barrels and washing machines.
18. Slipping into the buffer zone for a moment, you may find you can never leave contested space.

The theatre focuses on the nature of the Buffer Zone itself, which becomes the principal character in the performance. Rather than dealing with the tragic nature of this site and its history, in the tradition of magic realism this contested space is treated as an extraordinary and mysterious spectacle, a kind of 'wonderland' which, immersed in this confusion, plays the rational against the imaginary using architectural elements, objects, spaces, and geometries found in the Buffer Zone. Thus, those who have disappeared here during the last 35 years are merely the tools in a magic trick.

CONCLUSION

Enormous resources are invested each year in contested space and this has been the case for centuries. Architectural typologies for military control have developed, refinements have been made, and tools have emerged. Architecture has always been a powerful tool in war, social control, and the imposition of orders and hierarchies. No one would dispute that a wall can act as a form of exclusion or containment, defining the edges of contested space, reinforcing social divisions and separating communities. The watchtower is also clearly identifiable as another architectural device providing effective control over contested space. Yet most architects claim that architecture has no part to play in the arena of conflict resolution, or in the salvaging of community relations, or in the pursuit of social cohesion in contested space. Surely architectural typologies exist which can be used as tools to enhance communication in contested spaces? One thinks not only of bridges and tunnels, but also of marketplaces, cafés, streets and public squares. Or the street feasts held in London after the end of the Second World War to welcome the children home from their evacuation and other architectures of event. There is little research in this area of architectural and urban design. There is always more enthusiasm for the acquisition of control than there is for relinquishing it.

The invisible architecture studio has the tendency to cling to contested space. We are enthralled by its baroque tapestry, embroidering it with fictions, museums and memories as at The Desert[ed] Hotel. We like to manipulate, project and reflect contested space, as in The Berlin Cube project, concealing and releasing it as we transpose it across cultural boundaries. We like to expand and shrink it, and take home a specimen. We can also freeze contested space, thereby trapping, fragmenting and replicating it, and observing it for an eternity, as in the Nicosia projects. In doing so, we can see our image reflected and disappearing within it, and we lose the rational in discovering the imaginary. And then one day it melts and vanishes with us, and transforms itself back into 'uncontested space', once all memories of it are forgotten.

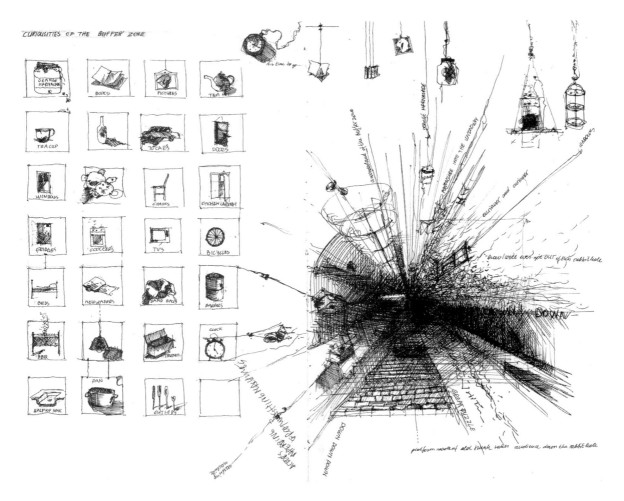

14.12 A Typology of Objects found in Contested Space or The Buffer Zone Cabinet.

ACKNOWLEDGEMENTS

With special thanks to: Stephanie Bahr, Mohammed Ennayet., Anam Hasan, Rasa Karuseviciene, Lina Lahiri, and Ali Qureshi whose projects are represented here (see *iNViSiBLe_architecture* weblink).

REFERENCES

Colomina, B. and Tschumi, B. 2005. Contested Territories, lecture at Tate Modern, London.

Deleuze, G. and Guattari, F. 1986. *Nomadology: The War Machine*. New York: Semiotexte.

Gregory, D. 2010. The City as Target, keynote speech at War + Architecture & Space, conference. Cork: University College Cork, September.

Gregory, D. The City-as-Target. Available at: http://web.mac.com/derekgregory/iWeb/Site/The%20city-as-target.html

Jones, S. 2000. *Darwin's Ghost: The Origin of the Species Updated*. New York: Random House.

Phillips, D. 1997. *Berlin: A Guidebook to Recent Architecture*. London: Ellipsis.

Tschumi, B. 1996. *Architecture and Disjunction*. Cambridge, MA: MIT Press.

Virilio, P. 1994. *Bunker Archaeology*. New York: Princeton Architectural Press.

15

Sketches of War: The Graveyards of Historical Memory

Jonathan Charley

TRYING TO REMEMBER

The need to objectify the memory of war and tragedy is a survival mechanism by which we distance the overwhelming reality that the history of civilisation is shadowed by barbarism. We feel obliged to build memorials, erect plaques, and preserve the remains of brutal episodes in which the act of remembrance is also a desire to forget. To be haunted on a daily basis by the knowledge that the history of capitalism is a history of conquest, enslavement, robbery, and murder is psychologically ruinous (Marx 1976: 874). Equally traumatic is the antithetical history of architecture as a *Natural History of Destruction* (Sebald 2004: 153).

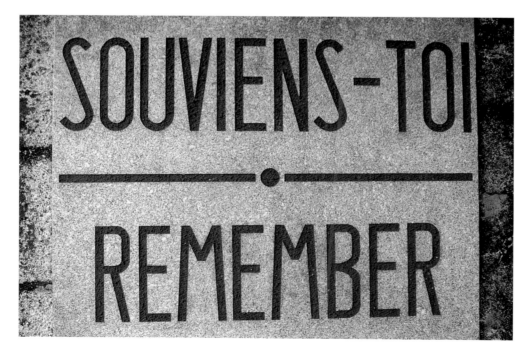

15.1   Entrance plaque to the memorial village, Oradour-sur-Glane, France.

One of my earliest architectural memories is of my family's hometown Plymouth. To the east of the bright new city centre planned by Patrick Abercrombie is located the Charles Church. It was left in ruins after 1945 as a permanent reminder of the 59 bombing raids that virtually destroyed the city. This physical expression of the relationship between 'hope in the future' and the 'memory of tragedy' was confusing as a child and remains difficult to resolve. This is why faced with the prospect of total historical amnesia philosophers asked three questions: 'Can there be poetry after Auschwitz? How do we address the fact that the curse of irresistible progress is irresistible regression?' (Adorno and Horkheimer 1989: 36). And how do we deal with the knowledge that the state of emergency in which we live is not the exception but the rule? (Benjamin 1969: 256–7). Two decades before in 1918 Kropp and Müller are talking in the German trenches:

"Albert, what would you do if all of a sudden it was peacetime?"
"There's no such thing as peacetime", replies Albert curtly (Remarque 1996).

WORD WAR

Albert was of course correct. I decided to construct a literary war machine to help me understand how this came to pass. The result was a formidable army. In the historical and theoretical frontline, I positioned Marx, Mandel, De Landa, Deleuze, Guattari, Virilio, Baudrillard, and Davis who were equipped with powerful narrative weapons on everything from the Permanent Arms Economy, to The Intelligent War Machine, Nomadology, and Urban Class War. The novels of Sebald, Mailer, Vonnegut, Heller, and Levi were evenly distributed to add polish, finesse and a

15.2 Gun shop in central Bucharest.

different sort of gravitas so that like soldiers and ordnance prior to conflict, the final assembly was spic, span, and ready for a photo shoot. I think about firing an opening salvo of anti-war poems by Sassoon and Owen, but instead I load the literary war machine with its first missile, Dwight D. Eisenhower's valedictory speech in 1961. 'My fellow Americans, we are compelled to create a permanent armaments industry of vast proportions'.

The cumulative power of such writings underline what we, like Albert already know. Far from being an aberration or an exception, war in all of its transferable configurations is ubiquitous. It permeates our everyday lives and built environment. Conquest breeds the privatisation of urban space; technological exchange permits the mass production of bombs and buildings; reconnaissance merges with civilian surveillance; and the fortress is reborn as the fortified condominium. If anything a non-militarised society at peace with itself and others, and the corollary, a peacetime city, would be the greatest departure from the social and economic reality of capitalist societies. In 1949, to commemorate this state of affairs, the Ministry of Truth declared that War was in fact Peace, and that cinemas should only show films of dismembered enemies.[1]

ANECDOTAL WAR DATES

In 1945, the Corporation of the City of Glasgow published a planning report (Bruce, 1947). Armed with benevolent zealotry, Robert Bruce described his plan to consign urban poverty, cholera, and unsanitary dwellings to history. The remedy was as simple as severing a gangrenous leg; the demolition of 95 percent of the Victorian City. Away with the marbled interiors of the City Chambers. Away with Greek Thomson and Macintosh. Away with it all, done in the name of the people. Out of the grimy ruins of the nineteenth century would rise a glittering collage of the Ville Radieuse, Broadacre City and other modern utopias. A cynic could be heard muttering on the backbench of the debating chamber:

> You see, what the Luftwaffe began, the urban planners will now complete. A timely trick of fate of which Napoleon's Baron von Haussmann would have been proud. Bulldoze the past as Aldous Huxley recommends, and in so doing conveniently relocate a potentially insurgent population to the periphery. "Job done", as they say. Job done.

In 1909, *Le Figaro* published the Futurist Manifesto for a new art and architecture. 'War is the world's only hygiene', Marinetti screamed. In his rabid imagination the Futurist city would be forged out of a toxic cocktail of militarism, patriotism and misogyny. Nothing was sacred, and if plans required the destruction of museums, academies and libraries, then so be it. 'Take up your pickaxes, your axes and hammers and wreck, wreck the venerable city, pitilessly' (Marinetti in Harrison and Wood 1993: 145–9).

In 1872, a year after the defeat of the Paris Commune, Zola published *The Kill* (*La Curée*). Saccard is looking out over Haussmann's boulevards and explaining to his wife Angele, the way in which necessary infrastructural improvement could help prevent proletarian insurrection.

> There it is laid out before us. Nothing could be simpler. "Paris slashed with sabre cuts, its veins opened, providing a living for a hundred thousand navvies and bricklayers, traversed by splendid military roads which will bring forts into the heart of the old neighbourhoods" (2008: 69).

15.3   Commemorative bullet holes in Berlin.

Somewhere, no doubt in a dusty cellar, an archivist catalogues the historical evidence of urbicide. He has been at it for centuries, but today his head is throbbing in an alarming manner as he finds it increasingly difficult to distinguish between the destructive tendencies of capitalist urban development and the retribution meted out by vengeful armies.

Accumulation by Dispossession

At the turn of the sixteenth century after the departure of the last Emir from Granada, pyromaniac ancestors of the Italian Futurists like Ferdinand II and the Grand Inquisitor Francisco de Cisneros, were still lighting ritual bonfires of Arabic texts in an effort to purify Spain and remove the traces of the scholarly traditions of the once great Islamic libraries. Meanwhile European philosophers and scientists were preparing an economic and philosophical revolution in which democratic reason would be merged with primitive capital accumulation. Rooted in the violent dispossession of others, maps became more valuable than gold, and in a stroke of malevolent cartographic genius the conquistadors and bandits of rival empires simply wrote, 'terra incognita' and 'terra inhabitus'. Court and ecclesiastical historians of the ancient world confirmed that these new lands bore no trace of civilisation.

A few centuries later the Frankfurt School assured us that since enlightenment had relinquished its own realisation and knowledge had abandoned truth, such prejudices would multiply and remain a permanent feature of everyday life.[2] Long before that Goethe's Gabriel warned us, 'paradisal brightness must swap with dreadful night'. So it was in the very heart of such a darkness that Leopold the Second's Palace of Justice was built whilst votes were denied to Belgian miners and his butcher mercenaries amputated the hands of recalcitrant Africans.

15.4 Abandoned croft on the Ardnamurchan peninsula, Scotland.

So it was that '*Liberté, Egalité* and *Fraternité*' that was etched into institutions devoted to law and money from Brussels to Paris did not extend to the revolutionaries on St. Domingue whose leader Toussaint L'Ouverture died in the Fort de Joux Prison.

And so it is that a ruined croft nestles into the west coast of Scotland and a mildewed stone fort perches on the coast of Brasil. They sit unhappily in landscapes whose picturesque qualities belie the fact that they have born witness to too much violence and hunger. Remotely located, there is only the occasional walker who stumbles by and momentarily glances at the fading structures, unaware that they can be read as memorials to the violent expropriation of the agricultural producer from the soil. At least that is what I saw. Piles of innocent stones that can tell a story, if you let them, about the unleashing of a class and racial warfare that destroyed the last traces of the ancient commune and turned the Highland and African farmer into landless wage labourers and slaves.

Cleared from the Glens by mercenaries wielding guns and fictitious legal documents and maps – tactics developed during the enclosure of common lands in England and perfected in imperial land grabs – for many highlanders there was only one option, emigration. Voyages away on the other side of the Atlantic whilst walking up the coast of Bahia, I remembered a documentary about slaving forts on the West African coast. It struck me as I looked back up the hill from the beach towards the arched doorway of a slave fort, that if you drew a line east from the entrance it would connect directly with the corridor of 'no return' at the Fort Elmina in Ghana, a tunnel of unimaginable misery that led straight out into the ocean. Taking photographs in such places feels reprehensible, a little like posing for a fashion shot amongst the broken headstones of the Jewish cemetery in Budapest. But that is what we do in order that moments of tragedy become postcards of our time, pretty pictures of flickering palmed sun and elegiac moor. Something for the flâneur to send home.

MILITARY VERNACULAR

We visit the camps, the cemeteries, the cells, and the war museums. We try to get a grip on how it is that the human brain can inflict misery and suffering with such imagination, and how it is that the scientific and architectural history of war, violence and punishment is as rich and ingenious as its antithesis. By reflex the camera shutter snaps the macabre landscapes, the painful machinery and the hostile buildings. This type of photography is therapeutic protection. Objectified in image form the historical event is distanced, somehow easier to handle. It is a dangerous game. Without an historical caption the surgery in Sachsenhausen concentration camp looks like any other white ceramic tiled laboratory. Without a caption the strange geometric turfed hillocks around Garelochead could be mistaken for the sculpted slag heap of a closed coal pit rather than the roofs of weapon's silos. Other structures from the history of human conflict are easier to deal with particularly those that technological revolutions in weaponry have rendered useless and transformed into photogenic monuments. A favourite for the 'war' tourist are the 'Expressionist' bunkers of the Atlantic Wall built by the Nazis that Virilio (1994) documented with the care of an archaeologist and which Ballard imagined as cryptic space age cathedrals designed to last a thousand years (2006: 14 and Hirst 2005: 211).

Not surprisingly for an island nation, the British coastline is a treasure trove for the military rambler. You can begin a tour with a visit to the Martello towers, the Napoleonic era fortifications that dot the coastline from Suffolk to Sussex and look like giant up-turned buckets. Some lie in ruins but others have been converted into homes and arts centres. Then there are the 28,000 Second World War pillboxes which, like the Martello Towers, have a website that maps them as a series of walks. On a tour of the military architecture of Fife in East Scotland I calculated that there were four generic types. Type One nestles on the beachhead. It is the first line of defence and is of the troglodyte variety. Carved straight into the cliff face, the front wall is built out of stone. Type Two sits amongst rocks on the headland. Constructed with stonewalls and reinforced concrete roof, it cannot make up its mind whether it should be

15.5   Type 4 Second World War bunker, Fife, Scotland.

hidden or exposed. Type Three is resolutely aggressive. Situated on top of the cliff and built out of cast in situ reinforced concrete, it is resilient enough to withstand incoming gunfire but not soil erosion. Type Four made of pink fletton brick capped with a concrete roof lies inland. Slowly enveloped by greenery, in time it will become indistinguishable from a funereal cairn. In the meantime, the pillbox doubles up as animal pen, homeless shelter, birdwatcher's hut and teenage hangout.

THE MACHINIC PHYLUM

Four thousand miles east on the same latitude as Glasgow, 56 degrees north, I spent weeks on end wandering through Moscow's concrete panelled housing estates – those that increase in density, height and territorial size as you move outwards from the centre to the periphery. In the rain soaked autumnal skies they stand erect like the totemic stones of long gone Neolithic societies. In brilliant sunshine they resemble a legion of alien machines. In reality the pre-fabrication of such vast quantities of housing is a monument to the victory of an economic and technological determinism that gripped the imagination of planners in both East and West. In the Soviet Union giant house-building combines – *domo-stroitelniyi kombinati* (DSK) – were to be the engine of this urban revolution that stretched from Berlin to Vladivostok. Staffed by anything up to 20,000 employees, workers were organised in cadres and brigades, largely replicating the centralised and concentrated power hierarchies of old school military structures. For nearly 40 years, without a pause, the DSK churned out concrete panels at the same speed as arms.

Soviet military planners and architect-engineers like their counterparts in the West had shared dreams. Employing similar materials, resources and machinery, the technocratic

15.6 Housing Estate, East Berlin.

imagination aspired to produce both weapons and buildings in automated processes that dispensed with human labour. Fast moving assembly lines would solve the housing crisis and transform building workers from 'manual combatants' to 'thinker creators'. Meanwhile in towns without grid references, scientists and engineers dreamt of the robotic production of smart weapons that eliminated the need for humans from both the factory and the battlefield. Any chance to minimise risk and uncertainty associated with combat-industrial labour must be grabbed. Work tools, weapons and the factory and military discipline of labour would become slowly indistinguishable from each other as if the same machinic phylum traversed both (Deleuze and Guattari 1996: 395).

The factory that produces cannons can also fabricate steel lintels. The first tanks and trams shared engines and tracks. The light bulb is pointed down to illuminate the street and up to spot aircraft. In 1906, Étienne Jules Marey invents the chrono-photographic rifle by merging the mechanics of 'repeater guns and repeater photography' (Virilio 1989: 96). Meanwhile on the building site, pneumatic drills and riveting guns gave birth to the Hilti Gun, laser guided drills and saws. There is, in fact, a constant traffic and transfer of materials, mechanical and 'dromological' technologies from one sphere of production into another. Speed of assembly, accuracy, efficiency, increasing lightness and mobility are of critical importance to both military and construction planners. The graphite bomb replaces the megaton bomb. The lightweight interactive façade replaces the heavy concrete panel.

PERMANENT ARMS ECONOMY IN MOSCOW

But new technology is useless without the right kind of organisation and planning. Tactics, strategy and logistics, are employed in both the War Machine and the Construction Industry to

15.7   Seventieth anniversary of Russian Revolution, Moscow.

extract some semblance of order out of the chaos and irrationality of both armed combat and building production, regardless of whether they are driven by the profit targets of capitalist firms or the plan targets of the State.[3] It is a vain exercise. One of the lessons from Mailer's *The Naked and the Dead* is that the only thing that could be organised with any real military precision were the folded tent flaps, duckboards and officers mess, none of which survived the first heavy rains. Similarly, for all the attempts to control what Marx and Engels called the 'anarchy' of capitalist production (Engels 1978: 331–9) and Schumpeter, the 'perennial gale of creative destruction' (2010: 70), the construction industry can no more escape economic crisis than General Cummings the unpredictable outcomes of jungle warfare.

So it was on returning from photographing the concrete panels of 24-storey tower blocks that I stood on a city centre Moscow street watching the SS20 missiles trundle past in celebration of the seventieth anniversary of the 1917 revolution. Spectators applauded with the same enthusiasm that they had once reserved for the miracle of hot water and modern domestic plumbing. By the early 1970s armament and military expenditure had become a permanent feature of the economic and political life of advanced industrial societies (Mandel 1999: 274). It was a military industrial alliance in which the mass production of the means of production and consumer goods was joined at the hip to the mass production of the means of destruction; a merging of the Welfare and Warfare State in which an administered population enjoyed improved living standards under the threat of annihilation (Marcuse 1986: 19). At the very moment when the British Prime Minister Harold Wilson was announcing that future prosperity would lie in the white heat of a scientific and technological revolution, it is estimated that the production of weapons 'amounted to nearly a half of gross investments the world over' (Mandel 1999: 275). By 1989, at the zenith of the 'total' industrialisation of the Soviet building industry, military expenditure stood at almost a third of GDP. It was the permanent arms economy par excellence that within two years had collapsed.

SECRET BUNKERS

It is probably difficult for people born after 1980 to understand the intense fear that periodically gripped the popular imagination after the bombing of Hiroshima and Nagasaki and the division of Europe into rival armed economies. I was three during the Cuban missile crisis and grew up in a generation for whom nuclear annihilation was not so much a distant possibility as a distinct probability. It was a culture of fear that spawned a mutant architecture devoted to secret weapons' development and underground seats of government such that in the event of a mushroom cloud some semblance of warrior life would continue. W.G Sebald described visiting an example of the former, the pagoda ruins on the isolated pebble beach at Orfordness that resembled a far eastern penal colony and where boffins dabbled in unspeakable forms of murder (Sebald 2002: 233). I went to an example of the latter madness, the Secret Control Bunker in Scotland built in the 1950s deep in the bowels of the earth where retaliatory orders would be given and martial law organised.

For some reason I imagined it as a facsimile of a rural village, a quaint reminder of a lost idyll that would help survivors cope with their underground incarceration. Accordingly I expected a cobbled street, a pub, a village church, post office, tartan wallpaper and maybe even a Macintosh tearoom. At ground level there is nothing to tell you about what lies underneath the grazing cows that wander around what looks like a farmhouse. But inside the gift shop at the front

15.8 Access corridor, Secret Bunker, Fife, Scotland.

door, a lift and then a steeply descending corridor take you down into a cavernous concrete mausoleum. The stench of unventilated claustrophobia hits the senses hard and reminded me of crawling along the passage to the inner chamber of the Great Pyramid of Khufu. In the event of nuclear war you might have acclimatised to the petrified atmosphere. But you would have remained lost in time and space, an increasingly rickety survival prisoner in permanent solitary confinement trying to smile in a spartan interior of insipid institutional paint that stinks of boiled cabbage.

Two floors, two corridors with rooms of varying sizes to either side, barrack bunk bedrooms, closets jammed with communications gadgetry, a decrepit theatre of operations which had none of the panache of Spectre's control centre, a pathetic box chapel, the one concession to the spiritual world, and the one concession to peace, a sad CND exhibition. We can be sure that our rulers are still planning for a subterranean escape in the event of Armageddon. They have always invested heavily in tunnels, hidden cellars and camouflaged escape routes. The difference nowadays is that so can we. For a few thousand quid you too can build yourself a bunker and stockpile cans of food and toilet chemicals. It is tempting to think that this abject fear of annihilation is mis-placed. Equally, it is tempting to think of the Secret Bunker as a dead world of dead time, a stuffed dummy reinforced by antiquated computer technology and the spectres of Woodbine smoking grey-blue uniforms. Like most historical theme parks, it presents the past as a crazed curiosity shop. The reality however, is that the ideological conflict that generated such paranoid architecture has not disappeared; it has simply been transformed and retargeted. This is not a place to dwell and I am glad that I would have been incinerated in the first seconds.

PICTURESQUE WARS IN MECHELEN AND ORADOUR-SUR-GLANE

I was participating in a workshop in Belgium on architectural memorials. Screwed to the yellow brick of the former Dossin barracks in Mechelen, there is a plaque that commemorates the

15.9   The 'high street' in Oradour-sur-Glane, France.

24,461 Jews who were deported from here to the German camps. In the basement of the four-storey block there is a museum founded in 1995 that documents some of the atrocities. It features harrowingly familiar black and white photographs of smiling victims snapped on summer days before the end. Alongside hang images of messianic Belgian Nazis, convinced that they were acting according to the laws of nature and history.[4] Inside the street level courtyard where prisoners were assembled, there is a garden with rose bushes, flowerbeds and trees. But this is not a garden of remembrance; it is a park for the residents who bought flats when the barracks were converted into accommodation, and who clearly do not believe in history's ghosts. Nothing I fear could be built or constructed to alter that. Maybe the barracks should have been left as a ruin, given over to nature and left to sleep. My only thought was to leave a placard on a piece of wood with the words, 'Nobody lives here'.

In contrast, the preserved in aspic village of Oradour-sur-Glane is uninhabited by the living. This is where the SS division *Der Führer* used a church as an oven to cook all the women and children. I had a horrible feeling that I was looking through the camera viewfinder at a film set composed of ruined yellow stonewalls, wired 1940s telegraph poles, abandoned cars and swaying sycamores. Birdsong was the only thing to break the silence. Kurt reminds me that this is to be expected. He says 'everything is supposed to be very quiet after a massacre, and it always is, except for the birds' (Vonnegut 2000: 14). I looked at the groups of bored school children being marched around and told stories of unspeakable horror. I wondered what they made of it? Did they think they were extras in a war film?

Theatrical Operations at Breedonk

I took a bus to Breedonk Fort which functioned as a prison and interrogation centre for Jews, political prisoners and resistance fighters. It was a brilliant winter day, perfect for taking

15.10 Entrance
to Breedonk
Fort, Belgium.

voyeuristic photographs of the traces of monsters that capture little but the rather kitsch and theatrical character of such places. Reality is suspended. Breedonk becomes a twisted theme park or a ready stage set for warped thespians. After all they speak of the Theatre of Operations and the Theatre of War. This was on my mind as I walked past the mannequin entrance guards standing in glass cases and the polished SS insignia in the mess room. The feeling of the inappropriate nature of this type of 'atrocity exhibition' deepened as I walked along the labyrinthine corridors, stopping to smell a musty cell, to stare at the butcher's hook from which prisoners were suspended, and to gawp at fetishised artefacts that masquerade as art installations.

No amount of facsimile can convey the reality of terror. The most frightening thing in the Stasi headquarters in Berlin is not the rubber-water torture chamber. It is the thoroughly mundane interview rooms that in their bureaucratic ordinariness reinforce Hannah Arendt's (1963) argument about the banality of evil. Like Walter Sebald, I trod around the perimeter of Breedonk trying to grasp exactly what part of the human imagination could have conceived, planned and built such a '… monstrous incarnation of ugliness and blind violence …'. A structure that seems disconnected from 'anything shaped by human civilisation, or even the silent relics of our prehistory' (Sebald 2001: 25).

But Breedonk is not exceptional. It is a footnote to the modern history of carceral architecture. This begins with the panopticon and continues to the ugly and disconnected warehouse prisons, barbed refugee centres, and labour camps of the twenty first century. It represents an unbroken linear history of the human imagination hard at work adapting the accumulated knowledge of how to instil terror. I remembered Goldstein who seemed to speak not just for Jews but for everyone:

> *No sacrifices were paid, no lessons were learned. It was all thrown away, all statistics in the*
> *cruel wastes of history. All the ghettoes, all the soul cripplings, all the massacres and pogroms,*

*the gas chambers, lime kilns – all of it touched no one, all of it was lost … There was nothing
in him at the moment, nothing but a vague anger, a deep resentment, and the origins of vast
hopelessness (Mailer 2006: 679).*

Clean Wars in Belgrade

*All of a sudden, between one and two in the morning, an almighty explosion shook Belgrade's
houses to their very foundations so that every window in every house from Dorcol to Cubura
was obliterated. A terrible panic gripped the civilians of Belgrade who had no idea what had
happened (Glenny 1999: 312).*

It was in fact a Serbian commander blowing up a bridge across the Sava to halt the advance of the
Austrians, who undeterred launched an artillery attack on the centre of Belgrade. It was similar
to the stories I had heard of the NATO bombardment that had started with incomprehension as
to how they could be attacking a Central European capital. In a German prisoner of war camp
Edgar Derby imagines a letter written to his wife: 'We are leaving for Dresden today. Don't worry
it will never be bombed' (Vonnegut 2000: 107). So thought Sasha and Mika on their way home
through central Belgrade. The sirens are wailing, but they surely wouldn't dare, and if they did
well, perhaps it won't be so bad. After all, computer video propaganda shows that the era of
indiscriminate carpet bombing has ended and a new type of warfare has begun – war in which
'strategic targets' can be bombed with spectacular accuracy.

The order was given and missiles slammed into the Ministry of Internal Affairs, the Ministry
of Justice and the Yugoslav Army HQ on Kneza Milosa. It was part of a ferocious NATO aerial
attack across the country that killed hundreds of civilians. In Belgrade alone, school buildings
were damaged, a hospital hit, and fires burned in a gynaecological clinic and a psychological
hospital. But the NATO press office had nothing to worry about for they have at their disposal a

15.11   Anti-War
camp opposite
the Houses of
Parliament,
London.

rich linguistic arsenal with which to camouflage such 'unfortunate incidents'; collateral damage; peacekeeping; friendly fire; operational security; legitimate target; false allegation and so on.

The information war had been launched with full force. It was after all a 'clean' war even though the idea of clean war, like that of a clean bomb or an intelligent missile is a sure sign of madness. Which is why the media resort to fables and just as in the mythological manned mission to Mars of Capricorn One, 'the day there is a real war you will not be able to tell the difference' (Baudrillard 2009: 43–59). There was no mainstream news of the curious lightning balls and exploding BLU-114/B graphite bombs that spread extremely fine carbon wires over electrical components. Seventy per cent of Serbia's power grid short-circuited. Amnesty subsequently found evidence of highly toxic and carcinogenic residues that could only have come from 'imaginary' depleted Uranium ordnance. In the 'hysterical trompe l'oeil' of carefully selected images pumped out by Western media there were no pictures of this dirty war or the environmental catastrophe at Pancevo 17 kilometres outside Belgrade where the Petro-chemical plant was destroyed. For days the smoking buildings emitted black and white clouds of a highly toxic mixture of ammonia, crude oil, liquid chlorine, hydrochloric acid and mercury that settled on the town and the surrounding fields and induced bursts of black rain. The costs to civilians of these poisonous winds and precipitation are incalculable.

In contrast, the reconstruction loans organised by the IMF and the World Bank to help the country back on its feet were easy to work out. As in previous military conflicts such as Vietnam and Iraq these loans were tagged to highly lucrative financial contracts with construction firms from approved NATO countries, amongst them Brown and Root a specialist in the construction of infrastructure and a subsidiary of ex-Vice President Dick Cheney's Halliburton group.

TOTAL WAR ON CIVILIANS

Twenty-five years ago I was stopped and questioned by police for walking along the pavements in Beverley hills. Perhaps because there was no-one else walking. Perhaps because I was taking photographs of signs normally reserved for covert military installations that had been domesticated on the front gates of a Tudor mansion: 'Warning, Approach with Caution. Armed Response'. Since then the City of Fear has been exported worldwide (Virilio 2005: 91). As dangerous as any contagious illness, the middle class in particular has been gripped by a form of siege psychosis. If it were a B-movie it would be listed as 'The Return of The City State – a paranoid fantasy in which your darkest fears of barbarian proletarians scaling the city walls and battering the gates come horribly true'.

All sense of perspective is lost in a very old fashioned way, a real and tangible fear of any 'other'. They can't head for the hills, so they head for real estate supplements that advertise *gulag* luxury towers in sparkling technicolour. In Moscow they want to build a totally sealed dome to protect inhabitants from all possible encounters with aliens. Ballard promises civil war. In Brasil they go straight for the heart. 'Come live in Liberty', the slogan says, 'Peace of mind for you and your family'. Helipads, crenellated walls, spiked fences, searchlights, cameras, and private security forces keep the home under observation. As well they might since many of the towers are nestled between favellas in which a different form of armed combat takes place – gangster against gangster, gangster against the police, gangsters armed not just with guns but hand held missile launchers with telescopic lenses and digital film recorders.

15.12   City Centre communication's tower, Bucharest.

Everything is held in camera by both sides. This reflects the fact that the science and techniques of both cinema and war – optics, cameras, screens, lights, tracking, mapping, reconnaissance, and shifting fields of perception and representation – are now fully employed in the contemporary city (Virilio 1989: 86). The merging of the audio-visual technologies and tactics of the modern war machine with urban life has helped create a 'martial landscape', a 'softly' militarised city that speaks of the archi-semiotics of class war (Davis 1990: 223). This is a price we seem willing to pay for the illusion of peace and security. And it is an illusion in which ideological deception and the mangling of a coherent sense of reality by the weapons of mass communication is essential to mask the reality of war and to convince us that living in a civilian maximum-security jail will conquer fear. As Virilio suggests:

> Full-scale annihilation of the sense of reality in which the weapon of mass communication is strategically superior to the weapon of mass destruction, whether atomic, chemical or bacteriological (2005: 34).

(To be continued …)

NOTES

1   This is of course a reference to George Orwell's novel *1984*, and his depiction of a society permanently at war governed by the omnipotent Ministry of Truth that declares 'War is Peace, freedom is slavery, ignorance is strength'.

2   For the theorists of the Frankfurt School, notably Adorno, Horkheimer and Marcuse, the fusion of rationality with the priorities of a capitalist commodity economy had transformed reason or rather 'rational thought' into a form of essentially violent instrumental rationality, such that: 'With the

abandonment of thought, which in its reified form of mathematics, machine, and organisation avenges itself on the men who have forgotten it, enlightenment has relinquished its own realisation' (Adorno and Horkheimer 1989: 41).

3   For De Landa, the machinic phylum runs through out natural and human history and refers to any process in which order emerges out of disorder. The War Machine understood as the historical accumulation of military knowledge and practice strives to produce order and discipline out of chaos (2001: 20).

4   In her discussion on ideology and terror in totalitarian dictatorships Arendt comments that: 'The rulers themselves do not claim to be just or wise, but only to execute historical and natural laws; they do not apply laws but execute a movement in accordance with its inherent law. Terror is lawfulness, if law is the law of the movement of some suprahuman force, Nature or History' (1976: 464).

REFERENCES

Adorno, T. and Horkheimer, M. 1989. *The Dialectic of the Enlightenment*. London: Verso.

Arendt, H. 1976. *The Origins of Totalitarianism*. New York: Harvest.

Arendt, H. 1963. *Eichmann in Jerusalem: A Report on the Banality of Evil*. London Faber and Faber.

Ballard, J.G. 2006. *The Atrocity Exhibition*. London: Harper Perennial.

Baudrillard, J. 2009. *The Gulf War Did Not Take Place*. Sydney: Power Publications.

Benjamin, W. 1969. *Illuminations*. New York: Shocken.

Bevan, R. 2006. *The Destruction of Memory: Architecture at War*. London: Reaktion.

Bruce, R. 1947. *First Planning Report to the Highways and Planning Committee of the Corporation of Glasgow*, Glasgow, Second Edition.

Davis, M. 1990. *City of Quartz: Excavating the Future in Los Angeles*. London: Verso.

De Landa, M. 2001. *War in the Age of Intelligent Machines*. New York: Zone Books.

Deleuze, G. and Guattari, F. 1996. *A Thousand Plateaus – Capitalism and Schizophrenia*. Minneapolis, MN: Athlone Press.

Engels, F. 1978. *Anti-Dühring*. Moscow: Progress Publishers.

Glenny, M. 1999. *The Balkans: Nationalism, War and the Great Powers, 1804–1999*. London: Penguin Books.

Harrison, C. and Wood, P. (eds). 1993. *Art in Theory, 1900–1990: An Anthology of Changing Ideas*. London: Blackwell.

Heller, J. 1996. *Catch 22*. New York: Simon and Schuster.

Hirst, P. 2005. *Space and Power-Politics, War and Architecture*. Cambridge: Polity.

Mailer, N. 2006. *The Naked and the Dead*. London: Harper Perennial.

Mandel, E. 1999. *Late Capitalism*. London: Verso.

Marcuse, H. 1986. *One-Dimensional Man: Studies in the Ideology of Advanced Industrial Society*. London: RKP.

Marx, K. 1976. *Capital*, Volume I. London: Penguin.

Orwell, G. 2004. *1984*. London: Penguin.

Remarque, E.M. 1996. *All Quiet on the Western Front*. London: Vintage.

Schumpeter, J.A. 2010. *Capitalism, Socialism, and Democracy*. London: Routledge.

Sebald, W.G. 2001. *Austerlitz*. London: Penguin Books.

Sebald, W.G. 2002. *The Rings of Saturn*. London: Vintage.

Sebald, W.G. 2004. *On the Natural History of Destruction*. London: Penguin.

Virilio, P. 1989. *War and Cinema – The Logistics of Perception*. London: Verso.

Virilio, P. 1994. *Bunker Archaeology*. New York: Princeton University Press.

Virilio, P. 2005. *City of Panic*. Oxford: Berg.

Vonnegut, K. 2000. *Slaughterhouse 5*. London: Vintage.

Zola, E. 2008. *The Kill (La Curée)*. Oxford: Oxford University Press.

Index